SHIFRA STEIN'S

DAY TRIPS®
FROM KANSAS CITY

D1227483

Help Us Keep This Guide Up to Date

Every effort has been made by the author and editors to make this guide as accurate and useful as possible. Many things, however, can change after a guide is published—establishments close, phone numbers change, facilities come under new management, etc.

We would love to hear from you concerning your experiences with this guide and how you feel it could be improved and kept up to date. While we may not be able to respond to all comments and suggestions, we'll take them to heart and we'll make certain to share them with the author. Please send your comments and suggestions to the following address:

The Globe Pequot Press
Reader Response/Editorial Department
P.O. Box 480
Guilford, CT 06437

Or you may e-mail us at:
editorial@globe-pequot.com

Thanks for your input, and happy travels!

Day Trips® Series

GETAWAYS LESS THAN TWO HOURS AWAY

SHIFRA STEIN'S **DAY TRIPS®**
FROM **KANSAS CITY**

Twelfth Edition

by

Shifra Stein

The
Globe
Pequot
Press

GUILFORD, CONNECTICUT

ISSN: 1538-4993
ISBN: 0-7627-2277-0

Manufactured in the United States of America
Twelfth Edition/First Printing

ACKNOWLEDGMENTS

Special thanks to Diane Lambdin Meyer whose invaluable help made this edition of *Day Trips® from Kansas City* a better one. I am grateful for all the help and assistance given to me by the chambers of commerce, state and regional tourism departments, and convention bureaus of the states of Kansas and Missouri. I am also indebted to photographer Bob Barrett, whose love of the prairie, back roads, and all things wild and beautiful made this book possible.

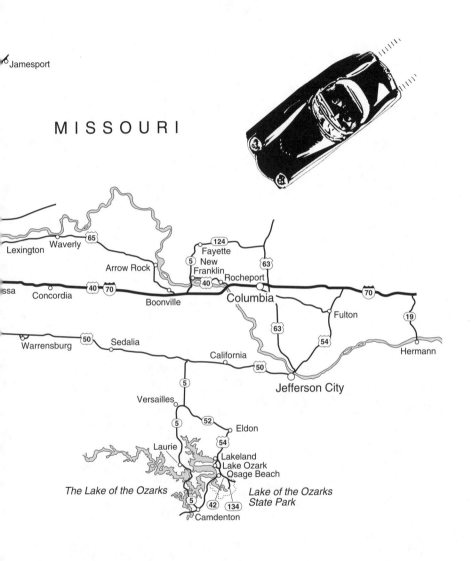

Jamesport

M I S S O U R I

Lexington Waverly 65
Fayette 124
Arrow Rock New 5
Franklin 63
Rocheport
ssa Concordia 40 70 40
Boonville Columbia 70
Fulton
19
Warrensburg 50 Sedalia 63
California 54 Hermann
50
Jefferson City
5
Versailles
5 52 Eldon
Laurie 54
Lakeland
Lake Ozark
Osage Beach
The Lake of the Ozarks Lake of the Ozarks
State Park
5 42 134
Camdenton

0   10   20   30 miles

Contents

WEST

NORTHWEST

DIRECTORY

PREFACE

Day Trips® *from Kansas City* has had a long and happy life. It was first published in 1980 and has been updated and revised ever since. Since that time, there have been letters and calls from people all over the country wanting to know when the book was going to be expanded to include more places. Well, it's time to toss away your old editions. You are holding in your hands a brand-new, chock-full-of-stuff publication that features sections devoted to the Lake of the Ozarks region; the Flint Hills; Tallgrass Prairie Preserve; Manhattan, Kansas; Columbia, Missouri; and other areas.

Many of you have written to tell me how much you love cheap eats, old-fashioned soda fountains, and great ice cream, so I took it upon myself to devour my way through Kansas and Missouri in order to provide you with the latest information on establishments that know no bounds when it comes to butterfat. (It was hard work, but somebody had to do it.)

I also expanded my pants by two sizes—all in the interest of research, mind you. I was forced to eat mini mountains of filet mignon and whopping twenty-two-ounce porterhouses and to gorge myself on homemade biscuits and gravy, real hash browns, and real mashed potatoes. It was terribly difficult for me to cram my mouth full of roast pork with honey-bourbon sauce and bouillabaisse while at the same time sampling fine wines from around the world. And, oh, the decadence of those desserts: chocolate cake topped with "evil fudge icing," peach praline pie, and homemade bread pudding with New Orleans bourbon sauce. Well, I hope you can appreciate to what lengths I went to make you the beneficiary of my gastronomic investigations.

Then there were those close encounters with the very exceptional and the very strange—what comedian Robin Williams might call "richly bizarre." Consider, if you will, hosting your wedding beside an eleven-million-pound steam shovel, or initiating a carp-feeding frenzy while munching on barbecued ribs. Who knows what adventures await as you frolic your way through a two-state region?

Armed with this book and a good map, you will find that you no longer have to trek to New Mexico, Arizona, or California to be in bed-and-breakfast heaven. Kansas and Missouri have sprouted so many superior new establishments that it was difficult to find space to include them all. Many offer upscale amenities, acres of land on which to stroll, and full gourmet breakfasts prepared by trained chefs. Some of these places have been touted in national magazines and newspapers; others are just about to be discovered.

Day Trips® holds plenty of breathtaking vistas, prairies, wildlife refuges, and places steeped in history. You'll travel pathways where settlers drove their conestogas through towns that marked the beginnings of the Santa Fe, California, and Oregon Trails. As you drive the back roads, you'll discover that the nineteenth century is still with us, in the elegant mansions, antebellum homes, and exquisite buildings that line the streets of small midwestern towns less than two hours from your doorstep.

The book's longevity attests to the fact that there is yearning in each of us for something that speaks to the heart. Kansas City borders a prairie that once grew soybeans and sunflowers. Today our burgeoning metropolis is crowding out the prairie and its fragile ecosystem. Wildlife is being decimated as we rip up fields to make way for business complexes, cinema multiplexes, strip malls, shopping centers, and gated residential communities. Chalk it up to "progress," but the fact is that we now must go farther and farther away from the city to find peace of mind and fresh air to breathe.

So prepare to detach yourself from the Internet, the fax, the Day-Timer, and the cell phone, and live life in the slow lane for a while. Join other readers who have already made *Day Trips*® part of their lives. As you read this book, you'll gain insights into what makes this part of America so special. There are maps to follow, but perhaps you'll seek your own roads to places you've never been before. Having seen them, you may grow to love them all the more because they are home.

Shifra Stein

USING THIS BOOK

Restaurant prices: Designated $$$ (expensive, $15 and over), $$ (moderate, $5 to $15), or $ (inexpensive, $5 and under).

Lodging rates: Designated $$$ (expensive, $100 and over per night), $$ (moderate, $50 to $100 per night), $ (inexpensive, $50 and under per night). Rates often change seasonally, so be sure to call first for current prices.

Credit cards: The symbol ☐ denotes that credit cards are accepted; (no cards) if the establishment doesn't take them.

Highways: Designated I– for interstate highways, U.S. for federal highways, and K– or M– for state routes. County and state roads are identified as such.

Hours: In most cases, hours are omitted in the listings because they are subject to frequent changes. Instead, phone numbers are provided for obtaining up-to-date information.

Handicapped accessibility: The designation ♿ is provided only for those attractions and services that feature outstanding amenities for the physically challenged. (*Note:* Attractions or services that emphasize amenities for the visually impaired are also designated as such.)

The prices and rates listed in this guidebook were confirmed at press time. We recommend, however, that you call establishments before traveling to obtain current information.

SMITHVILLE, MO

The small town of Smithville offers some shops and boutiques, but it is primarily known for being one of Kansas City's favorite weekend vacation spots for boaters, hikers, and outdoor enthusiasts.

WHERE TO GO

Smithville Lake and Clay County Parks (Camp Branch, Little Platte Park, and Crow's Creek Area). Two miles east of U.S. 169 on Northeast 180th Street, Smithville, MO 64089. Located amid rolling hills and grassland, the 7,200-acre lake is just 20 miles from downtown Kansas City and is surrounded by 27 miles of walking and horseback-riding trails. Clay County operates recreation areas on the lake, leasing nearly 5,500 acres from the U.S. Army Corps of Engineers. The recreation areas include more than 777 campsites for tents and RVs, 2 swimming beaches, 200 picnic sites, 11 shelter houses, and 2 full-service marinas. Favorites with fishermen are bass, walleye, crappie, and catfish.

Golfers are offered challenging play on two par-72, award-winning eighteen-hole championship golf courses.

The Kansas City Trapshooters Association offers the public a chance to do some of the finest trap and skeet shooting in the Midwest. This well-equipped facility includes twelve trapshooting pads, two skeet houses, five-man sporting clays, and a clubhouse. In addition to all campground rest rooms, Crow's Creek Area offers a

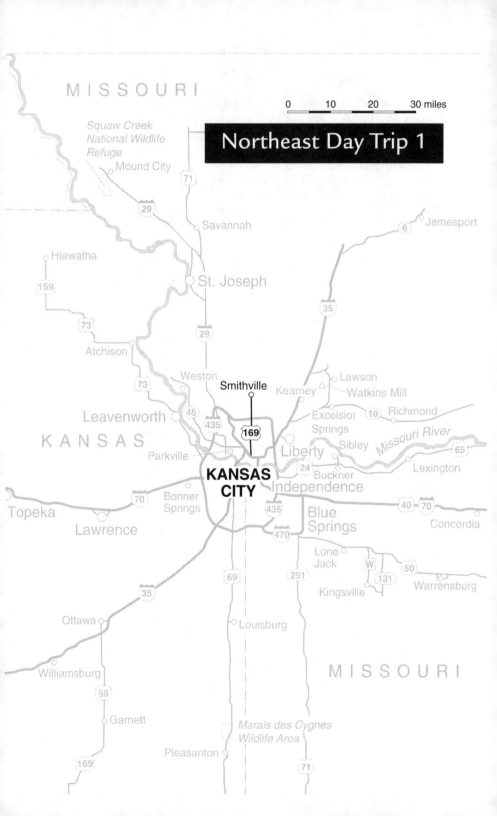

handicapped-accessible fishing dock and picnic shelter. Fee. &.
(816) 532–0803.

The Jerry L. Litton Visitor Center. M–92 east from Kearney or
U.S. 169 north from Kansas City to 16311 Highway DD (south end
of dam), P.O. Box 428, Smithville, MO 64089. Located inside the
park, the visitor center is named after the late sixth district con-
gressman; it offers exhibits and artifacts concerning the Missouri
Valley and the Native Americans who inhabited it. There's information about the lake and dam and on the life of Litton. The center also
has nature films, and you can schedule tours of the dam control
tower. Free. Call for hours. (816) 532–0174.

Woodhenge. Smithville, MO 64089. Located on the west side of
Smithville Lake in Little Platt Park, this is a working replica of the
only known square prehistoric Native American solar calendar. The
original site was flooded when Smithville Lake was created in the late
1970s. It's an interesting place to visit if you're already at the lake.
Open year-round. Fee. (816) 532–0803.

Comanche Acres Iris Gardens. 12421 Southeast State Route 116,
Gower, MO 64454. Travel about 4 miles north of Smithville on M–169,
then turn left on M–16 to the beautiful seventeen acres of Comanche
Acres Iris Gardens. Before the land was flooded to form Smithville
Lake, Jim and LeMoyne Hedgecock scoured the old homesteads for iris
rhizomes, which they replanted. They've bred nearly 1,000 new types of
flowers, which they sell around the world through a catalog company—and to anyone who happens by. Spring is the most impressive
time for a visit. You can wander through the flowers without charge
and enjoy the guinea hens, turkeys, and ducks that eat the bugs from
the blooms. (816) 424–6436; www.ccp.com/~comanche.

WHERE TO EAT

Lowman's Cafe. 505 South 169 Highway, Smithville, MO 64089.
This is where the locals come for a cup of coffee and to catch up on
the latest gossip. You can count on a great selection of cream pies
and the Lowman's special-recipe barbecue sauce on the ham and beef
sandwiches served seven days a week. Some locally made crafts and
beautiful handmade quilts decorate the cafe and are for sale. $; (no
cards). (816) 532–9000.

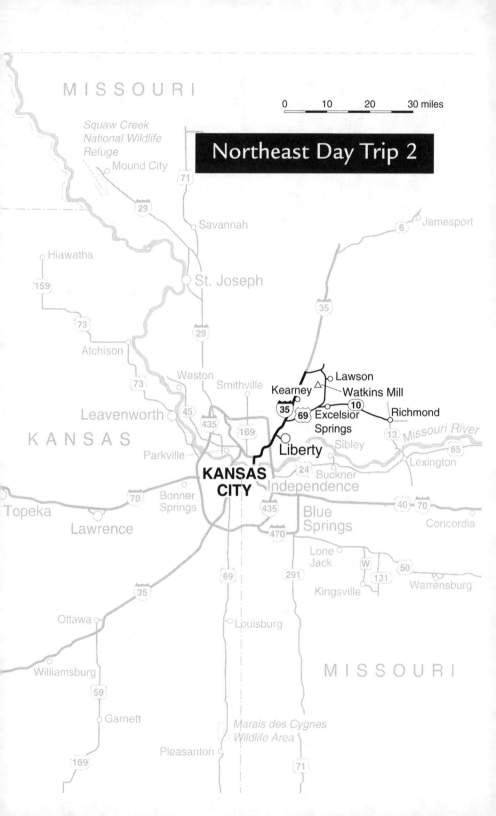

MISSOURI

Squaw Creek
National Wildlife
Refuge
Mound City

71

0   10   20   30 miles

Northeast Day Trip 2

29

Savannah

6 Jamesport

Hiawatha

St. Joseph

35

159

35

73

29

Atchison

Lawson

Weston

Watkins Mill

73

Smithville

Kearney

10 Richmond

Leavenworth

45

35

69 Excelsior
Springs

435

13 Missouri River

KANSAS

169

Parkville

Liberty Sibley

65

Lexington

KANSAS
CITY Independence

24 Buckner

70

Bonner
Springs

435

Blue
Springs

40 70

Concordia

Topeka

470

Lawrence

Lone
Jack

W

50

69

291

131 Warrensburg

35

Kingsville

Ottawa

Louisburg

MISSOURI

Williamsburg

59

Garnett

Marais des Cygnes
Wildlife Area

Pleasanton

169

71

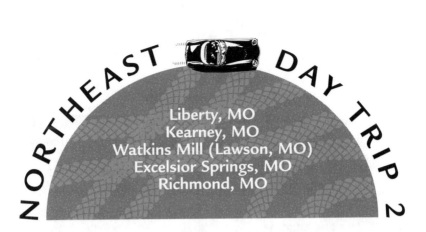

NORTHEAST DAY TRIP 2

Liberty, MO
Kearney, MO
Watkins Mill (Lawson, MO)
Excelsior Springs, MO
Richmond, MO

LIBERTY, MO

One of the most famous robberies attributed to the notorious James Gang was the daylight holdup of Clay County Savings in Liberty back in 1866. The robbers took $60,000 in gold and currency, and none of the money was ever recovered. Others who put Liberty on the map are Joseph Smith, the Mormon prophet, and Circuit Judge David Atchison, a Missouri senator credited with being president of the United States for one day. Colonel Alexander Doniphan took up the practice of law in Liberty in 1833. During his residence of thirty years, he became a leading citizen, orator, jurist, statesman, and soldier, eventually leading his famous expedition to Old Mexico in 1846–47—the longest military march ever made.

By 1820 Clay County was formed and named in honor of Henry Clay, the famed senator. Liberty, selected as the county seat, was established that same year. Two years later a college grew under the supervision of Dr. William Jewell, and today the lovely campus is still a fine center of higher learning. For more information contact the Liberty Chamber of Commerce, 9 South Leonard Street, Liberty, MO 64068 (816- 781-5200), or phone the Clay County Visitors Bureau's twenty-four-hour Family Fun Line at (816) 792-7691 for a Free Fun calendar of events in Clay County; www.ci.liberty.mo.us/.

WHERE TO GO

James A. Rooney Justice Center. Clay County Courthouse, 11 South Water Street, Liberty, MO 64068. Take a self-guided tour through the courthouse, which features outdoor ceramic murals depicting the county's history. If the court is in session, children can sit in, but they must be quiet. Free. (816) 792-7612.

Martha Lafite Thompson Nature Sanctuary. 407 North LaFrenz Road (0.5 mile southeast of William Jewell College), Liberty, MO 64068. This one-hundred-acre sanctuary is filled with wildlife that inhabit prairies, woodlands, meadows, and marshes. White-tailed deer, raccoons, foxes, squirrels, birds, and butterflies delight the eyes. The visitor center features educational exhibits for children and has organized activities such as wildflower and full-moon hikes. The visitor center is closed Monday. The hiking trails are open daily from 8:30 A.M. to sunset. Free. (816) 781-8598; www.naturesanctuary.com.

Clay County Museum and Historical Society. 14 North Main Street, Liberty, MO 64068. Housed in an 1877 drugstore, the museum collection focuses on Clay County history. It features a restored doctor's office, prehistoric Native American relics, toys, tools, arrowheads, and artifacts relating to the operation of a nineteenth-century drugstore. Fee. (816) 792-1849.

Jesse James Bank Museum. 103 North Water Street (the northeast corner of Courthouse Square), Liberty, MO 64068. Frank and Jesse James were responsible for the first successful daylight bank robbery during peacetime. The James boys made a bank "withdrawal" of $60,000 from the Clay County Savings Association on February 13, 1866. A William Jewell College student who witnessed the event was shot and killed. Nobody was ever convicted. Today you can take a glimpse into the workings of a nineteenth-century bank, along with a number of artifacts related to Jesse James. The original bank vault and a rare Seth Thomas calendar clock are part of the tour. The building is listed on the National Register of Historic Places. Open Monday through Saturday; closed Sunday. Fee. (816) 781-4458.

Historic Liberty Jail and Visitors Center (Mormon Jail). 216 North Main Street, Liberty, MO 64068. Mormon leader Joseph Smith was imprisoned here in 1838 for his beliefs. Built in 1833, the limestone jail eventually crumbled but was reconstructed by the

Church of Jesus Christ of Latter-day Saints in 1963. The jail has cut-away walls so that visitors can see what conditions were like more than 150 years ago. The center also teaches about the unfairness of perse-cuting those of different faiths. Guided tours include historical high-lights, exhibits, artwork, and interactive video displays. Open daily. Free. (816) 781-3188.

Liberty Farmers' Market. West side of Historic Liberty Square, Liberty, MO 64068. The Saturday farmers' market is open from May through October, and you can find a variety of produce here, in-cluding fruits, vegetables, flowers, bedding plants, and honey. There is also Farmers' Market on Wednesday, located next to Southerlands on M-291. The Saturday market opens early and closes at 1:00 P.M. The Wednesday market also closes at 1:00 P.M. Free. (816) 781-5105.

WHERE TO EAT

Hardware Cafe. 5 East Kansas Street, Liberty, MO 64068. Sterling Price Boggess opened his hardware store on Liberty's Historic Square on December 2, 1902. The Liberty landmark is now occupied by the Hardware Cafe, which offers a nice selection of lunch and dinner items, ranging from quiche, salad, and soup to prime rib, broiled trout, and baked pork roast. Many of the recipes are available in *The Hardware Cafe Cookbook,* available for sale in a number of gift and antiques stores in the area. Closed on Sunday and Monday evenings. $$; □. (816) 792-3500.

Cracker Barrel Old Country Store. 8225 North Church Road, Liberty, MO 64158. Breakfast is served all day at this popular chain restaurant. The menu is fun to read, and the food is fun to eat. Hearty breakfasts, lunches, and dinners are served. There's no skimping here: The plates are full, but your pocketbook's never emp-tied. Open daily. $$; □. (816) 781-1444.

WHERE TO STAY

Dougherty House Bed & Breakfast. 302 North Water Street, Liberty, MO 64068. Wake up to the smell of homemade biscuits and fresh-baked muffins at this restored 1880s home, graced by Oriental rugs and English Arts and Crafts and American Mission furnishings. A grand staircase with beveled and leaded glass leads to the upper floors that offer three bedrooms with private baths, modern jetted tubs, and antique accessories. Business travelers are welcome. Young children are not. $$-$$$; ☐. (816) 792-4888; www.doughertyhouse.com.

James Inn Bed and Breakfast. 342 North Water Street, Liberty, MO 64068. This unusual six-room bed-and-breakfast is located in a restored 1913 church. All rooms feature large Jacuzzi tubs, warm antique furnishings, and queen-size beds. Gothic windows allow the light to shine in through bath areas overlooking the bedrooms. A full breakfast is served in the dining room. Other amenities include a small meeting room and a gift shop. Advance notice is required if you want a massage therapist or in-room flowers or wish to hold showers, parties, or weddings. Rates differ for weekends and weekdays. $$-$$$; ☐. (816) 781-3677; www.thejamesinn.com.

KEARNEY, MO

The former home of outlaw Jesse James holds several attractions of historic importance. It also hosts a Jesse James Festival, complete with parade, rodeo, craft show, carnival, and barbecue cookoff, the second and third weekends of September. For information contact Jesse James Festival, P.O. Box 536, Kearney, MO 64060; (816) 628-4229; www.jessejamesfestival.com.

WHERE TO GO

Claybrook House Historic Site. 21216 Jesse James Farm Road (2 miles east of Kearney on M-92; west of the Jesse James Farm and Museum), Kearney, MO 64065. This pre–Civil War residence, built in 1858 by George Claybrook, was the home of Jesse James's daughter, Mary James Barr. The home is located across the road from the James Farm and was originally developed as a Southern-style plantation. Claybrook and nearby Jesse James Farm offer a glimpse of the contrasting nineteenth-century lifestyles of the very wealthy and the very poor. Civil War reenactments and fashion

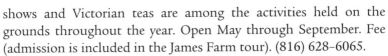

shows and Victorian teas are among the activities held on the grounds throughout the year. Open May through September. Fee (admission is included in the James Farm tour). (816) 628-6065.

Jesse James Farm and Museum. 21216 James Farm Road (2 miles east of Kearney on M-92), Kearney, MO 64060. This is the birthplace of Jesse James, where he and his brother Frank grew up during the mid-1800s. The house has been authentically restored, and there is a newly expanded museum, complete with an audiovisual display and a gift shop. The museum features the world's largest collection of James family artifacts. Open year-round. Fee (admission includes a tour of nearby Claybrook). (816) 628-6065; www.jessejames.org.

Jesse James Grave. Mount Olivet Cemetery, west end of M-92 on the way out of Kearney. Jesse's grave is located between two small evergreen trees on the cemetery's west side. Originally he was buried on the front lawn of the farm so that his family could protect his remains from grave robbers and curiosity seekers. For years Jesse's mother, Zerelda, sold pebbles off the grave to tourists. Later his body was moved to Mount Olivet. Open daily. Free.

Mount Gilead Church and School. 15918 Plattsburg Road, Kearney, MO 64060. This was the only school west of the Mississippi River to remain open during the Civil War. Third- and fourth-grade students are invited to take a class trip back to the 1800s, where they can experience an old-fashioned education. Lessons in history, reading, arithmetic, and spelling are taught by a schoolteacher in period attire. Experiencing school life in this one-room schoolhouse offers children a unique and unforgettable history lesson. Fee. Reservations required. (816) 628-6065.

Tryst Falls Park. Five miles east of Kearney on M-92. The Clay County Parks and Recreation Department runs this forty-acre park, which includes the area's only waterfall open to the public. It's a great place to picnic because of the many shelters and grills. Jesse James's father, a Baptist minister, baptized Walthus Watkins, owner of Watkins Mill, at Tryst Falls. Swimming is dangerous here because of the rocks and is not allowed. Fishing is no longer allowed. The park makes a sight-seeing stop in your tour of Jesse James Farm or Watkins Mill State Park. Open daily. (816) 532-0803.

WATKINS MILL (LAWSON, MO)

WHERE TO GO

Watkins Woolen Mill State Historic Site and Park. Located 6.5 miles north of Excelsior Springs and 7 miles east of Kearney, off M-92 at Highway RA, Lawson, MO 64062. This is the last nineteenth-century woolen mill in America with original equipment. The mill heralds the beginning of the industrial age and still contains sixty of the original machines and a steam engine. The Watkins home, smokehouse, summer kitchen, and fruit dry house, along with an octagonal school and a church, add interest. The 3,550-acre livestock farm had a sawmill, a gristmill, and a brick kiln as well.

The state park features picnicking, camping, hiking, fishing, and swimming in the lake. Bring your bike along and enjoy the bike/hike trail around the shoreline. Campsites are available. Bring food and drink; there are no concessions here and water is turned off from November 1 to April 1. Open daily. &. Free (fee for historic site). (816) 580-3387; www.mostateparks.com/wwmill.

EXCELSIOR SPRINGS, MO

A drive north on U.S. 69 will take you to Excelsior Springs in less than forty minutes. For information on what there is to see and do, call the Excelsior Springs Chamber of Commerce at (816) 630-6161; www.exsmo.com.

WHERE TO GO

Historic Hall of Waters. 201 East Broadway, Excelsior Springs, MO 64024. Long revered as a haven of health, Excelsior Springs has attracted thousands of people to its mineral waters since 1881. The Historic Hall of Waters was the central dispersal site of the five mineral waters found here and focused on the development of equipment for the use of water in therapeutic treatment. Siloam Springs remains today as the only natural supply of iron manganese mineral water in the country and is one of five recognized in existence worldwide. The mineral-water spa offers cardiovascular massage and therapeutic bodywork, including reflexology, acupressure, cranial-sacral technique, and deep-tissue neuromuscular massage. Between the steam baths, hot packs, and massages, you'll come away from this place as loose as a jellyfish.

At the Hall of Waters, you can belly up to the longest mineral-water bar in the world and sample the natural calcium mineral water or take home a bottle to drink. Bring your camera to photograph the beautiful Mayan Indian and Art Deco architectural designs. Baths are available year-round. Fee. (816) 630–0753; www.hallofwaters.com.

WHERE TO STAY

The Elms Resort & Spa. Regent Street and Elms Boulevard, Excelsior Springs, MO 64024. Touting itself as a unique retreat and conference facility for businesses and groups, The Elms Resort and Spa features tastefully appointed guest rooms and suites that include modern amenities such as voice mail, dataports, iron and ironing board, coffeemaker, and refreshment center. Choose from casual or fine dining options, or pamper yourself at The Spa, a 10,000-square-foot facility featuring therapists who wrap you in mud, seaweed, and aloe and massage you until you're jelly. A fitness center provides a swim track, jogging track, sauna, steam rooms, and equipment. There's also an outdoor pool, heated whirlpool, and hiking and biking trails. The Challenge Course, with its climbing wall, ropes course, and Burma bridge, is not for couch potatoes. A leadership center provides principle-based training and customized workshops that enhance personal, team, and organizational effectiveness. Call (800) 843–3567 for information on rooms, prices, and packages; www.elmsresort.com.

The Inn on Crescent Lake. 1261 St. Louis Avenue, Excelsior Springs, MO 64024. This country inn, which has earned a Mobil three-star rating, makes a great romantic getaway or a pleasant alternative for business people tired of the motel shuffle.

The three-story Georgian Colonial mansion is nestled on twenty-two acres and surrounded by two ponds and a lawn designed for strolling and relaxing. The innkeepers are graduates of the French Culinary Institute in New York and came here to unwind from the hectic pace of the Big Apple, so you can rest assured that your food will be interesting. A full breakfast might include quiches, scones, waffles, French toast, and other delights. The dining room is also available to guests of the inn for a three-course dinner (for an additional fee). The chef-owners will cook you up anything from rack of lamb to filet mignon, along with special meals on request.

Each of the seven guest rooms has a private bath, including whirlpool or claw-foot tub. The downstairs guest room is handicapped-accessible, with its own separate entrance, and is adjacent to the kitchen. The ballroom-size third floor can be reserved as a honeymoon suite. It features a king-size bed, a separate sitting area, and a whirlpool bath and custom marble shower big enough for two.

If that's not enough, there's an outdoor swimming pool where you can practice your backstroke on warm summer days. The ponds are stocked with bass and catfish, and the inn will supply you with a fishing pole and boat. The inn is available for private parties, weddings, and corporate retreats, with enough meeting space to accommodate up to fifty persons. $$$; ☐. (816) 630-6745; www.crescentinn.com.

RICHMOND, MO

Located 11 miles north of Lexington on M-13, Richmond, Missouri, touts itself as "The Mushroom Capital of the World." Time your trip so that it coincides with Richmond's annual mushroom festival the first weekend in May. This is when those hard-to-find morel mushrooms pop up, begging to be sautéed in butter and wine. The mushrooms are plentiful enough around here for a celebration in their honor. Richmond hosts a parade, plenty of food and craft booths, a model train show, a carnival, a beer garden, and other activities. Richmond folks will sell you some morels to take back home, but they won't reveal their secret mushroom spots. If you want to go searching in the woods, you're on your own. For information call the Richmond Chamber of Commerce at (816) 776-6916; www.richmondmissouri.com.

JAMESPORT, MO

In Jamesport, the Amish community offers a glimpse of a bygone era. These people are part of the Old Order Amish, who are direct descendants of the Mennonite Anabaptists, a group that developed during the Reformation in Germany and Switzerland. Today there are Amish settlements in at least nineteen states and Canada. In the early 1950s the Amish immigrated to Jamesport, now the largest settlement in the state. Currently about 2,000 Amish reside on the rich farmland of the area.

They shun the use of modern conveniences and travel by means of horse-drawn vehicles. Their peaceful lifestyle evolves around a close-knit family, their faith, and farming. These people may seem quaint to outsiders but are uniquely adapted for survival today. They beat inflation by living without the things we take for granted. They use no electricity, no cars, no televisions or radios. Their education ends at the eighth grade, and they don't seem to miss it. Many of the Amish farmhouses now have indoor plumbing, and most Amish families use oil furnaces, kerosene- or wood-burning stoves, and kerosene lamps. Their primary mode of transportation, the horse and carriage, is certainly more picturesque than automobiles.

Amish men are expert farmers who still use plows pulled by horses to till their fields. They dress modestly, in black broad-brimmed hats, white shirts, and black trousers.

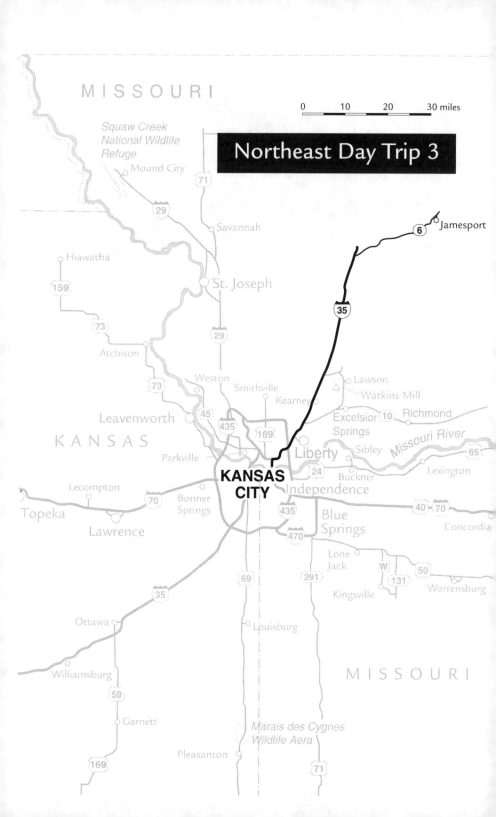

The women excel in the home arts, and anyone fortunate enough to attend an Amish quilting bee has a rare privilege in store, for every stitch sewn by these women is a perfect example of how well-made things used to be put together.

Usually a dozen Amish women attend a quilting bee. Seated at a large square table, they sew pattern blocks by hand and quilt them around a rectangular quilting frame. They wear plain, long cotton dresses held together with pins (they consider buttons worldly). On their heads they wear white prayer caps at all times. Their conversation often lapses into something called "Ferhoodled English," a combination of German, Dutch, and English.

Jamesport has prospered as a tourist attraction because of the Amish, and they in their practical way have taken advantage of public curiosity. If you're looking for authentic Amish foods, goods, and services, be aware that "Amish style" does not necessarily mean that something is Amish-made.

A visit to Jamesport can be fun if you tour it with the idea that there are two separate reasons for coming here. The first is to visit the Amish-owned stores, where you will find authentic Amish foods, quilts, and other items. The second reason is to enjoy the antiques, craft, and specialty shops, restaurants, and bed-and-breakfasts, most of which are *not* Amish-owned.

If you want to determine whether an establishment is Amish or Mennonite, check the days it is open; Amish shops close on Thursday and Sunday. The Amish are also fussy about having their pictures taken, since it violates their religious beliefs. As a courtesy, ask permission before you shoot.

You might try timing a trip to any one of a number of festivals, including the town's renowned Step Back in Time Christmas Craft Show, held the Friday and Saturday after Thanksgiving.

Free maps of the area are available at all the businesses and the Amish Country stores. Tours are available through Amish Country Bus Tours, P.O. Box 65, Jamesport, MO 64648; (660) 684–6776, and Hook & Eye Dutch House and Tour Service, Route 1, Box 9, Jamesport, MO 64648; (660) 684–6179.

For more information, contact the Jamesport Chamber of Commerce, P.O. Box 17, Jamesport, MO 64648; (660) 684–6682; www.jamesport-mo.com.

WHERE TO GO

Hook & Eye Dutch House and Tour Service. Route 1, Box 9, Jamesport, MO 64648. Excursions take in the Hook & Eye Dutch House, the only Amish house tour available in the area, plus a 30-mile junket through Amish farmland with stops at several Amish stores. A small fee is charged. (660) 684–6179.

WHERE TO SHOP

Balcony House Antiques. P.O. Box 223 (east of the four-way stop sign), Jamesport, MO 64648. This establishment features quality antiques and collectibles, Native American artifacts, books, and quilts. Open daily. (660) 684–6725.

The Barn Antiques and Crafts. P.O. Box 46, Jamesport, MO 64648. Come here for a large selection of antiques, collectibles, willow furniture, quilts, baskets, and Christmas decorations and crafts. Call for hours: (660) 684–6711.

Broadway Pavilion Mall. P.O. Box 58 (south of four-way stop), Jamesport, MO 64648. The mall has a large assortment of antiques, collectibles, furniture, glassware, pottery, records, old books, and more. Open daily. (660) 684–6655.

D & R Furniture and Home Furnishings. Two blocks west and 1 block south of the four-way stop, Jamesport, MO 64648. This Mennonite-owned shop offers a large variety of custom-built solid-oak furniture and wood crafts. Closed Thursday and Sunday. (660) 684–6707.

The Family Tree House. 100 North Broadway, Jamesport, MO 64648. Specializing in a decorative touch for every season, this fun shop offers custom floral arrangements, water fountains, fern stands, candles, and more. You'll find this creative store just one door north of City Hall. Closed on Sunday. (660) 684–6210.

Ellis Antiques. 3395 Livingston County Road 500, Jamesport, MO 64648. Open year-round, Ellis Antiques sells furniture and a general line of refinishing products. Open daily except Sunday, by chance or appointment. (660) 684–6319.

Colonial Rug and Broom Shoppe. Rural Route 1, Box 55 (2½ blocks west of the four-way stop on County Road F), Jamesport, MO 64648. See handwoven rugs, placemats, and brooms made daily. You can purchase them to take back home or ask the owners to design one to suit your own needs. Open daily. (800) 647–5586 or (660) 684–6211.

Kramer-Yoder Country Goodies. Kramer-Yoder Farm, Route 3, Box 59 (2 miles west on County Road NN), Jamesport, MO 64648. Natural farm-raised meats, homemade goodies, and crafts are sold at this Amish-owned store. Open Monday, Wednesday, and Friday. No phone.

Pastime Antiques. P.O. Box 102, Jamesport, MO 64648. Early country furniture and decorative items, plus original painted furniture, are sold here along with old-fashioned candy, antiques, and collectibles. Closed Sunday. (660) 684–6222.

This 'N That. P.O. Box 74 (1 block north of the four-way stop), Jamesport, MO 64648. A little bit of everything, including furniture, jewelry, and glassware, is sold here. Closed Sunday, except May through October. (660) 684–6594.

WHERE TO EAT

Anna's Bake Shop. Route 1, Box 34–A (west end of town), Jamesport, MO 64648. This Amish shop sells mouthwatering fresh-baked doughnuts, pies, breads, and cinnamon and dinner rolls. Closed Christmas through February 1. According to the owner, the phone works only "when the weather is above 20 degrees." Call for hours. $; (no cards). (660) 684–6810.

Country Bakery. Located 0.5 mile south of Jamesport on M–190, Jamesport, MO 64648. Leave room in your tummy and your car for some delicious, authentic Amish homemade baked goods. Closed Thursday and Sunday. $; (no cards). No phone.

Gingerich Dutch Pantry. P.O. Box 186, Jamesport, MO 64648. Located at the four-way stop in downtown Jamesport, this Mennonite-owned restaurant specializes in Mennonite cooking using Old Dutch recipes. Homemade pies, breads, cinnamon rolls, and other baked goods are featured. A buffet and a complete menu are available for individuals or large groups. Call for hours. $; □. (660) 684–6212.

J.J.'s Restaurant. P.O. Box 245 (downtown Jamesport), Jamesport, MO 64648. This friendly place features seating for up to one hundred people and specializes in bus/group package rates for its

Amish-style buffet. Step-on tour guides are available by reservation only. $; □. Closed Thursday. (660) 684–6608.

WHERE TO STAY

Bennett's Bed and Breakfast. 200 South Elm Street, Jamesport, MO 64648. A lazy afternoon swinging in the hammock of Barbara Bennett Schroeder's B&B is the perfect way to enjoy the Amish community. Or walk just 4 blocks to the many shops and restaurants of Jamesport. Your evening will be spent in the privacy of her queen bedroom with private bath. Barbara opens only in the spring and autumn months. And be sure to ask her about her daughter—an animator of Disney films. $–$$; (no cards). (660) 684–6022.

Country Colonial Bed and Breakfast. One block north and 1 block east of the four-way stop (downtown Jamesport), Jamesport, MO 64648. This 1800s restored home offers a veranda, three bedrooms with private baths, and a library of more than 500 books, some dating back to the nineteenth century. $$; □. (800) 579–9248 or (660) 684–6711.

Grand River Inn. Junction of U.S. 36 and 65, Chillicothe, MO 64601. Amenities here include a restaurant and lounge, along with comfortable rooms and a large pool with sauna and hot tub. Golf packages are available. The hotel can also arrange tours of the Jamesport area. $$; □. (660) 646–6590.

Painted Lady Bed and Breakfast. 403 North Locust Street Jamesport, MO 64648. Enjoy the full use of the 1900s Victorian cottage with two bedrooms and a complete kitchen. Or allow Linda Woodward to serve you a country-style breakfast before walking uptown to the attractions of Jamesport and a complimentary frozen custard at Woodward's Frozen Custard and Antiques. The malts are made with *real* malted flavorings! $–$$; □. (660) 684–6080.

EAST

DAY TRIP 1

Independence, MO
Sibley, MO
Lexington, MO
Waverly, MO

INDEPENDENCE, MO

To reach Independence from Kansas City, take I-70 East to I-435 North and the Truman Road exit; then take Truman Road east to Independence. Founded in 1827, Independence became known as the Queen City of the Trails, heading three dominant routes west—the Santa Fe, California, and Oregon Trails. (The Santa-Cali-Gon Festival, held annually on Labor Day weekend, commemorates the opening of these prairie pathways.)

Fortunes were made here during the westward expansion and Victorian periods, and many of the charming homes built during these times have been designated with historic markers. Today Independence is best known as the home of the thirty-third president, Harry S. Truman. Places related to his life here include his home, courtroom, and office, as well as the Harry S. Truman Library.

Just a few blocks from the Harry S. Truman National Historic Site (Truman home) is Independence Square, filled with restaurants and shops housing arts, crafts, antiques, and memorabilia. It's fun to go exploring around a historic area that has a great past. Smack in the middle of the square is the Jackson County Courthouse. Built in 1836, it was renovated in 1933 during the administration of Jackson County Judge Harry Truman.

On the east side of the courthouse is a full-size statue of Harry himself—the only one of its kind. *The Man from Independence*, a free multimedia show highlighting Truman's life before his presidency,

East Day Trip 1

is shown on the hour inside the courthouse. There are guided tours of the courtroom and office. A fee is charged. Call (816) 795-8200 for information and hours. While you're there, you can visit the gift shop, which features crafts made by senior citizens.

Independence Day tour packages are offered April through October and take in such attractions as the Bingham-Waggoner Estate, the Vaile Mansion, and the 1859 Jail, Marshal's Home, and Museum (see following listings). The normal tourist season runs April through October at many historic sites, so be sure to call before you go to make sure places are open. A walking-tour brochure of the area is available from the City of Independence Tourism Department, 111 East Maple Street, Independence, MO 64050; (816) 325-7111; www.ci.independence.mo.us.

WHERE TO GO

The Auditorium. 1001 West Walnut Street, Independence, MO 64050. This is the world headquarters for the Community of Christ. The 6,000-seat chamber features a world-famous 111-rank, 6,334-pipe Aeolian-Skinner organ, one of the largest church organs in the nation. Thousands of people use the building yearly for religious, cultural, and community-centered activities. Free organ recitals are offered daily from June through August and on Sunday the remainder of the year. Guided tours are available daily to the public. (816) 833-1000, ext. 3030; www.cofchrist.org.

Bingham-Waggoner Estate. 313 West Pacific Avenue, Independence, MO 64050. Built in 1855, this private home eventually became the residence of Missouri artist George Caleb Bingham, who lived here with his wife, Eliza, until 1870. In 1879 the home was purchased by Peter and William Waggoner, who remodeled the original structure. The house served as the Waggoner family home until 1976. The twenty-six-room residence is open to tour from April 1 to October 31. Fee. (816) 461-3491 or 325-7111; www.bwestate.org.

1827 Log Courthouse. 107 West Kansas Avenue, Independence, MO 64050. The first courthouse in Jackson County, this is the oldest historic site open to the public in Independence. Originally a county courthouse, it was used as a private residence in 1832. During the 1920s and 1930s, the structure housed the headquarters of the Community Welfare League, with Bess Truman (Harry's wife) as honorary vice-chairperson. In 1932 Jackson County Judge Harry S. Truman held court there while the main courthouse was being remodeled. Open daily April 1 to October 31. Fee. (816) 325–7111.

1859 Jail, Marshal's Home, and Museum. 217 North Main Street, Independence, MO 64050. Four buildings constitute this museum, operated by the Jackson County Historical Society. These include the jail that held the outlaw Frank James, the marshal's restored home, a one-room schoolhouse, and a county museum. Open daily April 1 to October 31. In March, November, and December closed on Mondays; closed completely in January and February. Fee. (816) 252–1892.

George Owens Nature Park. 1601 South Speck Road, Independence, MO 64057. The park has two fishing lakes stocked with bass, channel cat, bluegill, and bullheads. A fishing license is required for people ages fifteen through sixty-four. There are 4 miles of nature trails for hiking, as well as a nature center whose outdoor habitat is filled with live deer, bats, geese, and snakes. Films are offered on Saturday once a month. Group reservations must be made at least two weeks in advance. Open year-round. Closed Monday. Free. (816) 257–1760.

Harry S. Truman National Historic Site. 219 North Delaware Street, Independence, MO 64050. Located in the Harry S. Truman National Landmark District, this was the home of the former president and his wife, Bess Wallace Truman, until their deaths. Informative tours include a twelve-minute slide show at the ticket center and a fifteen-minute tour of the residence. Individuals must reserve their tickets in person on a first-come, first-served basis on the day of the tour, at the Truman Home Ticket and Information Center, 223 North Main Street, adjacent to Independence Square. Closed Monday, Labor Day through Memorial Day. Fee. (816) 254–2720; www.nps.gov/hstr.

Harry S. Truman Library. U.S. 24 and Delaware Street, Independence, MO 64050. One of ten presidential libraries administered by the National Archives and Records Administration, this library houses exhibits and memorabilia of the Truman years, as well as a research facility. An extraordinary Thomas Hart Benton mural greets you as you walk through the door. Permanent museum exhibits on President Truman's career include a replica of the Oval Office and a glimpse into his dramatic 1948 election victory over Thomas Dewey. Temporary traveling exhibits are often augmented with special program. The graves of President and Mrs. Truman are located in the library's courtyard. Open daily. Fee. (816) 833–1225 (information) or (816) 833–1400 (administrative offices); www.trumanlibrary.org.

Harry S. Truman Courtroom and Office. Independence Square Courthouse, Room 109, Main at Maple Street, Independence, MO 64050. This is where the thirty-third president of the United States began the political career that led him to the White House. You'll see Judge Truman's restored quarters and an audiovisual presentation about his life and courtship with Bess. Open Friday and Saturday; other days by appointment. Fee. (816) 881–4467.

Missouri Pacific Railroad Station. Grand Street and Pacific Avenue, Independence, MO 64050. This depot, which figured in Truman's 1948 "Whistle Stop" campaign, is listed on the National Register of Historic Places. There's daily Amtrak service into Kansas City. Round-trip group rates are available. Free (fee for Amtrak). (816) 421–3622.

Mormon Visitors' Center. 937 West Walnut Street, Independence, MO 64051. Operated by the Church of Jesus Christ of Latter-day Saints (Mormon), the center tells the fascinating story of the church in early Missouri history (1831–38) in slides, films, and artifacts. Open daily. Free. (816) 836–3466.

National Frontier Trails Center. 318 West Pacific Avenue, Independence, MO 64050. This acclaimed museum, library, and archival center is located at the principal jumping-off point of the Santa Fe, Oregon, and California Trails. It is the only interpretive center in the nation devoted to all three trails. The gripping story of the exploration and settlement of the American West is shown in an award-winning introductory film that prepares visitors for their interesting trip through the museum's many exhibits, which feature artifacts that include memorabilia and relics from the prairie pathways. The research library is the largest in the country devoted to the trails, and it houses many rare books. Open daily. Fee. (816) 325–7575; www.frontiertrailscenter.com.

Pioneer Spring Cabin. Southeast corner of Noland and Truman Roads, Independence, MO 64050. The austere two-room cabin was originally constructed in an Irish community known as Brady Town and moved to its present location in 1971. A spring outside the cabin has been re-created to represent the kind of welcome oasis that traders and emigrants may have found on their way west. Open daily April 1 to October 31. Free. (816) 325-7111.

Stephenson's Orchard. 6700 Lee's Summit Road, Kansas City, MO 64136. Stephenson's is the right place to come during apple- or strawberry-picking time. Just watch the newspaper to see when the orchard is open to the public. Once the fruit is picked, it's back home to bake the pie. Fall tours of the orchard, packing house, and cider mill are available to schools and organized groups by reservation only. Fee. (816) 373-5138.

The Temple. 201 South River Street, Independence, MO 64050. This unusual architectural structure is part of the Community of Christ World Headquarters complex and includes two visitor theaters, a lecture hall, and classrooms, plus a museum, a bookstore, a library, and a chapel with an adjacent meditation garden, along with administrative offices. Highlighting the building is a 1,600-seat sanctuary and a 102-rank, 5,686-pipe organ built by Casavant Frères Limitée of Quebec, Canada. Fashioned after the nautilus seashell, the 150-foot spire rises from the sanctuary and can be seen from many areas of the city. The public is invited to attend the programs dedicated to peace and reconciliation, along with a daily prayer for peace, offered in the Temple sanctuary at 12:30 P.M. Public organ recitals are offered at 3:00 P.M. daily June through August and on Sunday only the remainder of the year. Free. (816) 833-1000, ext. 3030.

Vaile Mansion–DeWitt Museum. 1500 North Liberty Street, Independence, MO 64050. One of the best examples of Victorian architecture in the United States, this 1882 mansion has a second-floor smoking room where woodwork is painted with dozens of little faces and animals. Open daily April 1 to October 31. Fee. (816) 325-7111.

WHERE TO EAT

Stephenson's Apple Farm Restaurant. U.S. 40 East at Lee's Summit Road, Kansas City, MO 64136. This family restaurant is famous for its hickory-smoked chicken, ham, and pork chops, apple cider, and luscious apple dumplings. Open for lunch and dinner and for Sunday brunch. Reservations recommended. $$; ☐. (816) 373-5400.

Courthouse Exchange Restaurant & Lounge. 113 West Lexington Avenue, Independence, MO 64050. This place features a full lunch and dinner menu offering everything from prime rib to homemade cinnamon rolls. The tenderloin sandwiches here are famous. This is a popular breakfast spot with all the fixings served until 10:30 A.M. The private banquet room can be reserved for groups. $-$$; ☐. (816) 252-0344.

Ophelia's. 201 North Main Street, Independence, MO 64050. Located on Historic Independence Square, this unusual restaurant offers American cuisine, with the highest quality seafood, steaks, chops, and pastas available for lunch, dinner, and Sunday brunch. $$-$$$ ☐. (816) 461-4525.

V's Italiano Ristorante. 10819 U.S. 40 East, Independence, MO 64055. This family-owned and -operated restaurant offers an Old World ambience and friendly service. Pasta, chicken, and seafood specialties are offered along with early-bird specials, as is a modestly priced Sunday brunch. $$; ☐. (816) 353-1241; www.vsrestaurant.com.

WHERE TO STAY

The Inn at Ophelia's. 201 North Main Street, Independence, MO 64050. Seven rooms and one suite afford the business or leisure traveler gracious accommodations, complete with private baths, voice messaging, modem capability, hotel amenities, and down comforters and pillows to make you feel at home. $$-$$$; ☐. (816) 461-4525.

Serendipity Bed and Breakfast. 116 South Pleasant Street, Independence, MO 64050. Housed in an 1887 home, this bed-and-breakfast features antique furnishings, along with Victorian children's books and toys, china figurines, glassware, and books for guests to peruse. The side porch provides a hammock and swing for peaceful relaxation. Accommodations include the carriage house, with king and twin beds, a kitchen, and a sitting room on the ground level, as well as two-room suites, one with a kitchenette. All have private baths. A full breakfast is served in the main dining room. The home also offers a Tour and Tea for a fee. $$-$$$; ☐. (816) 833-4719; www.bbhost.com/serendipitybb.

Woodson Guest House. 1604 West Lexington Avenue, Independence, MO 64052. This elegant nineteenth-century home features overnight accommodations complete with a full breakfast and evening hors d'oeuvres, plus a large two-room suite and two lovely guest rooms with private baths. The home sits on an acre of ground and is tucked away in an all-natural setting filled with trees, gardens, shrubs, and herbs. $$; ☐. (816) 254-0551; www.woodsonguest house.com.

Woodstock Inn Bed and Breakfast. 1212 West Lexington Avenue, Independence, MO 64050. Located near Independence's historic sites, this inn offers rooms with private baths and two elegant suites. You can choose from queen-, double-, and twin-bed accommodations. Breakfast is included and features gourmet waffles. $$; ☐. (816) 833-2233; www.independence-missouri.com.

SIBLEY, MO

It's the weekend and you're lying in bed daydreaming about places you'd rather be. You yawn and stretch, envisioning a drive through the Old South, with its historic homes and genteel manners. An instant later you picture yourself savoring a harvest of apples in New England. But a trip like that may cost more money than you want to spend. Besides, you've only got a day to relax—and this is it.

Not to worry. You could be out right now, picking apples in Missouri. Or taking in lunch at a lovely river town crammed full of historic homes and antiques shops. All this and more are within a forty-five-minute drive east of Kansas City on U.S. 24.

WHERE TO GO

Sibley Orchards. 4121 California Avenue, Sibley, MO 64088. Located 3 blocks from historic Fort Osage, the orchard offers blackberries and peaches in summer, along with sweet corn, tomatoes, and other seasonal vegetables. Peaches and apples are sold here in July. In fall apples, apple cider, and pumpkins are available. Evening hayrides are also offered and take visitors through the orchard. Open daily. (816) 650-5535.

Fort Osage. 105 Osage Street, Sibley, MO 64088. Drive 14 miles northeast of Independence and take U.S. 24 east to Buckner. Turn north at Sibley Street and follow the signs. Fort Osage is 3 blocks north of Osage Honey Farms. Built in 1808 by William Clark of Lewis and Clark fame, this first U.S. outpost in the Louisiana Purchase has lots of frontier buildings to explore, as well as Osage Indian artifacts and exhibits reflecting the area's early history. Closed Monday and Tuesday in summer; open Saturday and Sunday only November through April. Fee. (816) 650–5737.

LEXINGTON, MO

The historic town of Lexington can be reached by meandering along M–224, which takes you through the picturesque towns of Napoleon and Wellington, or you can zip here along U.S. 24.

Once one of the great river ports of this state, river trade made Lexington a fine commercial center and an outfitting point for those heading west. A U.S. land office was established in 1823, followed by a courthouse, a bank, churches, colleges, and more than 120 lovely antebellum and Victorian homes and buildings.

The cannonball embedded in one of the courthouse columns is a relic of the Confederate victory in the 1861 Battle of Lexington. The Anderson House, built in 1853 and located on the battlefield, was used as a field hospital and has been restored to its original elegance. For information: The Lexington Tourism Bureau, P.O. Box 132, Lexington, MO 64067; (660) 259–4711; www.historiclexington.com.

WHERE TO GO

Antebellum Homes. There are many examples of Greek Revival and Victorian homes in Lexington. The Vintage Homes Tour, held in September of odd-numbered years, allows the public a glimpse of the interiors of these elegant historic structures. Lexington has four historic districts on the National Register of Historic Places, and more than 120 antebellum and Victorian homes and buildings are listed on the register. For information on tickets, satellite parking, and shuttle-bus service for the event, contact the Lexington Tourism Bureau, P.O. Box 132, Lexington, MO 64067; (660) 259–4711; www.historiclexington.com.

Battle of Lexington State Historic Site and Anderson House. Northwest edge of town on Thirteenth Street, Lexington, MO 64067. Between September 18 and 20, 1861, Union forces suffered a major defeat at Lexington when the pro-Southern Missouri State Guard, commanded by former Missouri governor Major General Sterling Price, led 12,000 men against the Union outpost at Lexington. The siege ended when the Union troops ran out of food, water, and ammunition. This is one of the few Civil War battlefields that has never been cultivated, and outlines of the trenches are still visible on the self-guided walking tour. The visitor center is open daily and has a fifteen-minute film that brings the *Battle of the Hemp Bales* to life. For information: The Lexington Tourism Bureau, P.O. Box 132, Lexington, MO 64067; (660) 259–4711; www.dnr.state.mo.us/dsp.

Anderson House. On the grounds of the Battle of Lexington Historic Site. Built in 1853 by Colonel Oliver Anderson as a private home, Anderson House has been restored and furnished with antiques of that period. The house was used as a field hospital during the Civil War, changing hands from North to South three times. Battle damage is still visible both inside and outside the home. Guided tours are given on the hour, starting at the visitor center. Open daily. Fee. For information: The Lexington Tourism Bureau, P.O. Box 132, Lexington, MO 64067; (660) 259–4711; www.historiclexington.com.

Lexington Historical Museum. 112 South Thirteenth Street, Lexington, MO 64067. Built originally as the Cumberland Presbyterian Church in 1846, the museum contains an extensive exhibit on the Pony Express, along with Civil War artifacts from the Battle of Lexington, a coal-mining display, and a fine collection of early Lexington photographs. Open daily during summer; other times by appointment only. Fee. For information: The Lexington Tourism Bureau, P.O. Box 132, Lexington, MO 64067; (660) 259–4711; www.historic lexington.com.

Madonna of the Trail. At the corner of Highland Avenue and Cliff Drive, Lexington, MO 64067. This monument is one of twelve placed in every state crossed by the national Old Trails Road, the route of early settlers from Maryland to California. It honors the pioneer women who helped settle the west.

1830s Log House Museum. West end of Main Street, Lexington, MO 64067. This original log house was used as a home and business by several of Lexington's prominent early citizens and was also utilized as a tavern located on the Santa Fe Trail. Its pioneer furnishings provide a lesson in nineteenth-century life. Open Wednesday through Sunday in summer or by appointment. For information: The Lexington Tourism Bureau, P.O. Box 132, Lexington, MO 64067; (660) 259-4711; www.historiclexington.com.

WHERE TO EAT

Brass Eagle Restaurant. 907 Main Street, Lexington, MO 64067. Located in the historic Eagle Building, this refurbished restaurant boasts a varied lunch and dinner menu and turn-of-the-century decor that reflects the Victorian era. Open daily. $-$$; ☐. (660) 259-6668.

    Riley's Irish Pub and Grill. 913 Main Street, Lexington, MO 64067. This downtown gathering spot is located in a restored 1890s building complete with original tile floors, stained-glass window, pressed-tin ceiling, and back bar. Irish specialties such as mulligan stew are offered, along with sandwiches and Southern specialties such as sweet potato fries. Open Wednesday through Saturday. $; (no cards). (660) 259-4771.

    Peddler's Tea Room. 900 Main Street, Lexington, MO 64067. This quaint tearoom is located in one of Lexington's many antiques shops. It offers daily specials and plenty of hearty, country-style food. Try the warm bread pudding or fruit cobblers in season as you dine surrounded by the elegance of fine antiques. Lunch only. Closed Monday. Antiques shop is open Sunday. $; ☐. (660) 259-4534.

WHERE TO STAY

Inn on Main Street. 920½ Main Street, Lexington, MO 64067. Located in the downtown historic district, this 1840s building was renovated in 1998 and offers four king-size suites with private baths. Guests get a complimentary breakfast and a gift basket complete with coffee, champagne, and snacks. $$-$$$; ☐. (660) 259-3600.

    Iris Garden Bed and Breakfast. 1601 Franklin Street, Lexington, MO 64067. It's hard to decide which is more impressive at this 1840 antebellum home—the magnificent English garden complete with lily pond, or the lifelong collection of antiques by owners Iris Shepard and Garry Shulkind. The home's one guest room is the entire second floor and comes with its own private entrance. $$; (no cards). (660) 259-6974; www.irisgarden.micronpcweb.com.

The Lady of Lexington Bed and Breakfast. 905 Franklin Avenue, Lexington, MO 64067. This beautifully restored 1840s home is graced by leather wainscot and original hardwood floors. Three guest rooms are available. A backyard offers a gazebo, Jacuzzi, and fishpond. A deluxe breakfast is served; sherry, fruit, and seasonal flowers are placed in your room upon arrival. $$; ☐. (877) 894-6914 or (660) 259-4900.

The Parsonage. 1603 South Street, Lexington, MO 64067. This large, Queen Anne–style home was built in 1894 and served as the Methodist Church parsonage for many years. It features three nicely appointed guest rooms, a full breakfast, a hot tub, and a cafe area where cappuccino, tea, and wine are served. $$; (no cards). (660) 259-2344.

WAVERLY, MO

Missouri's Lafayette County contains numerous farms and orchards that lie along the site of the historic Santa Fe Trail. In spring, summer, and fall, roadside stands near the intersections of U.S. 24 and 65 sell delicious handpicked produce to passersby.

East of Lexington on U.S. 24 is Waverly, one of the Midwest's best fruit-producing areas, harvesting half the apple crop in Missouri. The town celebrates its fortune by holding the annual Apple Jubilee in mid-September. The jubilee features apple judging, entertainment, music, contests, and plenty of family fun. For information call (660) 493-2902.

The Santa Fe Trail Growers Association promotes tourism in this area and can provide you with a brochure that lists sixteen grower members that sell everything from "U-pick" and prepicked blackberries and asparagus to top-quality bedding and vegetable plants. If you would like an area map and a directory of the association members, or the association newsletter, send a self-addressed, stamped envelope to Santa Fe Trail Growers Association, Route 1, Box 131P, Waverly, MO 64096, or call (660) 252-0730.

WHERE TO GO

Peters Market. Located 1.5 miles east of Waverly on U.S. 65, Waverly, MO 64096. Homegrown yellow and white peaches, as well as nectarines, abound here in season, along with delicious fruit butters and locally grown farm produce. Fall brings crops of Red and Golden Delicious apples, together with the popular Braeburn, Fuji, Granny Smith, and Staymen Winesap varieties. Peters holds a flea market in October that offers utility-grade apples at ridiculously low prices. During fall harvest season, free tours of the market and orchard are offered to organized groups by appointment only. (660) 493-2368.

Schreiman Orchards. Two miles west of Waverly on U.S. 24, Waverly, MO 64096. This roadside market sells peaches in summer and apples in fall, along with homemade apple butter, honey, jams, jellies, apple-wood chips, cookbooks, and Amish-made foods. Open daily from mid-June through mid-November. (660) 493-2477 (pager).

Woelk's Blackberries. Two miles west of Lexington on the south side of M–24, Lexington, MO 64067. Blackberries are just one of the crops grown on these 116 acres. Apples have been grown on this land since before the Civil War, and Chris and Candy Woelk have added peppers, asparagus, and gooseberries. You can pick them yourself or stop by for those already picked. Call ahead to see which crops are available. (660) 259-2160.

East Day Trip 2

Conception Junction

Savannah

Jamesport

MISSOURI

Smithville Kearney Lawson Watkins Mill

Liberty Sibley

KANSAS
CITY Independence Buckner

Blue
Springs

Lone
Jack

Louisburg

Marais des Cygnes
Wildlife Area

Pleasanton

Ft. Scott National
Historic Site and
Museum

Frontenas

Pittsburg

Carthage

Savannah

Excelsior
Springs Richmond

Lexington Waverly

Concordia

Kingsville Warrensburg

Sedalia

Jamesport

Missouri River

Arrow Rock

Boonville

California

Versailles

Laurie

The Lake of the Ozarks

Camdenton

Fayette

New
Franklin Rocheport Columbia

Fulton

Jefferson City

Eldon

Lakeland
Lake Ozark
Osage Beach Lake of the Ozarks
State Park

Hermann

0   10   20   30 miles

EAST

DAY TRIP 2

The KATY Trail
Corridor and
Boonslick Country
Arrow Rock, MO · Boonville, MO
New Franklin, MO · Fayette, MO
Rocheport, MO · Columbia, MO
Jefferson City, MO · California, MO
Sedalia, MO

Worth More Time: **Fulton, MO · Hermann, MO**

THE KATY TRAIL CORRIDOR AND BOONSLICK COUNTRY

This trip encompasses cities and hamlets along the KATY Trail and Boonslick Country. You can begin your tour at Arrow Rock and make your way east on I–70, visiting Missouri River towns along the way. You can overnight in any one of a number of places or head home the same way you came. If time permits, travel south to Jefferson City along scenic M–179 instead of taking a quick trip on U.S. 63. From Jefferson City you can make the loop back to Kansas City on U.S. 50. Fulton and Hermann are the easternmost points on the trail. Although they lie closer to St. Louis than to Kansas City, they are included here because they are part of the KATY Central Consortium, a group of six communities that have banded together to promote the KATY Trail, one of several arms of the "Rails-to-Trails" program that is part of the National Trails System Act.

It's flat, free, and fun, and it snakes across the state for more than 200 miles from Sedalia to St. Charles. If you've never traveled the KATY Trail, you're missing some of the prettiest country in Missouri. The KATY Trail route can be traveled on foot or on wheels, and it parallels the Missouri River, with the water on one side and towering bluffs on the other. All along the way you can see glimpses of dense forests, wetlands, valleys, and rolling farm fields. In spring there are flowering dogwood and redbud trees. Fall brings crimson colors of maple and sumac, along with an abundance of wildlife that includes woodpeckers, red-tailed hawks, waterfowl, deer, and other creatures.

Trail users can meander through slices of rural history, some of which predates the Civil War. The section of trail between Boonville and St. Charles has been designated an official segment of the Lewis and Clark National Historic Trail, and the entire trail is part of the American Discovery Trail.

The KATY Trail is a common denominator that has revitalized many small towns that once flourished along the railroad. The Missouri-Kansas (MKT) Railroad, known as the KATY, ceased operation in 1986 and donated its right-of-way for the KATY Trail State Park. The Department of Natural Resources acquired the KATY Trail through the National Trails System Act—the "Rails-to-Trails" program that has helped turn inactive railroad corridors into recreational opportunities. Bed-and-breakfasts, restaurants, shops, and other services have prospered as a result.

Although the KATY Trail State Park has been designed specifically for bicyclists and hikers, campers or people on tight budgets may find themselves out in the cold, so to speak, for the small towns offer little in the way of inexpensive lodging as of this printing. One exception is the Katy Roundhouse in New Franklin, which provides camping, public rest rooms, a quick-stop shop, showers, and RV hookups. Larger cities, such as Columbia, Jefferson City, and Sedalia, offer inexpensive motels if that option suits your pocketbook better.

Transportation to and from lodging isn't a widespread trailside amenity yet. Some of the bed-and-breakfast establishments are very close to the trail. Morgan Street Repose in Boonville, for example, is only a block away. To ensure that you get where you want to go, it's best to call ahead and find out whether you'll have to hike or bike to your overnight lodging, or if you can arrange for a courtesy car to pick you up when you get there.

Although the trail is mostly flat, with a grade that seldom reaches more than 5 percent, it is very possible to overextend yourself, especially on a hot day. If you aren't an experienced hiker or biker, it might be best to drive to one of the trailside jumping-off points and pick up your bike there. Almost all the KATY Trail towns have bike-rental shops, and most offer a selection of mountain bikes, tandems, and toddler trailers for a modest hourly cost.

Six communities—Arrow Rock, Rocheport, Columbia, Jefferson City, Callaway County, and Hermann—have banded together to form the KATY Central Consortium, the purpose of which is to provide visitor information about the trail. Call (888) 441-2023 for information about these six communities. Dial (800) 652-0987 to talk with a person.

This book primarily features those communities that are an easy day trip from Kansas City, allowing you to make the journey in a couple of hours or so, see the sights, have dinner, and return home. If you wish, you can turn your visit into a lengthier sojourn and overnight at any one of a number of places along the way.

For more in-depth information on the KATY Trail State Park, get a copy of *The KATY Trail Guidebook* by Brett Dufur. An excellent resource, this book covers most of what you need to know when traveling the trail. Call (800) 576-7322 for a copy, or check your local bookstore. (Brett's Web site is www.pebblepublishing.com.) The Department of Natural Resources (800-334-6946) has brochures and information. Persons with hearing impairments can call (800) 379-2419 with a TDD. ☕.

BOONSLICK COUNTRY

Central Missouri's Boonslick Country was already beginning to enjoy a comeback long before the KATY Trail took shape. Happenstance would have it that the KATY Trail also passes near or through the Boonslick towns of Arrow Rock, Boonville, New Franklin, Fayette, Glasgow, Rocheport, Pilot Grove, Pleasant Green, and other communities. Something noteworthy to keep in mind is that many of the gorgeous old homes you'll find along the KATY Trail corridor and in and around Boonslick Country are listed on the National Register of Historic Places and offer bed-and-breakfast accommodations, as well as full country or continental breakfasts with all the trimmings.

As long as you're traveling the KATY Trail, you might as well visit the Boonslick region, which takes its name from a salt lick in southwestern Howard County that was worked, about 1805, by Nathan and Daniel Morgan Boone, sons of the famed pioneer and scout Daniel Boone. (The actual location of the salt springs is now part of Boone's Lick State Historic Site, located 8 miles northwest of New Franklin near Boonesboro.)

According to research provided by the Boonville Chamber of Commerce, Daniel Boone came to Missouri in 1779 at the request of the Spanish lieutenant governor. Boone was promised a grant of 1,000 arpents (an Old French unit of land equal to about an acre). He was to function as the commandant of the Femme Osage District as judge, jury, and sheriff. He died in Missouri in 1820 at the home of his son Nathan Boone near Defiance, Missouri.

The magic of the Boone name, plus the salt licks and fertile soil, drew early settlers to the area. There has been much speculation since that time as to why the *e* was left out of *Boonslick*. It may have been because then, as now, many people placed little importance on accurate spelling.

Boonslick Country is chock-full of history, for many of its towns brought politicians, land speculators, and entrepreneurs who later gained fame, such as Daniel Boone, painter George Caleb Bingham, and frontier scout Kit Carson.

If you have the time and the inclination, you might want to take a guided tour of Boonslick Country. For a self-guided tour brochure of the area, contact the Friends of Historic Boonville, P.O. Box 1776, 614 East Morgan, Boonville, MO 65233; (660) 882-7977; www. mid-mo-net/friendsart. For more information: Boonville Chamber of Commerce, Katy Depot, Spring and First Streets, Boonville, MO 65233; (660) 882-2721; www.mo-river.net.

ARROW ROCK, MO

As the state's first historic site, the Missouri River town of Arrow Rock is the western gateway to Boonslick Country. Located east of Kansas City, Arrow Rock can be reached by taking I-70 to M-41 North or traveling U.S. 24 East to M-41 South. Founded in 1829, it was an important Santa Fe Trail rendezvous point and home of several distinguished Missourians, including three Missouri governors, painter George Caleb Bingham, and Dr. John Sappington, who pioneered the use of quinine for treating malaria.

On their epic expedition upriver in 1804, Lewis and Clark made note of the area, and later William Clark termed it a "handsome spot for a town." Indeed, Arrow Rock was then, as it is now, a beautiful town, and it has somehow retained its peaceful country character and managed to keep the look and feel of nineteenth-century America.

Once a bustling frontier village with a population of 1,000, it has only seventy residents today. Each October during the annual Arrow Rock Craft Festival, that number increases as visitors come to enjoy historically authentic crafts interpreted in a period setting. Objects from the first half of the nineteenth century are explained by interpreters who demonstrate spinning, chair caning, corn grinding, rug braiding, and other old-time crafts; some of the products are offered for sale. The town hosts a variety of other events, including the Traditional Folk Music Festival in September and an antiques show in May.

If you're planning to overnight in Arrow Rock, be sure to make your reservations in advance at any one of a number of accommodations. Arrow Rock State Historic Site also offers several picnic places and a camping area on the limestone bluffs overlooking the Missouri River. Basic campsites and improved sites on the campground are available on a first-come, first-served basis through the month of October for a nominal fee. *Note:* Though the campsite is open year-round, there is no water from November to the end of March. A discount is available to seniors. Contact Arrow Rock State Historic Site, P.O. Box 1, Arrow Rock, MO 65320; (660) 837-3330.

For information on accommodations, restaurants, shops, tours, and events: Arrow Rock Merchants Association, P.O. Box 147-B, Arrow Rock, MO 65320 (660-837-3305); the Historic Arrow Rock Council, P.O. Box 23, Arrow Rock, MO 65320 (660-837-3335); and the Friends of Arrow Rock Walking Tours, P.O. Box 124, Arrow Rock, MO 65320 (660-837-3231); www.arrowrock.org.

WHERE TO GO

Arrow Rock Lyceum Theatre. Arrow Rock, MO 65320. The Lyceum is Missouri's oldest professional regional theater and the only professional theater serving rural Missouri. Popular, professional summer theater is presented here in rotating repertory from

May through August and into parts of October. Fee. (660) 837–3311; www.lyceumtheatre.org.

The Friends of Arrow Rock Information Center and the State Historic Site Interpretive Center. P.O. Box 124, Arrow Rock, MO 65320. Guides conduct tours of the village and historic structures that take in the George Caleb Bingham Home (1837), the Saline County Courthouse (1839), the Sites Home (1875) and Gun Shop (1844), and the Print Shop (1868). Fee. Tours are conducted daily Memorial Day through Labor Day and weekends in spring and fall. The interpretive center has fascinating displays that trace the westward expansion to the Boonslick region and its frontier life along the Santa Fe Trail. Tours: (660) 837–3231; hours: (660) 837–3330; www.arrowrock.org.

River Hills Llamas. Eleven miles south of Arrow Rock (call for directions), Arrow Rock, MO 65320. One of the world's oldest domesticated animals, llamas are bred and raised here as show-quality animals, pack llamas, sheep guardians, and pets. This is also the home of Kong, sire of one of the largest herds in the United States. If you're into browsing for llamas, this is the place to come. Call ahead for hours and fee information: (660) 846–2255; www.riverhillsllamas.com.

WHERE TO SHOP

Many Arrow Rock merchants and businesses operate seasonally, with hours that are frequently subject to change. It's always best to call ahead to find out what will be open the day you plan to visit.

Antiques Emporium. 6 Public Square, Arrow Rock, MO 65320. This shop has a diverse collection of eighteenth- and nineteenth-century furniture, along with china, silver, and glassware. (660) 837–3777.

Arrow Rock Antiques. Main Street, Arrow Rock, MO 65320. This shop features period furniture. Open May through September. (660) 837–3333.

Arrow Rock Country Store. Main Street (on the boardwalk), Arrow Rock, MO 65320. At this shop you can choose from a variety of gifts and collectibles, including Hummels, music boxes, crystal, unusual cards, educational toys and games, and more. Open year-round. (660) 837–3221.

Arrow Rock Craft Shop. Main Street (in the Masonic Lodge Building), Arrow Rock, MO 65320. Wood and fabric artwork, clothing, quilts, china, jewelry, and toys are offered here, plus breads, plants, confections, and seasonal produce. Open daily May through October and weekends only December and April. (660) 837-3384.

The House of Mary B. Main Street, Arrow Rock, MO 65320. Take a step back in time and browse through an assortment of quality handcrafted items of yesteryear, including baskets, brooms, dolls, imported Christmas ornaments, and more. (660) 837-3305.

WHERE TO EAT

Some Arrow Rock restaurants operate seasonally, with hours that are frequently subject to change. It's always best to call ahead to find out what will be open the day you plan to visit.

Evergreen Restaurant. M-41 and Main Street, Arrow Rock, MO 65320. Gracious dining with a European touch is offered in a restored 1840s home. A full bar and a selection of fine wines are featured. Catering and special-order baking for private parties are available. $$-$$$; (no cards). (660) 837-3251.

Grandma D's Cafe. One block south of Main Street, Arrow Rock, MO 65320. Enjoy dining surrounded by antiques and unique gifts. Sandwiches, salads, homemade soups, pies, and sweet breads are served daily, year-round. $; ☐. (660) 837-3335.

The Old Arrow Rock Tavern. Main Street, Arrow Rock, MO 65320. Built in 1834, the tavern continues to serve the public as it served those who drove their wagons over the Santa Fe Trail. The fare includes catfish, country ham, and fried chicken. Private parties and groups are accommodated. Call for reservations. $$; ☐. (660) 837-3200.

Old Schoolhouse Cafe. Main Street, Arrow Rock, MO 65320. The cafe specializes in homemade breakfast and lunch specialties. Small-group luncheons or dinners can be made by appointment. Open Monday through Saturday, Memorial Day through Labor Day; Saturday through October. $; (no cards). (660) 837-3331.

Ye Olde Ice Cream Shoppe. On the boardwalk, Arrow Rock, MO 65320. This place offers a variety of ice cream specialties, soups, sandwiches, and salads. $; (no cards). (660) 837-3364.

WHERE TO STAY

Some Arrow Rock bed-and-breakfasts operate seasonally, with hours that are subject to change. Call ahead for information and reservations.

Borgman's Bed & Breakfast. 706 Van Buren, Arrow Rock, MO 65320. This century-old home offers four rooms and three shared baths. A family-style breakfast is served in the kitchen and features the owner's home-baked items. Open year-round. $$; (no cards). (660) 837-3350.

DownOver Bed & Breakfast Inn. Main Street, Arrow Rock, MO 65320. This unusual establishment features six distinctively decorated guest rooms with private baths and a fully equipped guest cottage. A full breakfast is served daily. There are lounge areas for games and a front porch for relaxing. A bicycle built for two is available. $$–$$$; ☐. (660) 837-3268.

Kusgen Farms Bed & Breakfast. 6947 Lodge Lane (8 miles south of Arrow Rock), Blackwater, MO 65322. Located on a wooded bluff overlooking a fifteen-acre private lake, this newer home features spacious rooms; a quiet, comfortable atmosphere; and plenty of space for fishing and hiking. $$; (no cards). (660) 846-3061.

Miss Nelle's Bed & Breakfast. 633 Main Street, Arrow Rock, MO 65320. Located within walking distance of the shops, this restored 1853 home offers two comfortable guest rooms, one with a fireplace. A continental breakfast is served in the elegantly appointed dining room. $$; (no cards). (660) 837-3280 or (800) 795-2797.

Westward Trails Inn Bed & Breakfast. One block south of Main Street, Arrow Rock, MO 65320. This home has a private suite-size room that sleeps up to five and is equipped with an outside spa and patio, Franklin stove, and private bath and entrance. A full country breakfast is served. Open year-round. $$; ☐. (660) 837-3335.

BOONVILLE, MO

To reach the oldest surviving Missouri River town in the region, travel on M-41 south from Arrow Rock to I-70 and east to Boonville. The central gateway to Boonslick Country, Boonville was settled in 1810. The town still exhibits the cultural mix of original

Southern settlers, along with the influx of German immigrants who settled here in the mid-nineteenth century. Boonville's many restored historic buildings, restaurants, and bed-and-breakfasts make this a place worth visiting.

Boonville is also the county seat of Cooper County, the home of Kemper Military School and College, and the site of the first Civil War battle fought in Missouri (June 1861). South of Boonville are three interesting old plantation homes, including Ravenswood, Crestmead, and Pleasant Green Plantation House, that are open for tours.

Boonville was a town that made the transition from being a major river port to a booming railroad town. Many remnants of this era can still be seen in Boonville, including the restored MKT depot. You can pick up the KATY Trail State Park from Boonville eastward along the route of the Missouri River.

Named for Daniel Boone (as was the Boonslick region), Boonville prospered during the late 1820s. German immigrants arrived ten years later, and the river trade and Santa Fe Trail activity were the economic forces that sustained the town. The advent of railroads and the resulting confusion from the Civil War engagements fought in and around Boonville slowed the city's growth. Boonville today remains an important local center for transportation, tourism, and agribusiness.

The ongoing downtown revitalization program is strengthening the role of the central core as a business, cultural, and political center. Many of the historic buildings downtown are on the National Register of Historic Places. Indeed, Boonville contains seven National Register Districts and nineteen individual listed sites.

Boonslick Tours/Big Canoe Records offers excursions that relate to the culture, folklore, and history of central Missouri. Owned and operated by Bob Dyer, a local historian and folklorist as well as poet and musician-songwriter, Boonslick Tours offers an in-depth look at the region's history. In addition, Dyer has several music recordings that provide a satisfying glimpse into Missouri's rich and memorable past. Two Civil War recordings, "Johnny Whistletrigger" and "Rebel in the Woods," done in tandem with noted folk duo Cathy Barton and Dave Para, are masterpieces of Missouri lore. For information on tours, performances, and recordings, call (660) 882-3353.

For a self-guided tour brochure of the area, contact the Friends of Historic Boonville, P.O. Box 1776, 614 East Morgan, Boonville, MO

65233; (660) 882-7977; www.mid-mo-net/friendsart. For more information: Boonville Chamber of Commerce, Katy Depot, Spring and First Streets, Boonville, MO 65233; (660) 882-2721; www.mo-river.net.

WHERE TO GO

Many of the museums, homes, and attractions in Boonville have hours that are subject to change. The phone numbers are listed for your convenience, and it's best to call ahead to find out if these places are open on the day you plan to visit. You can also call the Boonville Chamber of Commerce for information: (660) 882-2721.

Cooper County Jail Museum, Jailers Residence, and Hanging Barn. Friends of Historic Boonville, P.O. Box 1776, 614 East Morgan, Boonville, MO 65233. Built in 1848, this venerable structure was the oldest continuously used county jail in Missouri until its closing in 1978. The last public hanging took place here in 1930, when a man named Lawrence Mabry was executed for a robbery and murder in Pettis County. This hanging was a factor in the elimination of capital punishment in Cooper County. The most famous prisoner held here was Frank James, brother of Jesse James. He was brought here on April 24, 1884, to answer a warrant for his arrest for a train robbery (what else?) that took place in 1876. Sympathetic citizens of Boonville raised his bond in a matter of hours, and the case was later dismissed for lack of evidence. Open by appointment. Fee. (660) 882-7977.

Crestmead. 7400 Highway A, Pilot Grove, MO 65276. Located 6 miles south of Pilot Grove, the Italianate mansion was built in 1859 by John Taylor, who operated his farm with slave labor until the end of the Civil War. The observatory at the top of the house was used to watch slaves working in the fields. The three-story home has a wide central hall that runs the length of the structure and features a massive octagonal newel post and sixteen rooms with 8-foot windows and period furnishings. Outbuildings include an ice and carriage house, restored slave quarters, and an old barn. The home has been owned since 1903 by the Betteridge family, who renamed it Crestmead, meaning "high meadow." The home is open to tour by appointment. Fee. (660) 834-4140.

Katy Depot and KATY Trailhead. Spring and First Streets, Boonville, MO 65233. The restored 1912 depot houses the KATY Trail offices and the Boonville Chamber of Commerce. (660) 882–8196.

KATY Trail State Park. (Cooper County trailheads in Boonville, Clifton City, and Pilot Grove.) This trail heads east from Boonville along some of the prettiest country in Missouri. For information and brochures about the KATY Trail from Boonville to Jefferson City, call the Department of Natural Resources. Free. (800) 334–6946.

Kemper Military School. 701 Third Street, Boonville, MO 65233. In 1844 Frederick T. Kemper opened his private school, which remains the oldest continuously operating military school in the state. The two-year college is also open as an educational facility for area residents. (800) 530–5600.

Pleasant Green. 7045 M-135, Route 1, Box 81, Pilot Grove, MO 65276. Located 9 miles south of Pilot Grove, this Federal-style brick mansion is built of handmade bricks and native stone. It was begun as a one-room house, with additions added from the 1830s through the 1870s, and was once a plantation of 2,500 acres. Settled by Winston and Polly Walker of Virginia in 1818, it survived Civil War raids and years of neglect. Florence Chestnutt, a sixth-generation descendant, is in the process of restoring the old homestead today. Many original furnishings are part of the home, and the facade has been returned to its 1877 appearance. The home is listed on the National Register of Historic Places and includes outbuildings that feature an old hexagonal barn, a curing shed, and restored slave quarters. The 1870 Pleasant Green Post Office building was moved here to serve as a mini gallery for local artists. The home is open to tour by appointment. Guides in antebellum dress serve coffee or tea in the dining room by advance request. Fee. (660) 834–3945.

Ravenswood Farm. Twelve miles south of Boonville on M-5, Bunceton, MO 65237. This impressive private home was built in 1880 by Captain Charles E. Leonard and his wife, Nadine. Five generations later it is still owned by Leonard descendants. Few changes have been made in the house: The furnishings and decorations are much the same as when it was built. Group and individual tours of the home are offered by appointment from March through November. Fee. (660) 882–7143 or (660) 882–2721.

Roslyn Heights. 821 Main Street, Boonville, MO 65233. This 1895 Queen Anne home features Romanesque Revival structures, towers, turrets, gable dormers, and a porte-cochere with Moorish decorative elements. Paneled front doors open from the front porch into a reception hall, and the entrance hall's original tile floor is intact. The house is graced by a geometrically designed stairway with motifs that illustrate the use of machinery during the Industrial Revolution. The parlor features a hand-painted ceiling and mahogany fireplace mantel. The other rooms in the home also have ornate designs and elegant antique furnishings. Tours are conducted on Sunday afternoon from April 1 through December 15. The home is open to the public for meetings, luncheons, receptions, and special events. Fee. (660) 882-5320.

Thespian Hall. Main and Vine Streets, Boonville, MO 65233. This restored Greek Revival opera house, built in 1857, is owned and managed by the Friends of Historic Boonville. It is the oldest theater still in use west of the Alleghenies and is on the National Register of Historic Places. If you can, time your visit to coincide with the music festivals held here. The Missouri River Festival of the Arts in August brings in fine performers, ranging from symphony orchestras and ballet companies to jazz, pop, and theater groups. The Big Muddy Folk Festival in April plays host to local and national musicians. Tours are available by appointment. For information: Friends of Historic Boonville, P.O. Box 1776, Boonville, MO 65233; (660) 882-7977.

WHERE TO SHOP

Boonville has many shops that offer a variety of antiques, crafts, and collectibles. For a complete listing contact the Tourist Information Center, Boonville Area Chamber of Commerce, Katy Depot, Spring and First Streets, Boonville, MO 65233; (660) 882-2721; www.mo-river.net.

WHERE TO EAT

The Settlers Inn. I-70 and M-135 (Arrow Rock and Pilot Grove exit), Boonville, MO 65233. For something very different, come and dine in this simple log home, where made-from-scratch food is cooked up in a small but mighty kitchen. The excellent family-style meals include main dishes such as beef and buffalo T-bone steaks, pheasant, country ham, game hen, buffalo brisket, smoked pork chops, and more. All dinners include salad, potato, vegetables, home-baked desserts, bread, and beverage. The cost is so reasonable you won't believe it.

Because the restaurant is small, you will need reservations. Call well in advance, especially if you have a large party. To expedite mealtime, the restaurant requests that you order your meat selection when you make your reservation. Seatings are at 5:30 and 7:30 P.M. on Friday and Saturday evenings. Special group bookings are available during the week. Closed Sunday. $$; ☐. (660) 882-3125.

The Stein House. 421 Main Street, Boonville, MO 65233. This friendly Boonville gathering place offers a variety of sandwiches, dinner plates, and beverages. Closed Sunday. $-$$; ☐. (660) 882-6832.

WHERE TO STAY

Lady Goldenrod Inn Bed and Breakfast. 629 East Spring Street, Boonville, MO 65233. On the National Register of Historic Places, this Queen Anne–style residence was constructed a century ago. Antiques grace the hallways and living areas. The upstairs bathroom is shared by hosts and guests and has a stained-wood floor and original claw-foot bathtub. A full breakfast is served. $; (no cards). (660) 882-5764.

Little Four Oaks Farm Bed and Breakfast. Four miles south of I-70 (call for directions), Boonville, MO 65233. This nineteenth-century farmhouse has been remodeled to retain its architectural integrity. It has a panoramic view of the countryside, though room space is limited. A continental breakfast is served daily, with a full country breakfast on weekends. Bring your horse for the weekend; they have boarding services. Call for hours and reservations. $$; ☐. (660) 882-8048; www.littlefouroaksfarm.com.

Morgan Street Repose. 611 East Morgan Street, Boonville, MO 65233. Built in 1869, this 5,000-square-foot, elegantly restored Boonville home lies only a block from the KATY Trail. It offers three interconnecting suites, with private baths, that can accommodate up to twelve people, making it convenient for biking or hiking groups. The home also makes a nice romantic getaway, featuring a private suite with a parlor, a sitting porch, and a garden view. A full gourmet breakfast is served with all the trimmings, including herbs and flowers. Call for hours and information. $$; (no cards). (800) 248-5061.

NEW FRANKLIN, MO

Campgrounds are a rarity along the KATY Trail. However, for tired travelers on tight budgets, New Franklin, 3 miles north of Boonville on M-5, provides an alternative to more expensive lodging. Campgrounds, public rest rooms, showers, and RV hookups are located adjacent to Trail Mile Marker 189 at the Katy Roundhouse. Once you bed down for the night, it's "happy trails" to you as you catch some Zs on famous ground "where the four trails meet": the KATY, the Santa Fe, the Boonslick, and the Lewis and Clark. For information: New Franklin City Hall, 130 East Broadway, New Franklin, MO 65274; (660) 848-2288; www.newfranklin.mo.org.

WHERE TO GO

Boone's Lick State Historic Site. Eight miles northwest of New Franklin, near Boonesboro. Take M-87 West from the northern approach to the Missouri River Bridge on M-5 to M-187, about 1 mile north of Boonesboro. Continue 2 miles west to the site of the salt springs, worked by the sons of Daniel Boone beginning around 1805. The state of Missouri has a kiosk here with information about the Boonslick region and the salt springs. A trail with informational signs winds through the woods by the remnants of the saltworks, and there's a shelter house with picnic tables, as well as public rest rooms. Free. (660) 848-2288.

WHERE TO EAT AND STAY

Katy Roundhouse. 1893 Katy Drive (KATY Trail Mile Marker 189), New Franklin, MO 65274. Located on the grounds of a century-old restored train depot, the Katy Roundhouse stands on the site of the former MKT Railroad switching yard. The area offers a full-service campground with spacious, secluded campsites for tent camping, including picnic tables, fire rings, and bike racks. In addition, there are full RV hookups, modern shower facilities, public rest rooms, a mini grocery, and tents for rent. Home-cooked dinners are served on Friday and Saturday evenings by reservation only. The steaks are fresh cut and broiled outdoors over an open grill. There are also a beer and wine garden and occasional live music for a small cover charge. $-$$; □. (660) 848-2232 or (800) 477-6605; www.katyroundhouse.com.

Rivercene Bed and Breakfast. 127 Country Road 463, New Franklin, MO 65274. Listed on the National Register of Historic Places, this fifteen-room mansion was built by Captain Joseph Kinney. The riverboat baron began construction in 1864 on the floodplain, leading locals to call the structure Kinney's Folly. Kinney was undaunted. Finding the highest flood point, he built the house 1 foot higher. Of course, he hadn't counted on the Great Flood of 1993. Jody and Ron Lenz purchased the home in 1992, only to be confronted by 4 feet of water in their living room during the flood, when Rivercene could be reached only by boat.

The couple has fully restored the mansion, incorporating the splendor of Kinney's original architectural masterpiece. The home has Italian marble for the nine fireplaces, black walnut for the front doors, and a hand-carved mahogany staircase. (A few years after Kinney completed Rivercene, the architectural plan was duplicated for the present Governor's Mansion in Jefferson City.)

Rivercene offers tours of the home, as well as overnight stays with queen-size beds and private baths, or you can take your choice of a two-room suite or a room with a whirlpool. A delicious breakfast is served in the large dining room, or you can have breakfast in bed. Group and individual tours are offered by appointment (fee). Rivercene can be rented for business retreats or meetings or for family reunions. Call for hours and reservations. $$-$$$; □. (800) 531-0862; www.rivercene.com.

FAYETTE, MO

WHERE TO GO

The Ashby-Hodge Gallery of American Art. On the Campus of Central Methodist College, 411 Central Methodist Square, Fayette,

MO 65248. Opened in 1993, the Ashby-Hodge Gallery holds a special collection of oil paintings, lithographs, watercolors, bronzes, graphite drawings, and acrylics representing the work of American regional artists. The gallery holds rare pieces by Swedish-born artist Birger Sandzén, lithographs by Jackson Lee Nesbitt, an ink and wash by Thomas Hart Benton, a rare egg tempera on panel by Charles Banks Wilson, and many other interesting pieces. This little gem of a place also features special exhibits throughout the year, often bringing in the artists themselves to greet guests at gallery openings. Call for a schedule of events. Open Tuesday, Wednesday, and Thursday from 1:30 to 4:30 P.M. Free. (660) 248-3391, ext. 563 or 300; www.cmc.edu.

ROCHEPORT, MO

WHERE TO GO

Rocheport is one of those tucked-away towns that is filled with history and memorabilia. From New Franklin you can head east on U.S. 40 to Route BB or head east from Boonville on I-70 to the Rocheport exit. The town is a perfect romantic getaway close to home, yet it also offers KATY Trail access for family outings. Antiques shops, an art gallery, cafes, a winery and bistro with a panoramic river-bluff view, and superior bed-and-breakfasts are part of its charm. Each summer the town's population swells from 225 persons to as many as 30,000 visitors, many of whom are KATY Trail travelers.

Located on the Missouri River, Rocheport was founded in 1825 and grew rapidly as steamboat transportation brought business to town. In 1849 fifty-seven steamboats made 500 landings at Rocheport. Nine years earlier the Whig Party held its convention in Rocheport and thousands of delegates arrived by carriage, wagon, steamboat, and horseback to support William Henry Harrison's presidential campaign.

Rocheport has survived disasters, including the Civil War and the Great Flood of 1993, when the 243-foot-long MKT Railroad tunnel, built in 1893, was filled with 4 feet of water.

Rocheport is on the National Register of Historic Places, and many of its residents live and work in restored nineteenth-century homes and buildings. The special blend of history and charm makes this town stand out as a great place to unwind from today's frenetic pace.

As the eastern gateway to Boonslick Country, Rocheport also affords one of the most beautiful views along the KATY Trail, parts of which wind along the river under the spectacular Moniteau Bluffs.

For more information on Rocheport, write the Rocheport Area Merchants Association, P.O. Box 44, Rocheport, MO 65279; (593) 698-2063 or (573) 698-3210; www.rocheport.com.

WHERE TO GO

Friends of Rocheport Museum. Moniteau Street, Rocheport, MO 65279. Museum displays include historic photographs and memorabilia of Rocheport as a nineteenth-century river and railroad town. Open Saturday and Sunday from 1:00 to 4:00 P.M. (573) 698-3701.

Trailside Cafe and Bike Rental. Rocheport, MO 65279. From KATY Trail Mile Marker 179, you can literally pedal into the parking lot of the Trailside Cafe. This nice little operation began as a small sandwich shop and eventually expanded into a dining room with an adjacent bike shop. The cafe is noted for its excellent pork tenderloin sandwiches that will feed two, plus fresh homemade baked goods. It also sells Gatorade for thirsty trail users, as well as spring waters and trail mix. New owners Nina Turner and Kathy Cobel have added fresh fruit to the trail offerings and grilled portabello mushroom sandwiches to the menu. They sell and rent bikes to fit everybody from a two-year-old to an adult. Child carts, tandems, and mountain bikes can be rented by the hour or by the day. You can also bring in your bike for tune-up or repair service. Closed in cold weather. Call for hours. $; ☐. (573) 698-2702.

WHERE TO SHOP

Rocheport is filled with plenty of places to browse and shop. Here are two of the more interesting places:

Flavors of the Heartland/Rocheport Gallery. 204 Second Street, P.O. Box 136, Rocheport, MO 65279. This unique store sells a variety of Missouri-made specialty and gourmet food products. You can choose from herb and fruit-infused vinegars, delicious apple and pumpkin butter, mustards, barbecue sauces, salsas, Boone County hams, and much more. The store features custom gift baskets filled with goodies like Caramel Satin and Chocolate Satin Dessert Sauces (ooooh!) and Lemon Satin Dessert Sauce (yum-yum!). The free samples are tempting. When you're through slurping and shopping, you can visit the adjoining gallery and ogle the original art. An artist reception is held the first day of each exhibit, and exhibits change every four to six weeks. (800) 269-3210 or (573) 698-2063.

Missouri River City Antique Shops. South of I-70 at Rocheport, on County Road BB, Rocheport, MO 65279. Antiques, furniture, and collectibles are sold at this complex of antiques shops. (573) 698-2116.

WHERE TO EAT

Abigail's. 100 West First (on the KATY Trail, adjacent to the Trail-side Cafe), Rocheport, MO 65279. Located at the KATY Trailhead in Rocheport, this restaurant offers wholesome fare in a restored historic church. The menu changes daily. There is a patio for outdoor dining and private parties. Hours vary. $-$$; □. (573) 698-3000.

Le Bourgeois Vineyards and Winery. P.O. Box 118 (1 mile north of I-70 on Route BB), Rocheport, MO 65279. This unique restaurant and winery makes a great place to unwind and enjoy a spectacular sunset from atop a river bluff. The land here offers rich soil and a microclimate that is ideal for grape production. Les Bourgeois produces red, white, and blush table wines from French hybrid grapes and native cultivars. The restaurant offers an outdoor wine garden and indoor dining featuring a variety of nicely prepared fish, chicken, and steak dinners, plus great desserts. $$-$$$; □. (573) 698-2300.

Trailside Cafe and Bike Rental. Rocheport, MO 65279 (see listing under Where to Go).

WHERE TO STAY

The small town of Rocheport offers some of the finest bed-and-breakfast accommodations to be found anywhere in Missouri, including the following:

Katy O'Neil Bed and Breakfast. 101 Lewis Street, Rocheport, MO 65279. This modest Victorian home was built in 1880 and is on the National Register of Historic Places. Katy O'Neil offers four rooms, including a converted railroad boxcar in the backyard that sleeps up to five and has a private bath, refrigerator, and cable television. The upstairs of the main house offers a family suite with a private bath, queen-size bed, and futon. There is a smaller bedroom downstairs with one double bed. Above the garage is a large rustic room with two beds and a sleeper sofa, which serves as a bunkhouse for cost-conscious travelers. $; □. (573) 690–2453.

Schoolhouse Bed and Breakfast. Third and Clark Streets, Rocheport, MO 65279. Touted as one of the country's top ten romantic inns, the Schoolhouse has been the subject of greeting cards and magazine articles. Large framed prints of the famous *Dick and Jane* primer grace the walls of this former schoolhouse. Elegantly refurbished, it now offers ten bedrooms with private baths, two of which have a "sweetheart" Jacuzzi. Each of the nicely appointed guest rooms is decorated in beautiful antiques. An upstairs dining room offers a full breakfast of coffee, fresh fruit compote, baked bread or muffins, and egg strata. $$–$$$; □. (573) 698–2022; www.schoolhousebandb.com.

The Yates House. 305 Second Street, Rocheport, MO 65279. Completed in 1991, the Yates House is a pretty reproduction of an 1850 roadside inn. Guests have a choice of two bedrooms and a suite, all with private baths. A back porch, a courtyard patio, and flower and herb gardens are yours to enjoy. The garden house next door has two bedrooms with private baths and a suite with fireplace and jetted tub. $$–$$$; □. (573) 698–2129; www.yateshouse.com.

COLUMBIA, MO

Leave your "girth control" pills at home and head east from Rocheport on I-70 to this college town. Recently touted by *Money* magazine as one of the best small cities to live in in America, this up-and-coming metropolis is located about two hours east of Kansas City on I-70. Columbia is enjoying an unprecedented boom as people relocate here to enjoy the high-quality, low-cost living it affords. The new growth has spurred a recent influx of young, innovative restaurateurs who have put a whole new spin on the word *homemade*.

Columbia is *the* place to head for thick, hand-cut Angus steaks; blue-plate specials; fine wines; eclectic and cross-cultural cuisine; and pies so good you'll think your own mama made 'em (if you had a mama who cooked at all). Plan a "dine-around" day at restaurants that offer unusual items ranging from satay quesadilla to pizza with cilantro, pesto, and artichokes. Dessert might be a double-dip cone of fresh, homemade Tiger Stripe ice cream, or pear strudel with Gewürztraminer caramel sauce (don't worry if you can't pronounce it; you can still eat it). If this is too rich for your blood, you might like a 1950s-style diner where you can get good home-style meals and great malts, or a venerable establishment that still serves everything from filet mignon to yellowfin tuna—at yesteryear's prices.

Columbia is home to the University of Missouri-Columbia, Stephens College, and Columbia College. However, you don't have to be a college student to enjoy yourself in this town. On any given summer night, you can listen to live jazz and blues outdoors or catch a concert by noted artists such as Joan Baez or Emmylou Harris at the Blue Note, one of the best live-entertainment venues in the state.

If you're looking for one-of-a-kind finds, visit downtown Columbia's arts-and-crafts shops, which sell everything from hand-made Brazilian tables, regional art, and rare books to items that reflect social, political, and environmental issues.

Within a 50-mile radius around Columbia are historic Missouri River towns, the nationally acclaimed KATY Trail, state parks, historic sites, antebellum mansions, and other Missouri treasures. The free *Columbia Visitors Guide* brochure lists several tours, as well as things to do, lodging, dining, nightlife, and other information. Contact the Columbia Convention and Visitors Bureau, 300 South Providence, Columbia, MO 65203; (573) 875-1231; www.visit columbiamo.com.

WHERE TO GO

The Blue Note. 17 North Ninth Street, Columbia, MO 65205. One of central Missouri's best live-entertainment venues is located in a restored vaudeville theater that features renowned blues, reggae, rock, and folk artists. Two full cocktail bars and an espresso bar are located on the premises. For tickets and information call (573) 874-1944.

MKT Trail. Fourth and Cherry Streets (downtown) to Scott Boulevard (Route TT), Columbia, MO 65201. Walk, jog, or bike on this 4.7-mile handicapped-accessible trail, which varies from an urban walkway to a densely wooded passageway. Parking is available at Stadium, Forum, and Scott Boulevard accesses. The MKT is Columbia's spur connection to the KATY Trail. The Martin Luther King Jr. outdoor amphitheater is located at the Stadium access. Free. &. (573) 874–7460.

Shelter Gardens. 1817 West Broadway, Columbia, MO 65218. Here's an insurance tip for you: This company has an award-winning, five-acre garden in the heart of town, with more than 300 varieties of trees and shrubs, as well as 15,000 annuals and perennials.

Particularly impressive is the outstanding architectural landscaping that fills the entire garden with sweeping color and beauty. Shelter Gardens is a place of repose within a busy metropolis. During spring and summer couples can be married here in the gazebo or near the waterfall. You can take your lunch on the lawn or enjoy a quiet walk through the tree-shaded paths. Public concerts are held on Sunday evenings in June and July.

What makes this garden particularly unique is the thinking and planning that went into it. It is handicapped-accessible and features an outstanding "Garden for the Blind" that can be experienced by both sighted and visually impaired visitors. The plants have been carefully laid out to allow you to smell, touch, and feel them. There's nothing like the sweet fragrance of a geranium leaf or the velvety softness of lamb's ears to impart nature's meaning.

The Garden for the Blind is elevated from the ground at waist level, so you don't have to keep bending over to enjoy it. There are signs in Braille, for those who can use them. You'll leave here with the delicious aroma of plants on your fingers—something that's better than store-bought perfume.

The grounds also include a Cactus Garden, where many varieties of prickly plants are grown to commemorate the soldiers who served in Desert Storm. There is also a rose garden, with more than sixty varieties of grandifloras, floribundas, and standard tea roses. In addition, there are a shaded pool and a stream featuring a waterfall—the sound alone is enough to calm you down after a rough day. Free. &. (573) 445–8441.

Twin Lakes Recreation Area. 2500 Chapel Hill Road, Columbia, MO 65205. This family-oriented facility offers swimming, boating, fishing, hiking, and nature study. The six-acre swimming lake has a deck, a diving platform, water slides, and a large sand beach. There's a water playground separate from the lake for small children. Fee. (573) 445-8839.

Stephens College. 1200 East Broadway, Columbia, MO 65215. Founded in 1833, Stephens College is the second oldest women's college in the nation. It offers programs in the arts, business, professional studies, and liberal arts and sciences. Its continuing education division offers weekend and independent study and short-format courses. The Firestone Baars Chapel features a unique four-foyer design created by Eero Saarinen, who also designed the St. Louis Gateway Arch. Tours are free. (800) 876-7207; www.stephens.edu.

Columbia College. 1001 Rogers Street, Columbia, MO 65216. This was the first institution of higher education for women chartered by a state legislature west of the Mississippi River. Founded in 1851, the coeducational school offers undergraduate degrees in liberal arts, sciences, and the professions. Located on twenty-six acres in the midst of the city, it features day and evening courses on the main campus and through its branch campuses located throughout the United States and Puerto Rico. Tours are free. (800) 231-2391; www.ccsi.edu.

University of Missouri-Columbia. The first public university west of the Mississippi River, UMC was founded in 1839. The 1,340-acre campus has an enrollment of nearly 24,000 students. Degrees are offered through its eighteen colleges and schools. UMC is one of the few institutions in the country that house journalism, law, medicine, agriculture, engineering, and veterinary medicine on a single campus. Missouri Tiger Athletics is renowned for its twenty-one sports, and Mizzou intercollegiate athletic teams compete in the prestigious Big 12 Conference.

The center of the campus is the historic Francis Quadrangle, at the entrance of Eighth and Elm Streets. This is the site of the Chancellor's Residence. Its eighteen surrounding buildings are on the National Register of Historic Places. The row of six Ionic columns that adorn the center of the Francis Quadrangle once supported the portico of Academic Hall, the first building erected on campus. The open area around the columns is the center of the cluster of redbrick buildings known as the Red Campus. It is modeled after Thomas Jefferson's design for the University of Virginia.

As a matter of fact, UMC houses the first monument erected for the grave of Thomas Jefferson. When Virginia decided to erect a new monument for Jefferson's grave and give the original away, UMC was first in line to grab the valuable castoff. Since President Jefferson was instrumental in acquiring UMC as the first state university in the Louisiana Purchase Territory, "Old Mizzou," as it is nostalgically called, was the logical choice to house the prized stone slab. (Virginia has since regretted its decision to give up the original grave marker, but UMC has no intention of returning it.)

UMC is spread out around Columbia and has several phone numbers and ZIP codes. To simplify things, write to one address for information. For information and tours: Visitor Relations, Reynolds Alumni Center, University of Missouri-Columbia, Columbia, MO 65211; (573) 882–2121 or 882–6333; www.missouri.edu. For professional meeting planning services: (573) 882–4349. For intercollegiate athletics schedule and ticket information: (573) 882–2386. To charge tickets: (800) CAT–PAWS. Some places you may want to visit on campus include the following:

Buck's. Eckles Hall, East Rollins and College Streets, UMC Campus, Columbia, MO 65211 (see listing under Where to Eat).

Hearnes Center. 600 Stadium Boulevard, Columbia, MO 65201. Musical entertainment with artists such as Whitney Houston and family shows such as Disney on Ice are offered throughout the year. For ticket and show information: (573) 884–PAWS.

The Museum of Art and Archaeology. Pickard Hall, University of Missouri-Columbia, Columbia, MO 65211. One of the best-kept secrets in the Midwest, this gem of a museum is worth the drive to Columbia. It houses 13,000 pieces of art and artifacts from six continents and is the third largest collection of its kind in Missouri. The Saul and Gladys Weinberg Gallery of Ancient Art is one of the most comprehensive in the state and features exhibits from ancient Egypt, Palestine, the Near East, Greece, Italy, and the Roman world. Religion, myth and art, and cultural connections are represented here and reflect the everyday life and teaching of ancient peoples from prehistory to the present. Pottery, metalwork, terra-cotta, glass vessels, coins, and stone sculptures are also featured.

Particularly noteworthy is the oldest piece in the museum, a

250,000-year-old ax handle that belonged to somebody's forefather, as well as a 4,000-year-old cuneiform tablet and case that afford a glimpse into an early form of human communication before computers and faxes. A Cypro-Archaic vessel, thrown before 600 B.C., is a reminder that the venerable craft of pottery is blessed with longevity, while coins and gaming pieces from Egypt, Alexandria, and Rome tell the story of leisure-time spending sprees long before riverboat casinos.

Other areas of the museum feature European and American paintings, sculptures, drawings, prints, and photographs from the fifteenth to the twentieth centuries. Lectures, symposia, gallery talks, film series, and educational programs are offered throughout the year. The museum encourages persons with disabilities to participate in its programs and activities. Don't forget to check out the gift shop. Closed Monday. Free. &. (573) 882-3591.

Museum of Anthropology. 100 Swallow Hall, University of Missouri-Columbia, Columbia, MO 65211. Like the Museum of Art and Archeology, the Museum of Anthropology is another one of those tucked-away-and-taken-for-granted places that don't get much fanfare. As early as 1885 UMC began accepting gifts of ethnographic materials, finally organizing them into a cohesive collection in 1902. The only anthropology museum in the state and one of the few in the Midwest, its archaeological collection is the largest holding of prehistoric Missouri artifacts in the world, including those dating from 9000 B.C. to modern times. In addition, the museum curates objects from many Native American cultures.

The Grayson Archery Collection housed here is probably one of the largest and most comprehensive collections of its kind in the world. Unusual thumb rings of carved jade used by Chinese archers represent only a fraction of the materials that are showcased at the museum's exhibit hall; the remainder lie in the Museum Support Center on Rock Quarry Road. Collections of archaeological and ethnological materials are available for use by qualified researchers, as well as students and faculty.

There are a number of Native American exhibits, dating from 11,000 years ago to the present. Works by Hopi artist Iris Nampeyo, plus Santa Clara pottery and authentic Hopi kachinas, are showcased. There is also a prehistoric section of Native American work that features Hohokam and Anasazi pottery. Another unusual display offers a glimpse into life on the plains after the Europeans introduced horses, guns, and glass beads. Imported primarily from Venice and Czechoslovakia, the beads were used by Native Americans in their art. Cloth ribbon, also introduced by Europeans, eventually replaced porcupine and bird quills. Both the museum exhibit hall and the exhibits at the Museum Support Center are open to the public. Tours are available by appointment. Open with advance reservations. Free. (573) 882-3764.

Rock Bridge Memorial State Park. 5901 South Highway 163. This 2,250-acre wooded park takes its name from the area where a stream flows beneath a natural rock bridge formation that was once a mill and is now the mouth of the Devil's Icebox cave. With more than 7 miles of passageways, this cave is Missouri's sixth longest. The park offers hiking trails, picnic areas, and a wilderness discovery area, but the most adventurous will want to go on a Devil's Icebox Wild Cave Tour. If you like to slosh around in dark, wet places, alternately paddle and portage canoes, and walk for six to twelve hours through passages involving slippery mud, steep banks, and rocky surfaces, then this cave is for you!

You'll get to stoop, squat, crawl, and climb through teeny, tiny passages that could be rather confining. The cave is closed from April 1 to August 31 to allow its colony of gray bats to breed and fly about making guano, which, in turn, supports whole ecosystems of unique organisms. Born spelunkers and fitness folks will love the experience; princesses who value a French manicure more than muddy fingers may want to avoid it. Call the park office to arrange a tour. The park is free; fee for cave tour. Open daily. (573) 449-7402; www.mostateparks.com.

The Walters–Boone County Historical Museum and Visitors Center and Maplewood Home. 3801 Ponderosa Street, Columbia, MO 65201. Located 3 miles south of the junction of State Highway 63 and I-70, the museum and visitor center are housed in a traditional family farmhouse. The museum contains the history of the area from prehistoric to present day in its 16,000 square feet of exhibition space. The Montminy Art Gallery located on site showcases the talents of mid-Missouri artists as well as the outstanding collection of a half a million photographic images that are part of the Boone County Historical Society Photo Archives, which date from the late 1800s to the mid-twentieth century. The museum also can be used for banquets, meetings, workshops, weddings, and receptions.

Just north of the museum is the Maplewood Home, a historic Victorian residence built in 1877 that is open to tour. The original furnishings include the latest innovations of the period. The home is listed on the National Register of Historic Places. Call for hours. Free to tour. (573) 443-8936.

WHERE TO SHOP

There's not enough room to list all of Columbia's shopping venues here. Major centers include Columbia Mall, Crossroads West, and the Forum Shopping Center, which features anchor stores as well as boutiques, shops, restaurants, eateries, and theaters. The thriving community also has many antiques shops that cater to every taste and budget.

Columbia's vibrant and bustling downtown is filled with fine restaurants, shops, galleries, bookstores, museums, and one-of-a-kind specialty stores that cover 45 square blocks surrounding Broadway. Some of the downtown establishments interconnect, making them easily accessible during inclement weather. For a free map and visitor's guide of downtown Columbia, contact Central Columbia Association Special Business District, 11 South Tenth Street, Columbia, MO 65201; (573) 442-6816. Below are just a few of the places you can visit:

A La Campagne. 918 East Broadway, Columbia, MO 65201. This interesting concept in building space features interior design ideas and furnishings for residences and businesses. Upstairs is a gallery featuring the work of Missouri artists. Downstairs holds fabrics, fine art, antiques, and other furnishings that showcase bold, unusual styles. Closed Sunday. Free to tour. (573) 815-9464.

Bluestem Missouri Crafts. 13 South Ninth Street, Columbia, MO 65201. This unusual store is actually a partnership of craftspersons who feature their own ceramic jewelry, weaving, pottery, and batik work. In addition, Bluestem is a showcase for an extensive collection of handmade functional and decorative work by other artists. Pottery, glass, wood, metal, and fiber art are represented here. Baskets, wooden boxes, toys, cards, and clothing made in Missouri and Missouri's contiguous states are part of the colorful displays. Open daily. (573) 442-0211.

Columbia Art League Gallery. 1013 East Walnut Street, Columbia, MO 65201. Art lovers will find real treasures at this cozy and intimate gallery, which features the work of local members, professionals, and nationally acclaimed artists. The league's annual "Sparkling Arts" exhibit, held from mid-November through early January, features one-of-a-kind art finds. Closed Sunday. Free. (573) 443-8838.

Columbia Books. 22 South Ninth Street, Columbia, MO 65201. If your idea of a bookstore is a laid-back, one-owner place in which to browse and buy, this bookstore may fit your needs. It offers a mix of 60,000 new and used books that include everything from rare publications dating back four centuries to the latest best-sellers. The store has a wealth of children's illustrated books, gardening tomes, and first editions. Open daily. (573) 449-7417.

The Candy Factory. 701 Cherry East Street, Columbia, MO 65201. This bright and cheery candy store is renowned for its delicious handmade chocolates, including chocolate-covered strawberries and scrumptious truffles. For real chocoholics, there's always "The Ultimate Pizza," a gourmet treat featuring one and a half pounds of deep-dish chocolate topped with fresh pecans, cashews, walnuts, cherries, and marshmallows, drizzled with white chocolate. Open daily. (573) 443-8222.

Cool Stuff. 808 East Broadway, Columbia, MO 65201. Globetrotting owner Arnie Fagan has a great sense of humor and an eye for the unusual. By his own definition, he seeks all things "cool, unusual, practical, and fun"—much of it from Africa, Asia, Central and South America, and parts of Europe and the Middle East. The place offers an eclectic mix of ethnic items that range from Southwestern sage smudges to Israeli dreidels. There are more than 4,000 varieties of beads and thousands of candles, plus toys, jewelry, accessories, and clothing. Unless he sells it prior to this book's publication, there's a one-of-a-kind Indonesian ricksha for sale with an asking price (don't ask) of $5,000. Open daily. (573) 875-5225.

Ice Chalet Antique Mall. 3411 U.S. 63 (at the junction of I-70 and U.S. 63 South), Columbia, MO 65205. More than 200 dealers, selling everything from antiques and collectibles to primitives and "junque," can be found here. A full-service cafe is located on the premises. Open daily. (573) 442-6893.

Latin World. 812 East Broadway, Columbia, MO 65201. The owners travel to Latin American countries to bring back uncommon items not found elsewhere. You can buy colorful signed Oaxacan wood carvings, horsehair butterfly pins, and handmade hammered-copper vases here. The shop also sells Brazilian marble tables containing inlaid jade and amethyst in the shapes of flowers, birds, and human figures. Woven, flexible Amazon baskets that can be folded into pot holders and lamp shades and Amazonian bows and arrows round out this curious assortment of colorful and cultural work. Open daily. (573) 874–5259.

Legacy Art & Bookworks. 1010 East Broadway, Columbia, MO 65201. This is Columbia's largest art gallery. It features the work of local and regional artists and holds special events and exhibits show-casing an array of two- and three-dimensional work. They also have fine crafts items for sale. Legacy is also committed to saving old books and documents. If you have family heirlooms or letters that need to be preserved, the gallery can provide information on how to do it yourself or the staff can do it for you. In addition, it may be worth a drive to attend one of the highly acclaimed weekend work-shops offered here. Rare-book conservator and book artist James T. Downey teaches a unique bookbinding class that allows students to create handmade, bound books. Seasonal workshops are given in paper marbling and softcover bookmaking techniques. There are also classes on papermaking and decorating papers, as well as a work-shop on making photo albums, memory books, and scrapbooks. Classes and dates vary with the season. Reservations are required. Fee for classes. (573) 442–0855; www.legacyart.com.

Poppy. 914 East Broadway, Columbia, MO 65201. Nominated as a Top 100 Retailer of American Crafts in the United States, this shop offers an excellent collection of artwork in clay, fiber, metal, wood, glass, and jewelry. Open daily. (573) 442–3223; www.poppydown town.com.

WHERE TO EAT

There was a time when Columbia offered little to stir the culinary imagination. That's not the case today. *Nation's Restaurant News* has touted Columbia as the best up-and-coming place to open a dining establishment. Several youthful restaurateurs have taken it upon themselves to impart fresh and vigorous menus that have boosted the city's image as a restaurant town. Columbia now has a wide variety of choices that range from low-priced cafes to upscale eateries. Espresso and cappuccino are found almost everywhere. So great is the demand for good wine and brews that you can find alcoholic beverages served at pizza houses, luncheonettes, sub shops, and inexpensive diners. Competition has spurred the upgrading of menus and ambience in order to keep pace with demand. Some of the best bets include the following:

Boone Tavern. 811 East Walnut Street, Columbia, MO 65201. Prime rib, fresh seafood, steak, pasta, sandwiches, and salads are served at this popular establishment, which also offers outdoor dining. Located next to downtown's Boone County Courthouse, the restaurant features large banquet rooms and has driver and escort service available for groups of forty persons or more. Open daily for lunch and dinner. $$; ☐. (573) 422–5123.

Broadway Diner. 225 South Fourth Street, Columbia, MO 65201. *USA Today* touted this venerable restaurant as "one of the ten great places to eat" in America. The working-class establishment opened in 1949 and is on the National Register of Historic Places. It features breakfast anytime and daily lunch specials for under $5.00. Come here for real hash browns and freshly mashed potatoes. Open daily for breakfast, lunch, and dinner. $; ☐. &. (573) 875–1173.

Buck's Ice Cream Place. Eckles Hall, East Rollins and College Streets (on the UMC Campus), Columbia, MO 65211. Under the supervision of UMC's Department of Food Science and College of Agriculture, Buck's is a student-run research, teaching, and service operation. It's also a gathering spot for aficionados of good ice cream. Old Mizzou's "Truman the Tiger" mascot is the inspiration for Buck's Tiger Stripe ice cream, a mixture of vanilla and chocolate, with some orange coloring thrown in to account for the tiger-like hue. It contains 12 percent milkfat, which is not as rich as butterfat, so maybe your thighs will be a little thinner from eating it. All ice cream is freshly made, is available in dipped and packaged forms, and weighs about 30 percent more per serving than most commercial products. Closed Sunday. $; (no cards). (572) 882–1088.

C.C.'s City Broiler. 131 South Tenth Street, Columbia, MO 65201. This excellent steakhouse is renowned for its corn-fed Black

Angus beef, hand-cut daily on the premises and cooked exactly as you like it. The signature item is a filet mignon, a mini mountain of meat, about 3 inches high, tender enough to cut with a fork, and accented with a special seasoning that makes the flavor sing. If you want something even bigger, there's a whopping twenty-two-ounce porterhouse that can fill you up fast. All steaks come with the restaurant's famous jalapeño twice-baked potato, burgundy mushrooms, salad or soup, and fresh, hot sourdough bread. On the lighter side, the chargrilled seafood is always fresh, and you can mix and match a meal of steak and shrimp, steak and oysters, or steak and lobster tail. The prime rib, served only on Friday and Saturday, sells out fast. There's a wall-to-wall wait on weekends, so come early. Dinner is served seven nights a week. $$–$$$; ☐. (573) 875-2282.

Cherry Street Wine Cellar. 505 Cherry Street, Columbia, MO 65201. Connoisseurs of fine wine and good food will enjoy a meal at this quiet, intimate bistro that features an ever-changing menu of eclectic and cross-cultural cuisine. You can choose from an interesting array of appetizers, entrees, and desserts, sample wines by the glass, or select from a number of superior bottled labels from around the world. The restaurant's "Flights of Wines" is a popular activity wherein patrons are offered three half-glasses of wine to sample with their meal. Depending on the day and the disposition of the chef, dinner can be a gravlax appetizer of cured salmon with pressed crackers, onions soaked in cranberry juice, capers, and a mustard dill sauce. Entrees like roast pork with honey bourbon glaze served with orange mashed potatoes and a corn cobette with sun-dried tomato butter or bouillabaisse—a fresh seafood stew of shellfish, fish, onions, tomatoes, wine, olive oil, garlic, saffron, and herbs—are not to be missed. Desserts are absolutely decadent. Call ahead to find out what's on the daily menu. Reservations recommended. Closed Sunday and Monday. $$–$$$; ☐. (573) 442-7281.

Ernie's. 1005 Walnut Street, Columbia, MO 65201. This venerable Art Deco storefront establishment has been in business since 1934 and was recently upgraded from a greasy spoon to a not-so-greasy spoon that even features a short wine list. It still serves up good food at great prices. Hearty breakfasts, classic sandwiches, and luncheon specials are offered here, as are espresso, cappuccino, and lattes. One of the best things about Ernie's is the ambience. The eclectic assortment of patrons ranges from babies to bearded octogenarians. Blue-collar workers elbow in side by side at the counters with college students and faculty. Don't be shocked by the menu prices: filet mignons, Delmonico steaks, K.C. Strips, and yellowfin tuna sell for under $8.00. Don't knock it until you try it. And, yes, dinners come with salad or soup, potatoes, and roll. Open daily. $; ☐. (573) 874–7804.

Lakota Coffee Company. 24 South Ninth Street, Columbia, MO 65201. This popular coffee roastery is located in the heart of downtown. The owner named the place for the Lakota Sioux, who loved the taste and smell of hot, strong coffee and who would, in their caffeine quest, raid wagon trains and steal the beans for their own coffee klatches. The establishment's lattes and cappuccinos are served in enormous Alice in Wonderland–size cups that must weigh in at around a pound. You can have your choice of scones, croissants, biscotti, and other edibles for dipping and sipping. The comfy chairs and laid-back ambience make the Lakota a perfect place to relax. The Lakota also sells coffee to take home and is especially proud of its hard-to-find varieties. Open daily. $; ☐. (573) 874–2852.

Le Petit Bouchon. 700 East Broadway, Columbia, MO 65201. This European-style bistro and bakery offers a strong variation on the commonplace. It offers a fine selection of wines by the glass or bottle in addition to a wonderful and unusual variety of poultry, meat, and vegetable dishes. For about the same price as an expensive burger, you can have frog legs with fresh Black Mission figs, pickled in balsamic vinegar and herbes de Provence, or grilled calamari with roasted red peppers for lunch. Dinner might be braised rabbit "aille" with wild mushroom risotto, or steak frites with white truffle oil, reggiano, Tuscan-style salted potatoes, and sautéed greens. Or you might choose an appetizer of escargots in an anisette and garlic butter or lobster salad with baby spinach, roasted pepper, and warm polenta. The wine list is excellent. Leave room for dessert. Open daily. $$–$$$; ☐. (573) 499–9463.

The Main Squeeze. 28 South Ninth Street, Columbia, MO 65059. Have you run out of energy? Then come here to jump-start your battery. Start your morning with a sixteen-ounce "Elvis Parsley"—a mixture made with beets, spinach, parsley, celery, carrots, and garlic—which provides the equivalent of five servings of vegetables. Have a smoothie (a blend of fruit and juice), or go for the homemade soups, hearty sandwiches, salads, or fresh baked goods.

There are no preservatives or artificial colors or flavors in anything you'll eat here. Breakfast can be free-range organic eggs, whole-grain pancakes, organic roasted potatoes, scrambled tofu, breakfast burritos, or biscuits with soy sausage gravy. There are also wheat-free nondairy entrees for vegans. Open daily 7:00 A.M. to 4:00 P.M. and for Saturday brunch. Closed Sunday. $; ☐. (573) 817–5616.

Peggy Jean's Pies. 1605 Chapel Hill Road, Columbia, MO 65201. Old-fashioned, deep-dish, homemade-from-scratch pies are offered here. This is not an assembly-line operation. Peggy Day and Jean Wagster started their pie-making establishment late in life and still put in sixteen hours rolling out the dough by hand and filling each pie, one at a time, with fresh ingredients. The secret piecrust recipe took three years to perfect. Baked in a deep *glass* pie dish, each pie serves between eight and twelve people. A $4.00 plate deposit is included—but if you return it, you get your four bucks back. Peggy Jean's also sells "Baby Pies" that serve two. There are plenty of fruit and cream pies from which to choose, including gooseberry, peach praline (a favorite), and sour cream cherry. Specialty pies range from chocolate bourbon pecan (Friday only) to Key lime. Open for lunch and dinner from 11:00 A.M. to 6:00 P.M., Tuesday through Friday. $–$$; ☐. (573) 447–1119.

63 Diner. 5801 State Route 763, Columbia, MO 65202. Remember the old neighborhood diner with its good food and soda fountain where you could always get super shakes and malts? Well, it's come back in the form of this 1950s-style diner, featuring neon lights, jukebox music, and the art and architecture of the era. Simple food and simple choices are offered here. The 63 Diner touts itself as a place that's "a little behind the times . . . when . . . grass was mowed, coke was a cold drink, and pot was a cooking utensil." Breakfast, lunch, and dinner are offered. Specialties include open-face roast beef and mashed potatoes, homemade ham and beans with grilled corn cakes, country-fried pork fillets, and country-fried chicken or pork cutlets with home-style gravy, mashed potatoes, and green beans. There's also a broccoli walnut casserole for those who swoon at the thought of ingesting too many calories. Sandwiches include almost any variety of burger known this side of Mars. Save room for homemade breads, rolls, pies, cobblers, and a hot fudge brownie sundae, complete with whipped cream and a cherry. Closed Sunday and Monday. $; ☐. (573) 443–2331.

Village Wine and Cheese. 929 East Broadway, Columbia, MO 65201. This European-style deli appeals to foodies who are looking for casual cuisine or something unusual to take home for dinner. The deli shelves are filled with things like organic, all-natural Boar's Head meats, along with Francis Ford Coppola's "Mammarella" pasta and cheeses from Neil's Yard Dairy, an importer of small artisan cheeses of unusual quality. You'll also find 250 wine labels from which to choose, along with unusual brews such as Chimay Ale, brewed at Scourmont Abbey by Trappist monks and bottled at Chimay, Belgium. If you choose to dine on the premises, you can imbibe the beverage of your choice and enjoy something different like a "Gunnison River Sandwich" made with tomato, green chilies, aioli, and pepper jack cheese, toasted and topped with red onion on sourdough bread. Open daily for lunch and early dinner, Sunday brunch, wine tastings, and special events. $$; ☐. (573) 442–1010.

WHERE TO STAY

Columbia is filled with hotels and motels to suit every budget. Best Western, Days Inn, Budget, Comfort Inn, Drury Inn, Econo Lodge, Holiday Inn, Ramada, and Motel 6 are just a few of the better-known accommodations. Bed-and-breakfasts, although not as plentiful, include some fine establishments, such as these:

The Gathering Place. 606 South College Street, Columbia, MO 65201. Built in 1905, the home was once a fraternity house. It has been completely renovated and features a grand front porch, black walnut stairs and floors, and rooms and suites filled with antique Missouri walnut, cherry, and tiger-maple furnishings. Three rooms have Jacuzzi tubs. The bed-and-breakfast caters to both business and leisure guests. Each room comes with a desk, a telephone with dataport, cable television, and a private bath. Fax and copy services are available. $$–$$$; ☐. (877) 731–6888 or (573) 815–0606; www. thegatheringplacebb.com.

Missouri Manor. 1121 Ashland Road, Columbia, MO 65201. This fabulous home offers all the charms of an English manor house and also serves as a gracious center for entertaining. Weddings, receptions, and meetings are held here on a continual basis. Built in 1930 and recently restored to its original elegance, this is one of the few surviving grand dwellings in the area. The cherry staircase, tile, fountains, and English perennial gardens have been lovingly maintained. Laura Ashley interior fabrics and wallpaper are used throughout the Manor, and the English oak table in the dining room was used in the Missouri Governor's Mansion in the early 1900s. The home can accommodate eighty seated guests for functions. The Manor serves a full breakfast, and guest rooms include private baths. There are two suites: One sleeps six, with two dressing rooms and a shared bath; the other is a bridal suite, available with private bath and dressing room. $$$; ☐. (573) 499-4437 or (888) 330-7885; www.missourimanor.com.

University Bed and Breakfast. 1315 University Avenue, Columbia, MO 65201. Close to downtown and within walking distance of UMC's campus, this turn-of-the-twentieth-century home offers midwestern hospitality and delicious gourmet breakfasts served in the dining room. Guest rooms are nicely appointed and come with their own private baths. Special rates are available for rental of the whole house. $$; ☐. (573) 499-1920; www.universityavenuebandb.com.

JEFFERSON CITY, MO

From Columbia you have a couple of ways to reach Jefferson City. Heading back west on I-70 to M-179, the road takes you through some pretty countryside that passes the Runge Nature Center on the way to Jefferson City. U.S. 63 South is faster and connects with U.S. 54, the mid-Missouri gateway to the Lake of the Ozarks region.

Like two sides of a coin, Columbia and Jefferson City are separated by less than 30 miles, yet there's a world of difference between them. Located south of Columbia on U.S. 63, Jefferson City is exactly opposite of Columbia with regard to atmosphere and ambience. Columbia is a liberal and laid-back college town with a high degree of tolerance for unconventional appearances and beliefs. Jefferson City is an old, conservative city that thrives on influence, politics, and power lunches, most likely taken at acceptable restaurants with acquaintances grouped according to social behavior and dress code. In Jefferson City moderate nonconformists fit in as long as no boats are seriously rocked.

Jefferson City is full of lovely residences and old refurbished homes, and a genteel, rather Southern influence permeates the town, which touts itself as a great place to raise a family. While Columbia places its emphasis on fun, food, and shopping, Jefferson City views history, architecture, and tradition as its most important assets.

Jefferson City's unique art and architecture are not to be found elsewhere. As the state capital, it holds the magnificent State Capitol Building, where the Missouri legislature convenes. The Governor's Mansion and Governor's Garden, Jefferson Landing State Historic Site, Cole County Museum, and other historic points of interest are also worth visiting.

Visitors can come to town along the KATY Trail. Binder Park campgrounds are the closest camping spot to the trailhead on U.S. 54 and State Road West. However, it still is a 10-mile ride by bike through traffic to the heart of the city.

If you decide to spend the night, you'll find a number of accommodations that cater to business and leisure travelers alike, as well as a smattering of good restaurants. Leave time for a visit to the Runge Nature Center and Missouri's most delicious secret, the Central Dairy. For information: Jefferson City Convention and Visitors Bureau, 213 Adams, P.O. Box 776, Jefferson City, MO 65102; (800) 769–4183 or (573) 634–3616; www.jeffersoncity.org.

WHERE TO GO

Cole County Historical Museum. 109 Madison Street, Jefferson City, MO 65101. Located across from the Governor's Mansion, the museum is housed in an 1871 building that features a collection of inaugural ball gowns of the former First Ladies of the state. Open for tours Tuesday, Wednesday, and Saturday. Call for hours. Fee. (573) 635–1850.

Governor's Mansion. 100 Madison Street, Jefferson City, MO 65101. This is the official residence for Missouri's First Family. Built in 1871, the mansion has an interior that is authentically restored to the Renaissance Revival period and includes a winding stairway, marble fireplaces, elaborate ceiling stenciling, and period furnishings. Portraits of Missouri's First Ladies are showcased on the walls. Docents in period costumes conduct tours of the first floor Tuesday through Thursday from 10:00 A.M. to noon and from 1:00 to 3:00 P.M. except during August and December. The grounds also hold the

Governor's Garden. Constructed in the late 1930s, it is filled with flowers, pools, and walkways and can be reserved for special events. Christmas Candlelight Tours are held at the mansion two evenings in December. Free. &. (573) 751-4141. The garden is also free to tour; (573) 751-7929.

Jefferson Landing State Historic Site (Lohman Building and Union Hotel). Jefferson and Water Streets, Jefferson City, MO 65101. The three-story Lohman Building, constructed of limestone in the mid-1830s, is thought to be the oldest structure in Jefferson City. It served steamboat passengers during the city's heyday as a busy river town. Charles Lohman, a native of Germany, operated an inn here at that time. A small museum on the premises depicts the history of the area. Adjacent to the Lohman Building is the Union Hotel. It was built in the 1850s, when the community was a busy center for rail and river traffic; it operated as a hotel following the Civil War and continued to do business until the decline of steamboating. The Elizabeth Rozier Gallery in the building is open for exhibits featuring Missouri's arts, artists, and cultures. An Amtrak station is located on the first floor of the Union Hotel. Both buildings are open daily. Call ahead for hours and information. Free. &. (573) 751-3475; www.dnr.state.mo.us/dsp.

Lincoln University. 820 Chestnut Street, Jefferson City, MO 65102. Established in 1866, the university is situated on fifty-two rolling acres and is a source for cultural events, sports activities, and continuing education. Free tours are available. (573) 681-5599.

Missouri State Capitol Building. West High Street, Jefferson City, MO 65101. Ranked number two among the nation's capitols for its art and architecture, the Missouri State Capitol sits on three acres of ground and rises 262 feet to the top of its dome. Completed in 1918, the Renaissance-style building is where Missouri's state senators and representatives meet from January through May to enact laws that govern the state. On Tuesday, Wednesday, or Thursday morning, you can watch the political process unfold from the visitors gallery. The Missouri Museum, located on the first floor, features exhibits of outstanding historical significance. The large state seal in the center of the first-floor rotunda is wrought in bronze and can be viewed from a higher location during a tour of the building. The guided tours, conducted by docents, take in the legislators' chambers, architecture and design, some unusual murals painted in such a way that they present an optical illusion for the viewer, and the Benton Mural. A color guide to the capitol and a booklet on the Benton Mural can be purchased at the information desk on the first floor. Tours are given daily, every hour on the hour from 8:00 A.M. to 4:00 P.M. except holidays. A Christmas concert is held annually the second Tuesday of December. Free. ᕪ. (573) 751-4127; www.jcchamber.org/dtsites.

The Benton Mural. House Lounge, on the third floor, west wing of the Missouri State Capitol. One of the most important and best reasons to visit the Missouri State Capitol is for the Thomas Hart Benton Mural, an expansive, stunning masterpiece that reflects the enormous genius behind it. You are welcome to return after the tour and sit in the lounge for a while and contemplate the painting from all angles. Of course, there will always be misguided critics who say Benton isn't a painter. The reference to Benton as anything less than a great artist is laughable. Come to think of it, the wily old iconoclast would have laughed all the way to the bank himself had he known that his mural, for which he cleared only $5,000, is now supposedly worth $26 million. That's irrelevant, for the painting is priceless, since it cannot be removed.

At one time the mural was seriously in danger of being destroyed by the very legislators who commissioned it. Painted in 1936, the work covers four walls with a breadth and scope that reflect the legends, history, landmarks, industry, and people of Missouri. According to the Missouri Department of Natural Resources brochure on the State Capitol, the Benton mural, entitled *A Social History of the State of Missouri,* offended many people because of its "lack of refinement." Refined, Benton was not, since he wanted to portray "activities that did not require being polite." His mural, in addition to its niceties, also depicts racist actions, hangings, and other messy and corrupt things that human beings—even Missourians—did in their zeal to build a state.

So enraged were the legislators by Benton's masterpiece that they deliberately defaced the mural, dashing out lighted cigars on it. They were about to whitewash it altogether when Benton's famous temper erupted. He took his case to the media and to the Missouri people, who backed him. The politicians relented and the painting stayed. There is no charge to see the restored work. Benton would have liked that. (573) 751-4127.

Runge Nature Center. M–179, c/o Missouri Department of Conservation, P.O. Box 180, Jefferson City, MO 65102. This 3,000-square-foot facility west of downtown is the Department of Conservation's showpiece. Missouri's habitats are explored in a variety of exhibits and dioramas that feature the state's wetlands, agricultural lands, rivers and streams, ponds and lakes, prairies, glades, forests, and caves. Hiking trails, outdoor demonstrations, and naturalist-guided programs are offered over 112 acres. Free. &. (573) 526-5544; www.conservation.state.mo.us.

WHERE TO EAT

A dining guide featuring area restaurant menus is available for a fee at local magazine racks and hotels or by writing Capitol City Dining, 1712 McKay Court, Jefferson City, MO 65109. In the meantime, here are some places to try:

Cafe DeVille. Located inside the Hotel DeVille, 319 West Miller Street, Jefferson City, MO 65101. Hand-cut Black Angus beef, fresh seafood specialties, pasta, a short but excellent wine list, and a selection of cordials, ports, brandies, and imported cognacs are featured in this elegant, intimate restaurant. The atmosphere is conducive to relaxing conversation, and the service is unobtrusive. Desserts are worth leaving room for, especially the Utterly Deadly Chocolate Cake, topped with Evil Fudge Icing. More Evil Fudge, please, and bring along some of that equally decadent and delicious Peach Crème Brûlée as well. Breakfast, lunch, and dinner are served daily. $$-$$$; ☐. (573) 636-5231.

Central Dairy. 610 Madison Street, Jefferson City, MO 65101. In Jefferson City the milkman still makes deliveries to your door twice a week, courtesy of Central Dairy, a mid-Missouri operation that sells products made in its plant from locally produced milk. The owner keeps his prices low at the ice cream store as a goodwill gesture to the community, so everybody can afford to come here. Cones still sell for around a dollar, including sales tax, and prices are minuscule for colossal blockbuster sundaes and splits so top-heavy with triple dips of ice cream, marshmallow, and hot fudge toppings and nuts that you'll need several napkins just to clean up. Try the Rock & Roll sundae, one of humanity's finest inventions, featuring vanilla, chocolate, strawberry, and black walnut ice cream, crowned with banana, marshmallow, pineapple, and strawberry toppings and nuts. Worry about cholesterol later. Central Dairy sells forty flavors of ice cream, including spumoni, Texas pecan, black walnut, cinnamon, caramel caribou, and other delights. This is a must-stop place for lovers of rich, creamy, homemade-on-the-premises stuff. Hand-packed pints and quarts are so affordable that serious aficionados will want to bring a cooler and plenty of dry ice to take some back home. The place never advertises: It doesn't need to. Call for hours. $; (no cards). (573) 635–6148.

Ecco Lounge. 703 Jefferson Street, Jefferson City, MO 65101. In 1838 the land on the corner of Jefferson and Dunklin was purchased for $32; in 1840 the back parking lot was bought for $26 more. The building was erected in 1858 and served as a "beer saloon." *Lounge* has replaced the word *saloon,* but beer is beer, and Ecco serves it up along with giant beer-battered onion rings and hefty burgers made from ground chuck and topped with blue cheese. Specialties are hot spiced shrimp, prime rib, and steak. The funky, working-class surroundings are fun. $; ☐. (573) 636–8751.

Das Stein Haus Restaurant and Lounge. 1436 Southridge Drive (off U.S. 54, next to the Ramada Inn), Jefferson City, MO 65101. German specialties here include beef rouladen, Wiener schnitzel, smoked pork chops with sauerkraut, sauerbraten, and bratwurst. Dinners also feature chateaubriand for two, veal medallions, frog legs, and Long Island Duckling Flambé, topped with orange sauce and served with spiced rice and red cabbage. The lounge features live music on Sunday evening. $$–$$$. ☐. (573) 634–3869.

WHERE TO STAY

Best Western Inn. 1937 Christy Drive, Jefferson City, MO 65101. Located off U.S. 54, this particular Best Western offers a family fitness center with an indoor pool, spa, and fully equipped fitness room; a guest laundry; two-room whirlpool suites; a full-service restaurant; free fax and copy services; and conference facilities. It has the advantage of being close to downtown but near enough to a pleasant park with a lake, a fitness trail, a playground, and fishing. $$; ☐. (800) 528–1234 or (573) 635–4175; www.bestwestern.com.

Capitol Plaza Hotel and Convention Center. 415 West McCarty (U.S. 50 and Missouri Boulevard), Jefferson City, MO 65101. The nine-story atrium setting and five-story waterfall set the scene for this pleasant hotel located in the heart of downtown. Nicely appointed rooms and suites open to the atrium, and there are king suite rooms for hosting meetings and interviews. Hospitality suites, banquet service for up to 1,200, state-of-the-art audiovisual equipment, and many other services are available for business guests. The hotel also offers a fully equipped exercise room, as well as restaurants featuring an array of items for breakfast, lunch, and dinner. $$-$$$; □. (800) 338–8088 or (573) 635–1234; www.jgh.com.

Hotel DeVille. 319 West Miller Street, Jefferson City, MO 65101. This small, moderately priced downtown hotel offers shuttle service to and from the KATY Trail. There are ninety-eight guest rooms equipped with coffeemaker, refrigerator, telephone dataport connector, and other amenities. One of the best reasons to come here is for breakfast, lunch, or dinner at the Cafe DeVille, located on the premises (see Where to Eat). $$; □. (800) 392–3366 or (573) 636–5231; www.devillehotel.com.

Jefferson Inn Bed and Breakfast. 801 West High Street, Jefferson City, MO 65101. Conveniently located near the Missouri State Capitol Building, the Jefferson Inn accommodates leisure and business travelers alike. Audiovisual equipment can be arranged for groups of up to fifteen persons. Continental breakfast is served for those on a tight schedule, while hearty midwestern fare is available for those who are traveling at a more relaxed pace. Spacious bedrooms and suites with private baths are decorated in Victorian elegance. Guests can also enjoy the use of a hot tub in the privacy of the light and airy Florida Room. $$-$$$; □. (800) 530–5009 or (573) 635–7196.

CALIFORNIA, MO

WHERE TO GO

Burgers' Smokehouse. Department 57–L, M–87 South, California, MO 65018. From U.S. 50 go south on M–87 a short distance to Burgers' Smokehouse. The eighteenth-century art of meat preservation is still used by this family-owned operation to smoke and cure turkeys, chickens, and meats the old-fashioned way. You can pig out on pork in the form of country-cured bacon and naturally aged smoked ham. The visitor center contains some interesting displays. There is a covered bridge, as well as dioramas with educational themes that point out the importance of the changing seasons as they relate to natural curing, drying, and aging of country-cured ham. Free tours are available. Open daily except Sunday, from mid-September through Christmas. (800) 705-2323 (tours) or (800) 624-5426; www.smokehouse.com.

SEDALIA, MO

From California head west on U.S. 50 to Sedalia, your first stop along the KATY Trail. The MKT (Katy) Depot was built in 1896 and used to house railroad offices and restaurants. Today the building is owned by the Department of Natural Resources and listed on the National Register of Historic Places. You can pick up the western-most entry point 3 miles northwest of Sedalia.

Sedalia's history dates back to 1857, when General George R. Smith decided to found a new town amid the prairie grasses. He envisioned a prosperous railroad city and named it Sedville, after his daughter's nickname. Friends eventually persuaded him to use the more mellifluous "Sedalia" to commemorate his progeny.

When the Civil War came along, Sedalia was in the thick of the fighting. Missouri, though a slave state, did not secede from the Union as did other slave states. Sedalia was captured and held by the Confederates, and later was made the seat of Pettis County.

The railroad, as Smith foresaw, did indeed play an important role in the town's growth. Sedalia flourished and drew new people with talent, such as Scott Joplin, who became known as the King of Ragtime. His sound spread across the country with compositions like the "Maple Leaf Rag," one of the finest pieces of ragtime music ever written. A historical monument was built at the Maple Leaf Club site in the 100 block of East Main Street, where Joplin lived and worked.

The Scott Joplin Ragtime Festival is held annually the first full weekend in June in Sedalia. The four-day event is the only classical ragtime festival in the world and commemorates the noted composer's work, bringing musicians and visitors from around the globe to the birthplace of ragtime. Food, crafts, and free performances on the Maple Leaf Club grounds are part of the fun.

Aside from its musical past, beautiful architecture can also be found in Sedalia. The old homes that line Broadway (U.S. 50), the buildings on the State Fairgrounds, and the downtown area are all of interest. There are also a number of shops and restaurants in the area. Brochures for walking tours are available from the chamber of commerce (located on the north side of the courthouse), 600 East Third Street, Katy Depot Historic Site, Sedalia, MO 65301; (800) 827-5295; www.visitsedaliamo.com.

WHERE TO GO

Bothwell Lodge Historic Site. 19349 Bothwell Park Road, Sedalia, MO 65301. Located 6 miles north of Sedalia on U.S. 65, this 180-acre park offers visitors scenic bluffs and wooded trails. It features picnic areas and Bothwell Lodge, a century-old lodge open for tours year-round. Fee to enter the lodge. (660) 827-0510.

Daum Contemporary Art Museum. 3201 West Sixteenth Street, Sedalia, MO 65301. Located on the campus of State Fair Community College, these five galleries exhibit paintings, drawings, prints, photographs, and sculptures by midwestern artists. Guided tours are available. Free. Closed Monday. (660) 530-5800; www.daum museum.org.

Downtown Historic District Walking Tour. 600 East Third Street, Katy Depot Historic Site, Sedalia, MO 65301. Stop by the chamber office downtown and get a copy of a free walking tour brochure. Many of the architecturally significant buildings house antiques and specialty shops. (800) 827-5295.

Liberty Center Association for the Arts. 111 West Fifth Street, Sedalia, MO 65301. This renovated 1920s theater in downtown serves as the center for performing and cultural arts in the area. Visual artists display their work at Gallery 111 and the Sedalia Community Theatre's all-volunteer troupe stages three productions a year. Stop in for a cup of coffee at The Bean Coffee Shop, located on the premises. (660) 827-3103.

Sedalia Ragtime Archives. State Fair Community College Library, 3201 West Sixteenth Street, Sedalia, MO 65301. The bar and stained-glass window from the Maple Leaf Club are housed here.

Ragtime buffs will enjoy browsing through letters, music, and other Scott Joplin memorabilia. Free. (660) 530–5800.

Missouri State Fair. State Fairgrounds, 2503 West Sixteenth Street, Sedalia, MO 65301. The 397-acre showplace for agriculture and industry comes alive with color and excitement in late August for ten days of shows, exhibits, and competitions, drawing nearly 400,000 people every year. Fee. (800) 422–FAIR or (660) 530–5600; www.mostatefair.com.

Paint Brush Prairie Conservation Area. Nine miles south of Sedalia, off U.S. 65 (watch for signs). This natural area captures the historic atmosphere at the time of homesteading. Unique plant species have been restored to the area, encouraging the return of native animals like prairie chickens, upland sandpipers, and Henslows' sparrows. Hiking trails wind throughout the area; visitors are welcome. (660) 530–5500.

WHERE TO EAT

Wheel Inn. 1800 West Broadway, Sedalia, MO 65301. If you like peanuts, you'll love the Wheel Inn. In business for more than fifty years, the Wheel Inn touts its claim to fame on its menu as a "Guberburger." This is a hamburger topped with melted peanut butter and garnished with fresh lettuce, tomatoes, and your choice of mayo, catsup, mustard, and onions. Some sage advice: Don't knock it before you try it. Why not be bold and surprise your taste buds with a Guberburger and a thick, rich peanut butter milk shake? Too much overstimulation? Not to worry: There are other popular items, such as fresh-squeezed limeades and lemonades, homemade chili, and the best foot-long chili dog in town. The Wheel Inn is the last of a dying breed—one of those rare and admirable restaurants that still have carhops, giving patrons the opportunity to dine inside or in the privacy of their cars. $; (no cards). (660) 826–5177.

WHERE TO STAY

Sedalia House Bed and Breakfast. 26097 County Road HH (2 miles east of U.S. 65), Sedalia, MO 65301. This elegant two-story Colonial-style home is situated in the midst of a 300-acre cattle ranch surrounded by ponds, woods, and rolling hills. You can relax on the beautiful pillared front porch or walk the trails to see bountiful wildlife. The accommodations offer six rooms, including a suite with private bath. A full country breakfast is served. Closed in winter. $$; ☐. (660) 826–6615.

WORTH MORE TIME: FULTON, MO, AND HERMANN, MO

FULTON, MO

Fulton, Missouri, is located east of Columbia on U.S. 54, within the "Kingdom of Callaway County." Fulton's distance from Kansas City is longer than a usual day trip, but as one of the communities in the KATY Central Consortium, it is included here. Callaway County calls itself a kingdom because of a Civil War treaty whereby Callaway County forces signed an agreement with Union troops that neither of them would invade the other. Since that day, when the sovereign United States dealt with Callaway County as an equal, Callaway County has been designated a kingdom by those who live there. Every June downtown Fulton hosts Kingdom Days, an event that offers food, crafts, a beer garden, parades, music, and more. For information on bed-and-breakfasts, dining, and other attractions: Kingdom of Callaway Chamber of Commerce, 409 Court Street, Fulton, MO 65251; (800) 257-3554; www.callawaychamber.com.

WHERE TO GO

Winston Churchill Memorial and Library. Westminster College, Fulton, MO 65251. Listed on the National Register of Historic Places, this is the site where Sir Winston Churchill gave his 1946 "Sinews of Peace" (Iron Curtain) speech. The memorial is the only museum of its kind in the world. However, there is a hefty admission fee for a self-guided visit that leaves much to be desired. If you've never been here before and know little about Churchill, it may be best to call ahead and arrange a tour with someone knowledgeable enough to discuss this famous church and British prime minister in depth.

The museum is housed inside the Sir Christopher Wren Church of

St. Mary the Virgin, Aldermanbury, which was brought over to the United States stone by stone and rebuilt on the grounds of the college. There are exhibits that mostly feature old photographs and newspaper articles relating to Churchill, along with stories about Gorbachev's 1992 visit to the college. Also housed here are some of Churchill's paintings, books, and other memorabilia. Located on the museum grounds is a sculpture created by Churchill's grand-daughter from eight sections of the Berlin Wall to symbolize the fall of the Iron Curtain. Open daily. Fee. (573) 642-6648; www.wcmo.edu.

HERMANN, MO

Located on picturesque M-19, just south of I-70, Hermann is outside the usual day-trip time frame, but it's included here because it is part of the KATY Central Consortium communities. Hermann is best known for having the state's oldest wineries, lots of antiques shops, and dozens of nineteenth-century homes, many of which have been converted to great bed-and-breakfasts.

Two historic homes—the Pommer-Gentner House on Market Street and the Strehly House on West Second Street—reflect the town's early German traditions. Hermann's popular wineries include Stone Hill, Adam Puchta, and Hermannhof, all offering tours and award-winning wines to sample. Hermann has a host of other attractions, including the Showboat Community Theater, open for live entertainment and tours; the Show-Stopper Revue, featuring a mix of Broadway and vaudeville fare; and the Historic Hermann Museum and Information Center, housed in an 1871 German school and featuring a number of educational displays.

Hermann also holds several renowned festivals and celebrations throughout the year. These include the Hermann Maifest, a May cele-bration of spring, complete with parades, German food, drink, arts, crafts, and music, and Octoberfest in fall, which offers music, food, and fun. There are daily Amtrak stops to and from Hermann. For more information on bed-and-breakfasts, attractions, restaurants, shopping, and festivals: Hermann Tourism Group, 312 Schiller Street, P.O. Box 104, Hermann, MO 65041; (800) 932-8687; www.hermannmo.com.

East Day Trip 3

BLUE SPRINGS, MO

The growth of this Kansas City suburb has been phenomenal. The high standard of living, good schools, and other amenities are a draw, along with popular parks and wildlife areas that bring people from around the region to this part of town.

WHERE TO GO

Burr Oak Woods Conservation Nature Center. 1401 Park Road (M-7 North and Park Road), Blue Springs, MO 64015. The center is nestled within 1,100 acres of mixed hardwood forest, prairies, glades, and limestone outcrops. Exhibits include hands-on displays of Missouri's fish, forest, and wildlife resources, including live animals. In addition, there are a 3,000-gallon aquarium stocked with native fish and reptiles, a 155-seat auditorium, and an indoor wildlife viewing area. Four outdoor hiking trails and wildlife food plots afford a glimpse of deer, turkeys, and raccoons. Two trails are wood-chipped, and two are paved. Picnic areas are available. &. Free. (816) 228-3766; www.conservation.state.mo.us.

    Burrough's Audubon Center and Library. Fleming Park (off Woods Chapel Road, near Lake Jacomo Marina), Blue Springs, MO 64105. You can learn all about nature at the center, which contains exhibits of birds' nests, insects, and butterflies. Outdoor feeders bring in a variety of birds to watch. The natural history library on site allows visitors to check books and videos out for four weeks. A gift shop on the premises sells birdseed, feeders, bird guides, and related items. Closed Monday, Wednesday, and Sunday. Free. (816) 795-8177.

Missouri Town 1855. Fleming Park, Blue Springs, MO 64105. Head east on I-70, then south on M-291; take a left at the Colbern Road exit to Cyclone School Road, then go left and follow the signs. This reconstructed 1850s farming community comprises more than thirty original structures that make up a charming village. Barnyard animals such as free-ranging chickens, sheep, and horses add an authentic touch. The volunteer staff, dressed in period attire, demonstrate chores done by frontier Americans. Closed Monday. (816) 795-8200.

CONCORDIA, MO

Located 53 miles east of Kansas City on I-70, Concordia is a sleepy little hamlet most of the time. Every September the town comes alive when it hosts a three-day celebration of its German heritage, complete with German brass bands, parades, cattle shows, and arts and crafts, along with plenty of German-style foods and imported German beers. Tourists come from around the state, swelling the population from 2,000 to as many as 5,000 in a single evening. For dates and times check newspaper ads, or contact the Concordia Chamber of Commerce, 702 South Main Street, Concordia, MO 64020; (660) 463-2454; www.concordiamo.com.

WHERE TO STAY

Mrs. G's B&B. One South East Fourteenth Street, Concordia, MO 64020. This ranch-style home affords a homestay experience and offers three rooms, each with private bath. One room is on the main floor and features a full-size bed and private bath; the other is located in the loft and has a full-size bed and rollaway. A third room is decorated in Scottish plaid with cherry furniture. A deluxe breakfast is served. Open weekends during the school year and full-time in summer. $; (no cards). (660) 463-2160.

EAST

DAY TRIP 4

Lone Jack, MO
Kingsville, MO
Warrensburg, MO
Sedalia, MO
Jefferson City, MO

LONE JACK, MO

A historic Civil War battlefield, one of the largest botanical gardens between Kansas City and Denver, a first-class bed-and-breakfast, and a dog that made national history back in 1870 are part of this unusual Day Trip that will acquaint you with this fascinating, yet relatively undiscovered, region.

WHERE TO GO

Lone Jack Civil War Battlefield and Cemetery. 301 South Bynum Road (1 block south of U.S. 50 at Lone Jack exit), Lone Jack, MO 64070. This is the site of the August 16, 1862, Battle of Lone Jack, where five hours of bloody, hand-to-hand fighting ensued. The event is depicted in dioramas, artifacts, and other displays that showcase what happened on this Civil War battleground. An annual commemoration is held the weekend closest to the original battle date. Open daily April through October; weekends November through March (donations suggested). (816) 566-2272.

    Bynum Winery. 13520 South Sam Moore Road (3 miles east of Lone Jack at the intersection of U.S. 50 and Sam Moore Road), Lone Jack, MO 64070. Sweet and dry varieties of Seyval Blanc, Villard Blanc, and Chancellor Noir are made here, along with apple, cherry, and other fruit wines in season. Fresh fruits and vegetables are also for sale in season. Open daily; call for hours. (816) 566-2240.

East Day Trip 4

KINGSVILLE, MO

WHERE TO GO

Powell Gardens. 1609 Northwest U.S. 50, Kingsville, MO 64061. Located 35 miles east of Kansas City, Powell Gardens is a not-for-profit, 915-acre botanical garden dedicated to beautifying and preserving the natural environment. Established in 1984 through a generous gift from the Powell Family Foundation, Powell Gardens is an outdoor paradise for gardeners and nature lovers, offering a changing palette of colorful flowers and plants throughout the year.

Powell Gardens utilizes horticultural displays, education, and research to serve the Kansas City community and surrounding areas. Gardens of annuals, perennials, native plants, ornamental grasses, and other seasonal plantings make up this spectacular facility.

Visitors may enjoy strolling through the Perennial Garden, Rock and Waterfall Garden, the Island Garden, and the Terrace Gardens at the Visitor Education Center. Other highlights include the magnificent structures designed by architects Fay Jones and Maurice Jennings. These include the Marjorie Powell Allen Chapel, the Visitor Education Center, and the Wildflower Pavilion.

Powell Gardens offers year-round special events, educational classes and environmental programs for children and adults, a lovely gift shop, and an excellent cafe where you can refresh and relax before or after your visit. Open daily. ♿. Fee. (816) 697–2600; www.powellgardens.org.

WARRENSBURG, MO

Located east of Powell Gardens at the intersection of U.S. 50 and M–13, Warrensburg has plenty of antiques stores, craft malls, specialty shops, restaurants, and cafes to visit. The town is the home of Central Missouri State University, known for its outstanding technology programs. Old Drum Days, held on the third weekend in September, honor the memory of Old Drum, the famous dog that was responsible for one of the strangest tales in the history of

Missouri's supreme court. For information: Warrensburg Chamber of Commerce, 100 South Holden Street, Warrensburg, MO 64093; (660) 747–3168; www.warrensburgmo.com.

WHERE TO GO

Central Missouri State University. Office of Admissions, Administration Building 104, Warrensburg, MO 64093. Founded in 1871, CMSU offers a wide range of academic programs in applied sciences and technology, arts and sciences, business and economics, and education and human services. The low student-faculty ratio on the 1,050-acre campus allows for quality, individualized attention. A well-known cultural center, CMSU offers opportunities to attend events and exhibitions of fine and performing arts, including those featuring celebrities in the entertainment and musical fields. The James L. Highlander Theater offers two main-stage or dinner-theater productions each semester. The CMSU Archives and Museum, located on the lower level of the Union Building, houses a diverse display of artifacts that changes themes monthly. The campus is free to tour. (660) 543–4677; www.cmsu.edu.

Downtown Warrensburg. c/o Main Street, Inc., 109 North Holden Street, Warrensburg, MO 64093. Spend a morning browsing along Main Street shops, services, and businesses, many of which are housed in venerable structures that are being restored and refurbished, thanks to the Warrensburg Main Street Program. The revitalization plan is helping to maintain the city's center through the context of historic preservation. (660) 429–3988.

Missouri Pacific Railroad Depot. 100 South Holden Street, Warrensburg, MO 64093. This century-old former railroad depot was rescued from physical decline and renovated for multiple uses. It houses the Warrensburg Chamber of Commerce and also serves as an Amtrak station. Two eastbound and two westbound passenger trains pass through here daily. You can take the Amtrak from Kansas City to Warrensburg and back, or head out to other locations, such as Jefferson City, Sedalia, Hermann, and St. Louis. You can purchase your ticket through a local travel agency or call (800) USA–RAIL for information on departure times and prices. (660) 747–3168.

Old Drum Monument. Market and Holden Streets (on the grounds of the Johnson County Courthouse), Warrensburg, MO 64093. In 1870 Senator George Graham Vest won a court battle and the hearts of dog lovers when he paid his famous tribute to the dog during the *Burden* v. *Hornsby* court case in 1870. That eulogy won the case for Charles Burden, whose favorite hound, Drum, was shot by Leonidas Hornsby, a neighbor. Burden sued for damages, and the trial became the focus of national attention, as each man became determined to win. After several appeals the case reached the Missouri supreme court. Vest's eulogy, in which he made in his final appeal to the jury, became a classic speech that reached the hearts of dog lovers around the world. He said, "The one absolutely unselfish friend that a man can have in this selfish world, the one that never deserts him, the one that never proves ungrateful or treacherous, is his dog." Who could resist a speech like that? Burden was subsequently awarded $50 in damages for the loss of this favorite dog. Free. (660) 747-3168.

WHERE TO STAY

Cedarcroft Farm Bed & Breakfast. 431 Southeast Y Highway, Warrensburg, MO 64093. Located on the 1867 John A. Adams Farmstead, now on the National Register of Historic Places, Cedarcroft has been beautifully renovated with modern comforts. The farm is surrounded by eighty acres of woods, creeks, and meadows. Wildlife—such as deer and wild turkey—abounds. The hosts provide guests with plenty of information about the area, including where to shop and how to find antiques and bargains galore. Guest quarters feature a two-room private suite with private bath. A guest cottage was added in summer 2001. There's also a parlor and gathering room. A large evening snack and a full country breakfast are included with your stay. $$; ☐. (800) 368-4944 or (660) 747-5728; www.cedarcroft.com.

SEDALIA, MO

(See East from Kansas City, Day Trip 2.)

JEFFERSON CITY, MO

(See East from Kansas City, Day Trip 2.)

Southeast Day Trip 1

0   10   20   30 miles

The Lake of the Ozarks, MO

THE LAKE OF THE OZARKS, MO

The enormity of The Lake of the Ozarks region begs an entire book, rather than a mere chapter. Because of the confines of this publication, however, the area has been condensed into a compact overview that covers primarily its western and eastern sides.

Located 165 miles from Kansas City, the Lake of the Ozarks is one of the Midwest's premier playgrounds. Because of the increased speed limit and the construction of new highways, it is a quick and easy day trip from Kansas City. The largest lake in Missouri, it offers 1,150 miles of shoreline (more than the entire state of California). Linking the east side of the lake to the west side is the new Lake of the Ozarks Community Bridge, a toll bridge that considerably reduces the drive time to get around the area.

The lake region covers 54,000 acres, and within its borders are one hundred marinas, dozens of waterfront restaurants and watering holes, and hundreds of shops, services, and businesses. Water activities abound from April through October. Average daytime air and water temperatures in spring run about 60 degrees, warming up to an average of 90 degrees in July and leveling off to about 70 degrees in fall. Off-season is a good time to go to the lake, because it's less crowded. Even winter provides things to do, from holiday festivities to romantic cold-weather getaways at large resorts that stay open at this time of year.

There are plenty of places to camp, with more than 900 private campground sites, ranging from rugged, wooded locations at the water's edge to paved parks with full hookups.

In addition, the Lake of the Ozarks is a prime fishing and golf destination, hosting prestigious tournaments such as Bass Masters and the PGA Club Pro Championship. As one of middle America's top golfing destinations, it has more than fifteen courses and 260 holes set amid the natural beauty of rolling hills, expansive forests, and dramatic bluffs.

The lake has a reputation for being the place where young people come to party. The weekends on the eastern side of the lake are crowded with speedboats, Wave Runners, and party cove revelers who come to rip around on jet cruisers and live it up. This part of the lake has lots of fast-food franchises, strip malls, go-carts, water slides, miniature golf, helicopter and seaplane rides, and excursion-boat rides, as well as plenty of shopping.

The west side of the lake offers some of the same amenities but is much quieter and more laid back. It draws less attention to itself but should by no means be overlooked. It features smaller resorts that cater to families and offers a variety of restaurants and shops, plus plenty of places to relax and contemplate life in the slow lane.

The Lake of the Ozarks may not seem as impressive as, say, the Atlantic Ocean, but it has its merits. When it was created back in 1931, it was considered the world's largest man-made body of water. The construction of Bagnell Dam was undertaken by the Union Electric Company, and the engineering feat was hailed as the most skillful of its day. The 2,543-foot-long dam's reservoir holds 650 billion gallons of water, covering parts of Miller, Camden, Morgan, Benton, Henry, and St. Clair Counties.

The enormous waterway is ringed by more than a dozen communities linked together by roadways in scenic succession.

On the lake's eastern edge above the dam are the tiny towns of Lakeside and Lakeland. Below the dam, on the Osage River, is the village of Bagnell, for which the dam is named. The first mile south of the dam is known to tourists as the Strip, which houses shops, arcades, amusements, and restaurants, along with family resorts, motels, and hotels.

South of the Strip are U.S. 54 and State Road HH. They lead to Horseshoe Bend's lush golf courses, resorts, restaurants, condominiums, and residential subdivisions. South of here is Lake Ozark, followed by Osage Beach, a popular 8-mile-long community of shopping malls, outlet stores, restaurants, country sampler shops, and many other attractions.

Following U.S. 54 south leads you across the Grand Glaize Bridge and State Road KK, the pathway to Turkey Bend. Here you'll find more golf, luxury estates, homes, condominiums, resorts, restaurants, and marinas.

Past State Road KK is Linn Creek, a residential community that is home to the Camden County Museum and Big Surf Water Park. South on U.S. 54 is Camdenton, the hub city of the area. It's bustling and crowded in the summer and offers shopping, restaurants, and plenty of family accommodations.

Camdenton is the dividing point between the west and east sides of the lake, where the small towns of Sunrise Beach, Laurie, and Gravois Mills provide a growing number of resorts, motels, campgrounds, and shopping and dining places.

North from here, at the crossroads of M–5 and M–52, is Versailles (pronounced *ver-sayles* by residents). It holds the Morgan County Historical Museum, retail shops, and the Hilty Inn, a bed-and-breakfast establishment.

Eldon—east of Versailles on M–52 as you drive southeast toward Osage Beach—boasts Fantasy World Caverns, shops, antiques stores, and eateries.

Most of the lakeshore is privately owned, and there is little public access to boating, swimming, or fishing. There are two public beaches, campgrounds, and boat-rental facilities at Lake of the Ozarks State Park. Both Osage Beach and Lake Ozark provide entrance to the park, the largest in Missouri. Ha Ha Tonka State Park, west of Camdenton off U.S. 54, includes unusual rock formations, castle ruins, and handicapped-accessible trails.

The *Lake of the Ozarks Vacation and Service Guide,* available from the Lake of the Ozarks Convention and Visitor Bureau (see address and phone below), can lead you to most of the better-known resorts, restaurants, and attractions. Be sure to call ahead if you're planning a winter visit; some lake area businesses close for the season. For information and a self-guided car tour brochure: Lake of the Ozarks Convention and Visitor Bureau, P.O. Box 1498, Osage Beach, MO 65065; (800) 386-5253; www.funlake.com.

WHERE TO GO

BOAT RENTALS, MARINAS, AND SCENIC CRUISES

One way to enjoy the lake is on a boat. With more than one hundred marinas, it's impossible to list all the facilities here. Most of the resorts and campgrounds have their own boat rentals and marinas. Houseboating is also an option (see Where to Stay). For a complete rundown, get a copy of the latest edition of the *Lake of the Ozarks Vacation and Service Guide,* available from the Lake of the Ozarks Convention and Visitor Bureau, P.O. Box 1498, Osage Beach, MO 65065; (800) 386–5253; www.funlake.com.

Celebration. Pier 17, P.O. Box 1650, Osage Beach, MO 65065. If you prefer to have someone else take the stern, you might try a ride aboard the *Celebration,* the most elegant cruise ship on the lake. The 80-foot yacht features open-air decks and climate-controlled interior salons. All-day packages include dinner cruises and family scenic cruises. Daily excursions are available, as are special private charters for corporate functions, weddings, and groups. Reservations required. Fee. (800) 669–9296 or (573) 302–0023; www.pier17osagebeach.com.

Tropic Island Cruises. The Lodge of Four Seasons, State Road HH, Lake Ozark, MO 65049. This 75-foot luxury motor yacht sponsors daily scenic cruises. It can also be rented for special events, such as family reunions, weddings, business meetings, and parties. It holds 149 passengers, and food service and catering are available. (573) 348–0083; www.tropicislandcruises.com.

BUTTERFLY GARDENS

House of Butterflies. Route 2, Box 3192, Osage Beach, MO 65065. Located in the heart of Osage Beach, on the north side of Lake Road 54–63, this off-the-beaten-path attraction is a good educational experience for children and their parents. The 3,600-square-foot enclosure houses many varieties of lovely butterflies and provides a tranquil setting in the midst of the hustle and bustle of Osage Beach.

Owners Henry and Ruth Weinmeister have put many years of research, planning, and hard work into their dedication to preserving butterflies. The Weinmeisters enhance public understanding of the plight of butterflies with regard to encroaching development that is decimating the insect's populations.

Henry Weinmeister loves to go into detail about the saving and raising of butterflies, especially if parents and children are willing to listen. A natural-born teacher, he readily points out that butterflies need more than pretty flowers to feed on. All are plant-specific, he will tell you, meaning they need certain plants to reproduce. According to Weinmeister, these insects, which add much beauty to our lives, are in peril. He points out that hybrid plants have little nectar and do not attract butterflies, and that many butterflies need common weeds, wildflowers, and certain trees to live. However, these plants and the butterflies that are dependent on them are quickly disappearing to make way for parking lots and strip malls.

You'll come away from the Weinmeisters' garden feeling that you've learned something important. Communing with butterflies makes you understand why these fascinating creatures are worth keeping in this world. Open late April through late September; hours vary. Fee. (573) 348-0088; www.houseofbutterflies.com.

CAVES

Renowned as the Cave State, Missouri has more than 5,000 registered and mapped caves, with 300 "wild" caves in the three counties surrounding the Lake of the Ozarks. There are four show caves located within 30 miles of one another. A 93-mile triangular drive around the lake takes you from cave to cave through tree-lined roads. The caves are open to the public for tours and feature paved walkways, handrails, and lights. They include the following:

Bridal Cave. Thunder Mountain Park, 526 Bridal Cave Road, Camdenton, MO 65020. Located north of Camdenton off M-5 on Lake Road 5-88, this forty-six-million-year-old cave is the oldest cave in the area and one of three most scenic caves in America. It is the site of a legendary Indian wedding ceremony held in the early 1800s. More than 1,800 couples have been married in the cave's breathtaking Bridal Chapel. The cave is accessible by car or boat. Open daily year-round; hours vary. Fee. (573) 346-2676; www.bridalcave.com.

Jacob's Cave. 23114 Highway TT, Versailles, MO 65084. Off Route TT, north of Gravois Mills, this is the largest cave in the area and the only walk-through cave in Missouri that is handicapped-accessible. The cave, known for its depth illusion, features the world's largest geode, reflective pools, musical stalactites, prehistoric mastodon bones, and unusual strawlike formations. The rock shop on the premises features a black-light rock display, along with native minerals, crystals, and geodes for sale. Open daily year-round. &. Fee. (573) 378-4374; www.jacobscave.com.

Fantasy World Caverns. Route 3, Eldon, MO 65026. Located seven minutes east of Bagnell Dam off U.S. 54, this three-level cave offers guided tours of its natural waterfalls, canyon passages, and large domed ceilings. Before it was returned to its natural state, it was used as a dance hall and skating rink. Open daily Memorial Day through Labor Day; weekends the rest of the year. Hours vary. Fee. (573) 392-2115; www.fantasyworldcaverns.com.

Ozark Caverns. Lake of the Ozarks State Park, Route 1, Box 371, Linn Creek, MO 65052. This state-owned cave is located outside park boundaries, off U.S. 54 on Route A. Visitors are given handheld lanterns as guides take groups through the spectacular highlighted sights, which include Angel's Shower, a continual flow of water that falls from the rock ceiling into two massive stone basins below. Closed in winter. Hours vary. Fee. (573) 346-2500; www.mostateparks.com.

COUNTRY-WESTERN MUSIC SHOWS

There are several country music palaces in the area. Scheduled shows normally run from April until October, with Christmas shows in November and December. Two of the most popular in Osage Beach are the following:

Lee Mace's Ozark Opry. P.O. Box 242, Osage Beach, MO 65065. Located a quarter mile west of U.S. 54, this country music showcase opened in 1953 and is the first family music theater of its type in the country. Family entertainment is the hallmark here, with music that runs the gamut from country to sentimental favorites and gospel, with plenty of comedy thrown in to keep the show fast-paced and fun. Open April through October. Hours vary. Reservations. Fee. &. (573) 348-2270; www.leemaceozarkopry.com.

Main Street Music Hall. 1048 Main Street, Poverty Flats Village, Osage Beach, MO 65065. Toe-tapping country music, as well as sentimental favorites from the 1950s and 1960s, is performed here. Open May through October; hours vary. Also open in late November to the Saturday before Christmas; hours vary. Reservations. Fee. (573) 348–9500; www.lakemusichall.com.

FISHING

The Lake of the Ozarks offers excellent fishing year-round. Bring your deep-diving crankbaits, jig 'n frog lures, and top-water lures and drop in a line for large- and smallmouth bass, Kentucky bass, black and white crappie, bluegill, white bass, channel and flathead catfish, and hybrid stripers. If you're lucky, you might hook a rare spoonbill paddlefish (see Osage Catfisheries, below). The Missouri Department of Conservation provides regulation and stocking of the lake, which has brought in record catches, such as a 91-pound blue catfish and a 134-pound paddlefish! Fishing licenses are required for all persons except Missouri residents over sixty-four and youngsters under sixteen. Fee. For information: Missouri Department of Conservation, *Wildlife Code of Missouri*, P.O. Box 180, Jefferson City, MO 65102; (573) 751–4115.

Osage Catfisheries. Nichols Road (on the grounds of Sycamore Creek Golf Club—no kidding!), Osage Beach, MO 65065. It isn't every day that you find a golf course featuring lakes and ponds that serve as combination water hazards and spawning pools for catfish. Adjacent to the course is Osage Catfisheries, which raises catfish, bass, and bluegill and is the only licensed producer of spoonbill paddlefish in the country. The oldest fish in North America, the paddlefish has the distinction of producing an excellent black roe that is second only to the beluga caviar of the Russian sturgeon. Osage Catfisheries ships paddlefish caviar both domestically and internationally. Although the catfishery itself is not open to the public, if you play golf you can enjoy a walk around a challenging course featuring zoysia tees, Bermuda fairways, lovely residential homes, and ponds that are unlike any others. Tours can be arranged with advance reservations. (573) 348–9593 or 348–2305.

GOLF COURSES

The Lake of the Ozarks offers excellent and affordable places to hit the links. Tan-Tar-A Resort and the Lodge of Four Seasons were ranked among the top fifty golf resorts in the world in a 1996 *Condé Nast Traveler* readers' poll. In excess of 260 holes and fifteen courses varying in length, degree of difficulty, elevation changes, water hazards, and strategic layouts make the courses appealing for all levels.

Major players, including Arnold Palmer, Lee Trevino, and Tom Watson, have lent their skills to numerous tournaments. The Junior Golf Program gives boys and girls the opportunity to participate in various golf clinics, and McDonald's Junior Golf Tournaments are held June through August. Reduced rates are offered at participating courses.

The Lake of the Ozarks has some enticing "Golf-a-Round" packages to encourage visitors to play here. You can make hotel reservations and schedule tee times at any of the associated courses with a single phone call. All the resorts and golf clubs offer packages for their individual properties, and you can contact your favorite property for arrangements. Most of the lake's courses are open daily year-round, weather permitting. Call for hours. Courses include the following:

The Lodge of Four Seasons Championship Golf Resort & Spa. P.O. Box 215, Lake Ozark, MO 65049. There is a pro shop on site, along with golf instruction, custom practice facilities at the "Golf University," numerous golf packages, and three courses. The Lodge's Championship Course is a classic Robert Trent Jones, Sr., design that features rolling fairways, large greens, and spectacular par 3s. The design of this eighteen-hole, 6,567-yard, par-71 course utilizes land that juts out into the lake, creating challenging golf and some of the most beautiful scenery in the Midwest. *Golf Digest* and *Golf* magazine consistently rank it among the top five courses in the state. Two other courses, the Executive and Seasons Ridge, offer challenging layouts for beginning or advanced golfers. Seasons Ridge, ranked by *Golf Week* as the fifth best course in Missouri, is one of the top public courses in the state. (800) THE-LAKE or (573) 365-3000; www.4seasonsresort.com.

Old Kinderhook Golf and Marina Community. Lake Road 54-80, P.O. Box 1050, Camdenton, MO 65020. This 638-acre recreational community has it all—cottages, patio homes, garden villas, and condos, some of which are resort rentals. Amenities include a Tom Weiskopf championship golf course complete with undulating zoysia fairways, large bent-grass greens, four elevated tee boxes on each hole, and natural rock waterfalls. The 6,855-yard, eighteen-hole, par-71 design makes this one of the best crafted and most uniquely playable courses in the Midwest. (573) 346-4444; www.oldkinderhook.com.

Osage National Golf Club. P.O. Box 1300, Lake Ozark, MO 65049. Nestled between the lake and the lush Osage River Valley, the first Arnold Palmer–designed course in Missouri boasts a lovely course that incorporates wandering creeks, several lakes, and greens ranging from 29 to 47 yards in depth. The par-72, twenty-seven-hole, 7,150-yard layout is challenging for all skill levels and offers three possible eighteen-hole combinations. (573) 365–1950; www.osagenational.com.

Sycamore Creek Golf Club. Lake Road 54–56 at Dude Ranch Road, 1270 Nichols Road, Osage Beach, MO 65065. Catfish, caviar, and golf are part of this unusual success story by a remarkable family-owned company that is responsible for some of the most ingenious use of property and resources in the country. Fish-filled ponds serve as combination golf course water hazards and spawning pools for catfish! The eighteen-hole golf course and catfishery are located on a wooded, 300-acre valley surrounded by gorgeous upscale homes. Amenities include a snack bar, a lounge, and rental clubs. There are zoysia tees, midiron Bermuda fairways, Crenshaw bent-grass greens, and, of course, catfish. (573) 348–9593; www.sycamorecreekgolfclub.com.

Tan-Tar-A Resort, Golf Club, & Spa. P.O. Box 188, State Road KK, Osage Beach, MO 65065. The resort has consistently been awarded *Meeting & Conventions* magazine's prestigious Gold Key Award. It offers the John Jacobs Golf School, special packages, rental equipment, driving ranges, two pro shops, a staff PGA pro available for consultation, and two courses. The Oaks Course, designed by Bruce Devlin and Robert Von Hagge, is a masterful eighteen-hole, par-71 layout, with 6,432 yards of demanding approaches, nine water hazards, and more than sixty sand traps along a tight terrain. In 1994 this was the host headquarters course for the PGA Club Pro Championship. Another course, Hidden Lakes, offers nine holes, par 35, and fairways set amid stunning lake views and difficult sand traps. Other amenities include racquetball, waterskiing, five pools, a health spa, horseback riding, tennis, a full-service marina, and more. The resort boasts several restaurants and lounges that serve everything from seafood and steaks to pizza and burgers. (800) 826–8272 or (573) 348–3131; www.tan-tar-a.com.

Other courses in the area include the Lake Valley Country Club, the Dogwood Hills Resort and Golf Club, and the Bear Creek Valley

Golf Club in Osage Beach; the Eldon Country Club in Eldon; the Bay View Golf Course in Linn Creek; and the Indian Rock Golf Club in Laurie. For a complete list and golf package information, contact the Lake of the Ozarks Golf Council at (800) 490-8474; www.golfing missouri.com

MUSEUMS

Morgan County Historical Museum. Old Martin Hotel, Versailles, MO 65084. As the seat of Morgan County, Versailles has a history that dates back to 1833. Much of the town's memorabilia has been preserved by members of the Morgan County Historical Society, who staff the museum inside the old Martin Hotel. Historical treasures found here include a library with bound volumes of Morgan County newspapers from 1877, a century-old square grand piano, and an old beauty shop with artifacts from yesteryear, plus a barbershop, a weaving room, a war relics room, and more. Closed Sunday. Fee. (573) 378-4401.

SHRINES

Mary, Mother of the Church Shrine. M-5 between Versailles and Camdenton, on the grounds of St. Patrick's Church, Laurie, MO 65038. Dedicated to Mary, Mother of the Church, this remarkable shrine is housed in a natural grotto on the premises of St. Patrick's Church. Mary, Mother of the Church Shrine is surrounded by a terraced amphitheater that seats several thousand worshippers and Mother's Wall of Life of polished black granite. A three-tiered super-structure of steel towers over the altar, and fountains and waterfalls add to the stately setting. The project was designed by Frank Grimaldi of Kansas City and the epic statue that personifies Mary is by sculptor Don Wiegand. Available for viewing daily year-round. Free. (573) 374-6279; www.mothersshrine.org.

STATE PARKS

Ha Ha Tonka State Park. Route 1, Box 113-M, Camdenton, MO 65020. Accessible by water or land; located between Mile Markers 14 and 15 in the Big Niangua Arm. By car it's just west of Camdenton off U.S. 54 on State Road D. By boat, be aware that the park's famous ruins are up a 300-step staircase from the docks below. The ruins are of an early 1900s castle and estate, conceived and developed by Robert McClure Snyder, a Kansas City businessman who acquired 2,500 acres of land and built his private retreat, importing Scottish stonemasons to ensure authentic construction techniques. Kansas City architect Adrian Van Brunt designed the three-and-a-half-story European-style castle, complete with a stone stable, an 80-foot-tall water tower, and nine greenhouses.

Construction began in 1905. Unfortunately, Snyder was killed in an automobile accident on Kansas City's Independence Boulevard a year later. The interior of the castle was completed in 1922 by Snyder's sons, who were eventually forced to sell Snyder's natural-gas supply business to eastern interests. As Union Electric's Lake of the Ozarks project began encroaching on the natural spring-fed lake at the foot of Ha Ha Tonka cliff, the owners were forced to lease the property out as a hotel. Finally, in 1942 Ha Ha Tonka burned, the fire caused by a spark from one of its many fireplaces. The castle was gutted, and what remains today are the outside walls. The state of Missouri purchased the estate in 1978 and opened it to the public as a state park. The 3,527-acre grounds feature scenic trails, and there are natural bridges, caves, and other geologic wonders to be found here. Open for day use only, year-round, dawn to dusk. Free admission; no camping. ♿. (573) 346–2986; www.mostateparks.com.

Lake of the Ozarks State Park, P.O. Box 170 (U.S. 54 to M–42, east to M–134), Kaiser, MO 65047. Missouri's largest state park offers 17,000 acres and 89 miles of shoreline. The park provides rare public access to two beaches, plus boat-launching areas. There's even an on-site airport, with a 6,500-by-100-foot runway, plus terminal building, parallel taxiway, and fuel and tie-down service. Hiking trails, horseback riding, and four organized youth camps are offered. The free sand beaches provide swimming opportunities, and nearby picnicking and hiking areas are available. You can also reserve a picnic shelter here for large groups. Open daily, dawn to dusk, year-round.

Along the park's lakeshore is the Ozarks Aquatic Trail, designed for boaters, with stops marked by buoys. A free booklet keyed to the buoys is available at the park office. Naturalists present programs in an open-air amphitheater during the summer; the park also provides guided hikes and a variety of other programs. Information is available on site about the park and its nine trails. Free admission. Fee for reserving picnic shelter. Fee for camping; reservations required. ♿. (573) 348-2694; www.mostateparks.com.

WATER PARKS, PARKS, MINIATURE GOLF, AND GO-CARTS

Big Surf Waterpark. U.S. 54 at State Road Y, Linn Creek, MO 65052. Located between Osage Beach and Camdenton, this family-oriented park features twenty-two acres of fun, with a wave pool, rapid rides, body flumes, and a "Bubble Beach" for young children. Open daily, Memorial Day through Labor Day. Hours vary. Fee. (573) 346-6111; www.bigsurfwaterpark.com.

   Big Shot Family Action Park. U.S. 54 at State Road Y, Linn Creek, MO 65052. Adjacent to Big Surf Waterpark, this attraction offers racers, bumper boats, go-carts, an arcade, kiddie rides, and miniature golf. Open daily March through October. Hours vary. Fee. (573) 346-6111; www.bigshotraceways.com.

   Miner Mike's Indoor Family Fun Center. Located across from the Factory Outlet Mall, U.S. 54, Osage Beach, MO 65065. This indoor family fun center offers bumper cars, a roller coaster, a Ferris wheel, games, miniature golf, and more. Hours vary. Fee. (800) 317-2126 or (573) 348-2126; www.minermikes.com.

WHERE TO SHOP

The Lake of the Ozarks has hundreds of shops, ranging from a factory outlet mall to strip malls, antiques and craft shops, and specialty stores. The number of places at which to browse and buy are too numerous to list here, but we've included some of the better-known malls and a few unique shops that are worth a visit.

MAJOR SHOPPING AREAS

Factory Outlet Village. U.S. 54 off I-70, Osage Beach, MO 65065. This sixty-one-acre factory mall is Missouri's largest. It features more than 110 manufacturer outlets, including Van Heusen Direct, Polo/Ralph Lauren, Brooks Brothers, Donna Karan, Laura Ashley, Tommy Hilfiger, Dansk, and Lenox. You can find quality and bargains in clothing, housewares, shoes, children's wear, jewelry,

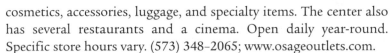

cosmetics, accessories, luggage, and specialty items. The center also has several restaurants and a cinema. Open daily year-round. Specific store hours vary. (573) 348-2065; www.osageoutlets.com.

Main Street Village. Off U.S. 54 West, Osage Beach, MO 65065. This quaint Victorian-themed village offers an assortment of nicely appointed shops, boutiques, and eateries. Open daily year-round. (573) 348-5101.

Stone Crest Mall. U.S. 54 East (0.25 mile north of the junction of U.S. 54 and 42), Osage Beach, MO 65065. If you're looking for an unusual gift to take home, this enclosed shopping center offers a variety of retail and gift shops and restaurants. Open daily year-round. (573) 348-3106.

UNUSUAL BOUTIQUES, SHOPS, AND GALLERIES

Class Act. 5513 U.S. 54 (1 mile southwest of Grand Glaize Bridge), Osage Beach, MO 65065. Self-proclaimed as "the ultimate boutique," this shop specializes in women's clothing, jewelry, shoes, hats, etc. It also features lotions, candles, body scrubs, and an on-site interior design business. Open daily year-round. (573) 348-0090.

Country Crossroads. 1 Palisades Village, U.S. 54 and State Road KK, Osage Beach, MO 65065. Bear lovers will love the name brands sold here. The store is a Gold Key Dealer for Department 56 treasures and has current additions to collectibles, such as Heritage Village, Dickens Village, and other selections, as well as accessory pieces that go with them. Candles, quilts, afghans, and nautically themed gifts are also featured. Open daily year-round. (573) 348-0606.

Lisa Frick Art Gallery. 2840 Business 54, Lake Ozark, MO 65049. This unusual gallery is definitely worth a stop. The owner-artist offers her paintings for sale, along with unique collections of jewelry, fine art, pottery, and sculpture from around the country. Open year-round. Closed Tuesday. (573) 365-7270; www.lisafrickgallery.com.

Ozark Bar-B-Que and Boutique. M-5 to State Road F to State Road TT, Sunrise Beach, MO 65079. Devour plates of excellent ribs, fries, and pies at the adjacent barbecue eatery (see also Where to Eat) and then go shopping at this unique store that sells a variety of clothing, sun gear, and souvenirs. The boutique specializes in hilarious T-shirts and hats. There's everything from glitzy sequined caps to comical berets such as the "Carmen Miranda," complete with bananas and other assorted fruit. The upstairs and downstairs provide buyers with a wide array of beautiful handmade clothing, soft and gauzy dresses from Indonesia, and swimsuits to fit every figure. Downstairs there is plenty of fun sportswear, beach necessities, and kids' stuff. Open April through October. Hours vary. (573) 374-7769.

WHERE TO EAT

More than one hundred restaurants are located on the lake, and some have access by both water and land. The fare ranges from fast food to gourmet, with most of the restaurants offering broad menus that give you a taste of everything, from Italian and Mexican to French and American, along with Ozark-style delicacies such as catfish, trout, and barbecue. Sunday brunch is served at several restaurants, and many establishments offer hearty breakfasts and refreshing drinks. Because of space limitations, we can mention only a few of the many dining establishments we found to be good choices. Many restaurants close in fall and winter, so be sure to check before you go. For a complete rundown of local eateries, write for your copy of the *Lake of the Ozarks Restaurant Guide,* available from the Lake of the Ozarks Convention and Visitor Bureau, Box 1498, Osage Beach, MO 65065; (800) 386-5253.

Black Bear Lodge. Tan-Tar-A Resort, Golf Club, and Spa, State Road KK, Osage Beach, MO 65065. The lodge offers casual family dining in a hunt-club atmosphere for breakfast, lunch, dinner, and Sunday brunch. You can dine outdoors in warm weather, and children eight and under eat for free from 5:00 to 6:00 P.M. when accompanied by an adult. $$; □. (800) 826-8272 or (573) 348-3131.

Captain's Galley. Lake Road 5–89 at Mile Marker 31, P.O. Box 1104, Camdenton, MO 65020. Open for breakfast, lunch, and dinner, this floating restaurant is accessible by boat or car. The lunch and dinner menu features an assortment of nicely prepared sandwiches, salads, steaks, and fish. Breakfast can be omelettes, homemade biscuits and gravy, pancakes, or waffles. Open daily March through January 1. $–$$; □. (573) 873-5227.

HK's Steak House. The Lodge of Four Seasons Championship Golf Resort and Spa, P.O. Box 215, Lake Ozark, MO 65049. Rated one of the top steak houses in the state by the Missouri Beef

Industry Council Beef Backers, this restaurant prepares fine cuts of certified Angus beef over an elevated charcoal grill. $$$; ☐. (800) THE-LAKE or (573) 365-3000; www.4seasonsresort.com.

Ozark Bar-B-Que and Boutique. (M-5 to State Road F to State Road TT), Sunrise Beach, MO 65079. This is a rather unusual lakeside family restaurant, boutique, and market; it is basically a one-stop place to eat, shop, and feed fish. If you haven't had the experience of dining on great barbecue while watching an onslaught of deranged carp in a feeding frenzy, well, here's your chance. The restaurant will provide you with carp food as well as human food. Start off your morning with biscuits and gravy or eggs Benedict; for lunch or dinner try hickory-smoked ribs, chicken, pork, or beef, and finish off with a piece of tasty homemade pie for dessert. Afterward drop by the adjacent Ozark Bar-B-Que Boutique (see Where to Shop) for souvenirs. Open daily, May through September. $-$$; ☐. (573) 374-7769.

Peace & Plenty Cafe. 5837 U.S. 54 at Main Street Village, Osage Beach, MO 65065. After shopping in the Village, you can have lunch in this small restaurant, which offers sandwiches, homemade breads, and desserts. Open daily for lunch year-round. $-$$; ☐. (573) 348-1462.

Traditionally Stewart's Restaurant. 1151 Bagnell Dam Boulevard (U.S. Business 54), Lake Ozark, MO 65049. If you're looking for a place that isn't upscale, trendy, or themed, try Traditionally Stewart's. You don't have to spend a lot of money to get a lot of food at this unpretentious down-home restaurant. Located on the blue-collar side of the lake, Traditionally Stewart's has great appeal for people looking for something different.

For breakfast try the "Hungryman": two biscuits and gravy for a little more than four bucks. The "biscuits" are mammoth-size, mouthwatering, miniloaves that weigh about a pound each. If they didn't taste so good, you could probably use them for ballast.

While you're stuffing yourself, the person you're with can feast on an elephant-size cinnamon roll big enough for three or perhaps snarf down a "Number 6"—country pork tenderloin, two eggs, country chunk potatoes, and, yes, a biscuit and gravy.

So, do the math: If you divide a total of three of Traditionally Stewart's biscuits between two normal-size people, add a cinnamon roll, meat, and potatoes, you will get a couple of overfed gourmands whose pants don't fit properly. This is OK because you're on vacation. You can also return for lunch or dinner. Then you can choose from simple, tasty offerings such as salads, sandwiches, and entrees like fried catfish and Ozark sugar-cured ham. $–$$; (no cards). (573) 365-2400.

Toledo's. The Lodge of Four Seasons Championship Golf Resort and Spa, P.O. Box 215, Lake Ozark, MO 65049. *Wine Spectator*'s Award of Excellence went to this restaurant, which offers one of the most outstanding restaurant wine lists in the world. In addition, it offers a mixture of Southern French, Italian, Greek, Spanish, and Moroccan food. Live entertainment is presented Tuesday through Saturday. Open daily. $$–$$$; □. (800) THE-LAKE or (573) 365-3000; www.4seasons.com.

The Wharf Restaurant. P.O. Box 85 (M-5 at the north end of the Niangua Bridge, 8 miles north of Camdenton), Camdenton, MO 65020. The house specialty here is prime rib, roasted to perfection in a blend of seasonings and served with salad and potato. The Wharf is open for breakfast, lunch, and dinner from late May through early September. Closed Tuesday. $$; □. (573) 873-3520; www.thewharf restaurant.com.

WHERE TO STAY

There are numerous places to stay at the Lake of the Ozarks—from no-frills fishing cottages and motel rooms to upscale family resorts, houseboats, and beautiful condominiums and homes with a view. Many places are family owned and offer waterfront housekeeping units and playgrounds for the kids. The east side of the lake is the more frequented, with plenty of places to stay and resorts large enough to hold huge conferences. The west side is less crowded, with fewer places to stay but with more natural beauty to see. The list is much too long to print here, but you can find what you're looking for by calling (800) FUN-LAKE (386-5253) for your copy of the *Lake of the Ozarks Vacation Guide*. In the meantime, here's a sampling of some accommodations you may find to your liking:

Country Club Hotel and Spa. State Road HH and Carol Road, P.O. Box 1599, Lake Ozark, MO 65049. This world-class resort and racquet club offers luxurious amenities, unique services, and European decor that appeals to upscale tastes. Guests are treated to scenic lake views from their spacious rooms, suites, or villas at the only AAA four-diamond hotel in central Missouri. They can take advantage of amenities such as an excellent health club and fitness facility, indoor and outdoor swimming pools, tennis courts and a Van Der Meer Tennis University, racquetball courts, a restaurant and lounge with live New Orleans–style jazz, and more. In addition, the resort features 20,000 square feet of state-of-the-art meeting and banquet facilities. Individual and group packages are available. $$$; ☐. (800) 964–6698 or (573) 964–2200; www.countryclubhotel.com.

Forever Resorts. Lake of the Ozarks Marina, M–5 North at the Niangua Bridge (north side of bridge and west side of M–5), Box 3229, Camdenton, MO 85020. If you're thinking about staying aboard a houseboat, you can rent one here. These floating homes range from 56 to 65 feel long and are equipped with everything you'll need, including four staterooms, a sofa bed, a dining area, a full kitchen with two refrigerators, a gas stove, and a microwave. There's even a television equipped with a VCR in case you get bored. All houseboats come with full-size sundecks, built-in water slide, and gas barbecue grill. Your kitchen equipment, towels, and linens are provided. There are two bathrooms in case you bring along the whole family. A houseboat costs a bit more than a hotel but can sleep up to ten people, so you can split the cost.

Although the boat is big, it's easily maneuverable, with dual 130-horsepower engines that can allow you to chug along at a sensible speed. You can spend the night tied up at any one of a number of marinas, or you can overnight along the shoreline. A few places you can put in are quieter than others, but be aware that much of the shoreline is privately owned and not accessible to the public. The houseboat company can guide you to the quieter and less frequented places. For the most peace and privacy, come during the week or in the off-season. Open daily March through November, weather permitting. $$$; ☐. (800) 255–5561; www.foreverresorts.com.

Hilty Inn Bed and Breakfast. 206 East Jasper, Versailles, MO 65084. This elegant, historic Victorian home offers a change from resort condominiums and cabins. Accommodations include four guest rooms with private baths and a special bridal suite. A full breakfast is served. A tearoom offers English high tea and gourmet dinners by reservation Monday through Friday. Open year-round. $$; ☐. (800) 667–8093 or (573) 378–2020.

Inn at Grand Glaize. P.O. Box 969, Lake Road 54–40, Osage Beach, MO 65065. Located in the heart of Osage Beach, it offers 150 guest rooms and suites, a pool, a fitness center, and 13,000 square feet of meeting space under one roof. A marina, complimentary boat slips, and a restaurant and lounge with live entertainment are available to guests, along with a prime rib buffet and Sunday brunch. Special vacation packages and condominium rentals are available. Open year-round. $$–$$$; □. (800) 348–4731 or (573) 348–4731; www.innatgrandglaize.com.

The Lodge of Four Seasons Championship Golf Resort and Spa. Horseshoe Bend Parkway, P.O. Box 215, Lake Ozark, MO 65049. Named to *Condé Nast Traveler*'s "50 Best Golf Resorts," The Lodge is one of only five resorts in the Midwest to be so designated. Opened in 1964, it offers forty-five holes of championship golf, including a Robert Trent Jones, Sr., signature course. The resort offers more than 65,000 square feet of meeting space that can accommodate up to 1,800 persons. It also has a full-service marina, four swimming pools, (one indoor/outdoor), a world-class spa, children's video arcade, and more. If that's not enough, there are a variety of shops, a cinema, and beautifully landscaped Japanese gardens to stroll through. Several restaurants on the premises feature wines, fresh specialties, and lake views. Fine dining can be had at HK's Steak House, which features certified Angus beef. You can choose from a variety of accommodations that offer two- and three-bedroom condominiums and guest rooms, many with lake views. Golf, spa, family, fun, romance, and nautical adventure packages are also available. Open year-round. $$$; □. (800) 843–5253 or (573) 365–3000; www.4seasonsresort.com.

Lone Oak Point Resort. #1 Lone Oak Road, Sunrise Beach, MO 65079. The nicest resort on the west side of the lake can be reached by taking M–5 south from Versailles to Route F; then go left on State Road TT and follow the signs. Located on a wooded, nine-acre peninsula with a superb lake view, Lone Oak Point is owned by an environmentally aware couple who have maintained its architectural integrity by preserving the land around it and not overbuilding. The resort has an enclosed fitness spa with indoor pool, sauna, and exercise room. Other amenities are an outdoor pool, a wading pool, an enclosed fishing area, and covered boat stalls.

Accommodations range from cottages and duplexes to two-story units. With the exception of the motel rooms, all have complete kitchens, and most feature microwaves, trash compactors, garbage disposals, ice makers, television, and a deck and patio with a grill. All kitchens come complete with cooking utensils, dishes, and silverware, a coffeemaker, a toaster, and a vacuum. Lone Oak Point is quiet, peaceful, and lovely, but you do have to bring your own bath and dish towels and soap, and there is no maid service or telephone in the room. Reservations from mid-June to mid-August are accepted in multiples of seven days only; there is a two-day minimum stay before or after that time. Open March through November. $$–$$$; ☐. (573) 374–7992; www.funlake.com.

Millstone Lodge. State Road O, Box 1157, Laurie, MO 65038. The largest resort on the west side of the lake, Millstone caters on weekends to a younger crowd, who come here for skiing, boating, and getting a great tan. The resort offers reasonably priced rooms, rental boats, free slips and boat launching, group meeting facilities, nearby golf, and an outdoor pool. Accommodations range from kitchenettes and suites to motel units. The on-site restaurant is open for breakfast, lunch, and dinner. Open March through December. $$; ☐. (800) 290–2596 or (573) 372–5111.

Tan-Tar-A Resort, Golf Club & Spa. P.O. Box 188, State Road KK, Osage Beach, MO 65065. Open for more than thirty years, Tan-Tar-A is a 420-acre resort housing more than 930 guest rooms, 185 suites, and meeting space totaling 93,000 square feet. Tan-Tar-A offers the John Jacobs Golf School, special packages, rental equipment, driving ranges, two pro shops, a staff PGA pro available for consultation, and two courses (see Golf Courses, in Where to Go). Other amenities include racquetball, waterskiing, five pools, a health spa, horseback riding, tennis, a full-service marina, and more. The resort boasts several restaurants and lounges and offers special amenities for children and parents, including in-room baby-sitting, a children's playhouse, and a summer kids' camp. Open year-round. $$–$$$; ☐. (800) 826–8272 or (573) 348–3131.

South Day Trip 1

CARTHAGE, MO

Founded in 1842, Carthage (drive south on U.S. 71) was the site of the first major land battle of the Civil War after the U.S. Congress formally declared war against the South on July 5, 1861. Events of the battle are highlighted in a kiosk of text and graphic illustration near Carter Park. The town was destroyed by guerrilla warfare in 1864. After the Civil War, Carthage drew investors and entrepreneurs, and by the end of the nineteenth century, it is reported to have had more millionaires per capita than any other U.S. city. Much of the wealth came from mining. There were rich deposits of lead, zinc, and a gray marble for which Carthage is famous. Elaborate Victorian architecture still stands to mark the heyday when the town had unlimited prosperity.

Recently Carthage has had a taste of that prosperity once again. Precious Moments Chapel brings thousands of visitors here annually. The Maple Leaf Festival, held in October, is another draw; it features a car show, a dog show, crafts, food, entertainment, a homes tour, a parade, a petting zoo, a quilt show, and the biggest parade in southwest Missouri.

You can take a driving tour of several of the Victorian homes in the area, all erected between 1870 and 1910. Many of them were built using Carthage marble, and a number of them have been converted to bed-and-breakfast accommodations. A self-guided-tour brochure is available. For a complete listing of things to see and do, contact the Carthage Chamber of Commerce, 107 East Third Street, Carthage, MO 64836; (417) 358–2373; www.carthagenow.com.

WHERE TO GO

"Battle of Carthage" Civil War Museum. 205 East Grant Street, Carthage, MO 64836. The museum features authentic artifacts and information about the battle. An elaborate, detailed mural of the event, painted by local artist Andy Thomas, and a diorama depicting the battle are showcased here. Open daily. Free. (417) 358–6643.

George Washington Carver National Monument. 5646 Carver Road, Diamond, MO 64836. The original cabin where this great African-American was born no longer stands, although a plaque marks the spot. This park pays tribute to Carver's achievements and distinctions as one of America's great scientists, educators, and humanitarians. It's open every day. Free. (417) 325–4151.

Jasper County Courthouse. Between Third and Fourth Streets, 2 blocks east of Garrison Street, Carthage, MO 64836. Designed in 1894 by Maximilian Orlopp of New Orleans, the Romanesque Revival structure was constructed of native stone quarried by the Carthage Stone Company. It was completed in 1895 at a cost of $100,000 and is on the National Register of Historic Places. The public is free to visit. A free walking-tour brochure of the Courthouse Square Historic District is available from the Carthage Chamber of Commerce. (417) 358–2373; www.carthagenow.com.

Precious Moments Chapel. 480 Chapel Road, Carthage, MO 64836. This is Samuel J. Butcher's "gift of thanksgiving to the Lord." Murals covering 5,000 square feet depict scenes from the Old and New Testaments. The Precious Moments Art Gallery showcases the history behind Precious Moments, original pieces of art by local artists, and personal family memorabilia. The visitor center is patterned after a European village. Cottage- and castlelike structures within the village house several shops. Gospel and bluegrass music shows are presented several times daily. The Precious Moments Collectors Christmas Weekend, held the first weekend in December, features a candlelight service, dinner, classes, and tours of the Butcher home. Open daily. Admittance is free. (800) 543–7975; www.preciousmoments.com.

WHERE TO STAY

Grand Avenue Bed and Breakfast. 1615 Grand Avenue, Carthage, MO 64836. This Queen Anne Victorian home features spacious and elegant rooms with amenities that range from rooms with queen-size beds and private baths to a room with king-size bed and large private bath with Jacuzzi. A full breakfast is served in the formal dining room. There's also a pool available for guests. Group discounts are available with the rental of four or more rooms. Special packages and murder mystery weekends are also offered. $$; ☐. (888) 380-6786 or (417) 358-7265; www.grandavenue.com.

    Harmony Heights Bed and Breakfast. Deer Run Estates (call for directions), Carthage, MO 64836. It's a little hard to find, but it's worth the drive to stay at this rustic cabin located footsteps from a flowing creek. It offers a fully furnished kitchen, bath, bedroom in the loft area, woodstove, air-conditioning, television, and VCR. The natural setting is perfect for relaxation. Grab a fishing pole and canoe downriver, or just watch ducks and geese swim by from the front porch. A hot or cold breakfast is delivered to your doorstep every morning. This is a great romantic getaway for two, but children are welcome if you want to bring them. $$; ☐. (417) 359-9136 or (417) 358-1445.

    The Leggett House. 1106 Grand Avenue, Carthage, MO 64836. Completed in 1901, this Victorian Carthage stone house offers six large rooms, an elevator, private or shared bath, and full breakfast in the formal dining room. The decor features beveled and leaded curved windows, an open staircase, paneled entry hall, and mosaic-tiled solarium with marble fountain. $$; ☐. (417) 358-0683; www.leggetthouse.com.

Southwest Day Trip 1

When sojourning in southeast Kansas, remember that people here like things simple, especially food. Fried chicken or chicken-fried is the featured cuisine in many places. Simply surrender yourself to iceberg lettuce rather than radicchio and don't expect Chez Panisse, and you'll be quite happy here.

Southeast Kansas is filled with stores that tout themselves as antiques shops but in actuality are crammed wall to wall with flea-market "junque." Just as long as you know what to expect, it's fun to browse and you might discover an occasional treasure, but don't expect a Sotheby-style find.

Southeast Kansas does have unexpected charm. In small towns, such as Chanute, tree-lined cobblestone streets, gorgeous old homes, and whole city blocks have been preserved. Southeast Kansans take pride in their historic heritage, and the area holds many architecturally significant structures—including one of singularly weighty importance called Big Brutus.

LOUISBURG, KS

WHERE TO GO

Louisburg Cider Mill. P.O. Box 670, Louisburg, KS 66053. Take U.S. 69 to K–68, then travel west for 4 miles. If the idea of cold apple cider, fresh-baked bread, and homemade cider doughnuts intrigues

you, this is the place to go for a quick getaway. The store displays cider products and natural foods in old-time barrels and cases to give the feeling of a country emporium. The warm, friendly atmosphere makes you want to linger all day. While you're there, don't forget to sample the doughnuts. These cakelike goodies, made with cider, have a marvelous texture. You can watch the doughnuts being made and then take home the results.

The cider mill is also the home of the Lost Trail Root Beer Company. This special root-beer brew is refined in eastern Kansas from a family recipe passed down through generations to the present owners. The soft drink is a real thirst quencher on a Kansas scorcher.

Apples are pressed every day except Friday and Sunday from September through November. The store is open from 9:00 A.M. to 6:00 P.M. seven days a week except Thanksgiving and Christmas. Free tours are available in fall. (800) 748–7762 or (913) 837–5202; www.cidermill.com.

Powell Observatory. Just off 263rd Street and U.S. 69 (3 miles northwest of Louisburg, KS), c/o Astronomical Society of Kansas City, P.O. Box 400, Blue Springs, MO 64015. Run by the Astronomical Society of Kansas City, Powell Observatory houses a 30-inch computer-controlled telescope for public viewing of the night skies from May to October. Located in Lewis-Young Park, the facility has a heated classroom (with rest rooms) attached to the 20-foot domed observatory, where star-observing parties are held twice a month. There is also a Junior Astronomers Group for kids ten to seventeen. Children should be at least 36 inches tall to use the big scope and old enough to understand what they're seeing. Free. (913) 837–5305.

MARAIS DES CYGNES WILDLIFE AREA (LA CYGNE, KS)

Those who have an eye for the unexpected can find wonder in the beauty of the Marais des Cygnes Wildlife Area. Located outside La Cygne in the picturesque floodplain of eastern Kansas, the refuge occupies more than 7,000 acres of man-made marshes rippling with natural lakes and laced with miles of rivers and creeks.

The most wonderful thing about Marais des Cygnes, other than its natural beauty, is that it is only an hour south of Kansas City on U.S. 69. The area is a resting place for migratory waterfowl and other birds. Primitive camping is available, as well as hunting and fishing with the proper license.

The refuge takes it name from the Marais des Cygnes River, meaning "marsh of the swans," a title bestowed by the early French trappers who discovered it. Ironically, there is a good chance that what the trappers saw were not swans, but white pelicans that migrate through the area each spring. Flocks of these graceful, long-billed creatures can be seen floating in the water in early May and their presence in the marsh pool, tinted a rosy amber by the setting sun, creates a surrealistic splendor not unlike that found in the marshes and swamps of the southern United States.

Ducks, geese, herons, egrets, and birds of prey can be spotted in the marshy area. During spring and fall migration, the temporary population of migrating ducks may reach 150,000. So far, 300 species of birds have been sighted at Marais des Cygnes, and about 115 species, including mallards, blue- and green-winged teal, and Canada geese, nest here.

As for fishing, it's plentiful in spring when crappies and catfish abound. At this time of year, you can often see huge spawning carp leaping out of the water, courting each other in happy twosomes. They're wonderful to watch but not so good for angling—they're so wrapped up in each other that dangling bait holds little appeal.

The fishing draws people who stand along the marsh banks for much of the day, hoping to catch their evening meal. Those driving campers park alongside the water and sit in lawn chairs, casting in their lines at twilight.

Across from the refuge on U.S. 69 is Trading Post, a spot that played an important role as a rendezvous for a pro-slavery gang in the 1850s. In fact, the entire Marais des Cygnes area figured prominently in the Kansas struggle for statehood from 1851 to 1861. Here the pro- and antislavery forces fought over whether the territory should enter the Union as a free or slave state. In 1858 a gang of pro-slavers massacred eleven free-state men near Trading Post. The men became martyrs to the abolitionist cause, and the site of their deaths is a registered National Historic Landmark called the Marais des Cygnes Massacre Memorial Park. It's 5 miles east of U.S. 69 at Trading Post in Linn County.

Marais Des Cygnes Wildlife Area is free to tour and is open daily. It's managed by the Kansas Department of Wildlife and Parks, 16382 U.S. Highway 69, Pleasanton, Kansas 66075. The Marais Des Cygnes Refuge office number is (913) 352–8941; call ahead for the bird count before you go.

Adjacent to the state wildlife area is the Marais des Cygnes National Wildlife Refuge. Managed by the U.S. Fish and Wildlife Service, it's unique for its abundance of large tracts of bottomland hardwood forest. Common species are pin and burr oak, pecan, walnut, and hickory. More than thirty-five species of warblers have been documented during the spring migration. The best viewing is usually in May in forested areas. Open daily. Free. (913) 352–8956; www.r6.fws.gov/maraisdescygnes.

Cedar Crest Lodge. P.O. Box 151, Pleasanton, KS 66075. If you can't get enough of the natural beauty of the great outdoors of this region, spend the night with Matt and Laura Cunningham at Cedar Crest Lodge. Their 7,000-square-foot home is situated on 113 acres of rolling hills, trees, and ponds. Their eleven guest rooms reflect their love of travel, and Laura is a great cook, preparing a breakfast you will remember for a long time. If you like to paint and decorate, ask them about their painting seminars. Matt and Laura have children, so they will welcome your well-behaved children as well. $–$$ ☐. (913) 352–6533 or (866) 233–2700; www.cedarcrestlodge.com.

FORT SCOTT, KS

All along the Overland Trails, U.S. Cavalry forts, such as Fort Scott, sprang up to defend western settlement. Between 1838 and 1845 a military road was constructed through the Indian Territory to connect Fort Leavenworth in Kansas and Fort Gibson in Oklahoma. Throughout the years the road was traveled by soldiers, immigrants, Native Americans, outlaws, and traders.

Today the old military road no longer exists, but modern U.S. 69 and other connecting pathways located near its original route have been designated the Frontier Military Scenic Byway. Fort Leavenworth and Fort Scott, two of the remaining historic Kansas forts that lie along that route, are open to tour today.

Located 75 miles south of Kansas City on U.S. 69, Fort Scott has been called "one of the best-kept travel secrets in the Midwest" by some of the nation's top travel writers.

Once a sleepy Kansas town, Fort Scott has awakened, wide-eyed and bushy-tailed, to welcome its burgeoning tourist industry. The authentically restored military fort and National Historic Site is, of course, the main attraction.

From April to December the fort hosts a series of special events featuring activities that portray a vivid picture of life on a frontier post during the nineteenth century. In June the annual Good Ol' Days celebration takes place. Selected by the American Bus Association as one of the top one hundred events in North America, the Good Ol' Days hosts a whirlwind of activities for the entire family, with plenty of food, fun, crafts, and entertainment.

From April 1 through mid-December, the Fort Scott Tourist Information Center (located off the U.S. 69 bypass adjacent to the fort) offers refreshments, along with information about theme weekends, special living history programs, and seasonal celebrations. It also features Dolly the Trolley tours, which take visitors through the historic city, including Fort Scott National Cemetery. The tours are completely narrated and leave hourly from the center, beginning at 10:00 A.M. You can also inquire about bus tours for schools, churches, and youth or civic organizations. For information: Fort Scott Chamber of Commerce, P.O. Box 205, Fort Scott, KS 66701; (800) 245–FORT; www.fortscott.com.

WHERE TO GO

Chenault Mansion. 820 South National Avenue, Fort Scott, KS 66701. Little has changed since the Chenault banking family built this elegant mansion in 1877. Beautifully appointed with the owners' extensive antiques collection, the mansion was designed with striking stained glass and unusual woodwork and is open to tour daily. The mansion also operates as a bed-and-breakfast. Fee. (620) 223-6800.

Historic Trolley Tour. Fort Scott Tourist Information Center, off U.S. 69 adjacent to the fort, Fort Scott, KS 66701. You can start your sight-seeing here with the guided Trolley Tour, which leaves every hour on the hour, 10:00 A.M. to 4:00 P.M. except at noon. The tour takes you past historic attractions, striking architecture, and landmarks. The trolley runs from mid-March through mid-November. Fee. (800) 245-FORT.

Fort Scott Jubilee. Memorial Hall, Third Street and National Avenue, Fort Scott, KS 66701. Regional and national performers take the stage every Saturday night for an exciting, fun show that is great country music entertainment. Bus tours are welcome. (913) 883-2006.

Fort Scott National Historic Site. Old Fort Boulevard, Fort Scott, KS 66701. The restored 1842 Frontier Military Fort was built to keep peace between the Indians and the settlers. The troops wound up policing the plains, supplying Union armies during the Civil War, and protecting railroad workers in the 1870s. A major tourist attraction that brings visitors from around the world, Fort Scott is the only completely restored frontier fort of the pre–Civil War period in the United States. Now designated a National Historic Site, the fort is located right in the center of the city, within walking distance of many shops and dining establishments.

Fort Scott's eighteen structures, including a hospital, a guardhouse, a bakery, and barracks, tell the story of the mounted Dragoons, "bleeding Kansas," and the Civil War. Open for self-guided tours year-round; closed Thanksgiving, Christmas, and New Year's Day. Fee. (620) 223-0310; www.nps.gov/fosc.

National Cemetery. Get directions to the cemetery from the Fort Scott Tourist Information Center, off U.S. 69 adjacent to the fort, Fort Scott, KS 66701. The National Cemetery is older than Arlington and just as historically important. Indian scouts buried here include many with memorable names and histories. Soldiers interred on these grounds include black infantrymen from the country's first Colored Volunteer Infantry. Free. (800) 245–FORT.

Ralph Richards Museum and Annex. 117–119 South Main Street, Fort Scott, KS 66701. You can tour this seven-room Victorian residence and see displays that include railroad memorabilia, old tools, quilts, and a fully stocked general store. Open Friday through Monday. Fee. (800) 245–FORT.

Victorian Downtown. From Old Fort Boulevard to Sixth Street. Walking-tour information is available from the Fort Scott Tourist Information Center, off U.S. 69 adjacent to the fort. The 6-block downtown area is on the National Register of Historic Places. Buildings from the period 1860 to 1919 have been restored and are the architectural showpiece of the city. Many homes feature ornate woodwork designs of gingerbread, stained and leaded glass, turrets, hitching posts, and stepping-stones for carriages. (800) 245–FORT.

WHERE TO SHOP

The Country Cupboard. 12 North Main Street, Fort Scott, KS 66701. The largest gift and craft shop in the area, this store sells country crafts, collectibles, and gift items. The adjacent Victorian Charm annex features new Victorian-inspired merchandise. Closed Sunday. (620) 223–5980.

Junk & Java. 20 Scott Avenue, Fort Scott, KS 66701. Nestled under awnings in the historic district, this Norwegian-style coffee shop offers a sidewalk cafe in warm weather. Inside is an assortment of antiques, paintings, gifts, gourmet foods, coffees, and collectibles for the hunter and fisherman. Open daily. $; ☐. (620) 223–0366.

Sekan Occasion Shops. 2210 South Main Street, Fort Scott, KS 66701. Gifts galore can be found here, from wedding gifts and Cherished Teddies to Precious Moments memorabilia and flowers. Closed Sunday. (620) 223–5190.

WHERE TO EAT

Shawnee Trails. 101 State Street, Fort Scott, KS 66701. Home-style cuisine is served here, with menu offerings that vary from stacked sandwiches and barbecue items to salads, steaks, and specialty entrees. Daily specials and senior specials are also featured. Open daily. $–$$; ☐. (620) 223-0124.

WHERE TO STAY

The Lyons' Victorian Mansion. 742 South National Avenue, Fort Scott, KS 66701. Gracious hospitality is the hallmark here. Guest suites can accommodate couples, families, business travelers, and anyone looking for a home away from home. Seven guest rooms, some with claw-foot whirlpool tubs, are spacious. A full breakfast is served complete with country-fresh eggs, garden herbs, and produce. Other amenities include an in-room telephone with dataport, dedicated computer lines, fax, copier, and answering service.

Lyons House loves to package its product. The "Sweet Suite Retreat" features two nights, a complimentary bottle of champagne, a bag of fine chocolates, and a bouquet of long-stemmed roses. It includes a breakfast basket in your room, or you can join guests in the dining room.

The Lyons' Victorian Mansion specializes in event planning for business and social occasions, ranging from birthday parties and teas to sumptuous nine-course Victorian feasts for groups of up to fifty. Business retreats, murder mystery weekends, an on-site spa, and educational tours are also offered. $$–$$$; ☐. (800) 78–GUEST or (620) 223-3644; www.lyonsmansion.com.

PITTSBURG, KS

The "Fried Chicken Capital of Southeast Kansas," Pittsburg has several chicken emporiums from which to choose. It is also famous for being the jumping-off point for the attraction known as Big Brutus, a sixteen-story-high, one-of-a-kind mining shovel located just southwest of Pittsburg near West Mineral, Kansas.

Pittsburg is also known as the "Gateway to the Ozarks" and is located south of Fort Scott on U.S. 69. At first glance you might not know that this town has a lot of Old World drama behind it. Pittsburg was actually an early-twentieth-century settlement of Europeans who came to work in the coal mines. Those who live here today are the descendants of people who traveled to this part of

Crawford County from Sicily, Austria, and Bohemia.

Pittsburg, along with the tiny town of Frontenac, which borders it to the north, were Crawford County mining communities that appealed to those who wanted to escape poverty, oppression, and political injustice. Lured by the promise of work, the immigrants who toiled in the mines brought an unusual mix of cultural and ethnic backgrounds to southeast Kansas. Between 1880 and 1940 more than 31,000 people from fifty-two countries flocked here to begin deep-shaft mining, the most dangerous method of digging coal out of the earth.

It was hard work, with little pay, but those who endured caught the attention of the Socialist Party in the early 1900s. The European miners, who tended to be pro-labor, vigorously supported the unions, strikes, and socialism that became closely tied to the coal industry. Eventually the area became known as the Little Balkans region because of the number of Europeans who settled here.

Crawford County's colorful past is celebrated with a number of festivals. Little Balkans Days, held every September, features boccie ball, a parade, polka music, arts-and-crafts booths, and ethnic foods. For information: Crawford County Convention and Visitors Bureau, 117 West Fourth Street, P.O. Box 1115, Pittsburg, KS 66762. (800) 879-1112 or (620) 231-1212; www.morningsun.net/cvb.

WHERE TO GO

Big Brutus. Six miles west of the junction of K-7 and K-102 and 0.25 mile south, West Mineral, KS 66782. You, too, can host a wedding, reception, private party, or family reunion outside—or inside—an eleven-million-pound Bucyrus Erie 1850 B mining shovel called Big Brutus. Just imagine how many hors d'oeuvres might fit inside Big Brutus's dipper, which is large enough to hold 150 tons! The behemoth reaches a height of sixteen stories and is the second largest electric shovel in the world.

New technology in 1960 made surface mining economical. The Pittsburg & Midway Coal Mining Company purchased Big Brutus at a cost of $6.5 million—not to dig coal but to remove the dirt and rocks covering the coal seams. From 1962 to 1974, more than nine million tons of coal were gouged out of the dirt, laying bare the land and leaving hundreds of "strip pits" behind. In 1974, when it was no longer cost-effective to operate Big Brutus, the steam shovel was shut down.

The legacy of Big Brutus could have been an environmental disaster; instead, it is a rare instance of a mined land reclamation success story. The Pittsburg & Midway Coal Mining Company donated the area surrounding Big Brutus to the Kansas Department of Wildlife and Parks, which, in turn, has reclaimed the 14,250 acres of land as a haven for hunting and fishing.

The Big Brutus Visitors Center has displays and information surrounding the colorful history and heritage of the region. You can take a self-guided tour or climb up Big Brutus's boom, but you have be at least thirteen years old. There are primitive camping facilities and RV hookups on site, plus picnic tables and hot showers to meet the needs of campers and visitors. Open daily. Fee. (620) 827–6177; www.bigbrutus.org.

Crawford County Historical Museum. Atkinson Road and Twentieth Street on U.S. 69, Pittsburg, KS 66762. The colorful history of Crawford County is featured in interesting exhibits that include vintage clothing, coal-mining and farming artifacts, photographs, and horse-drawn vehicles. Outdoor displays include a one-room schoolhouse, an authentic neighborhood grocery store, and a coal-mining steam shovel. Open Wednesday through Sunday. Free. (620) 231–1440 or 231–3794.

Hotel Stilwell. Seventh Street and Broadway, Pittsburg, Kansas 66762. Built in 1880, the historic hotel has hosted guests who have included William Jennings Bryan, Eugene Debs, Susan B. Anthony, and Theodore Roosevelt. The building was restored in 1997 by the Stilwell Heritage and Educational Foundation in partnership with MetroPlains Development, Inc., and is on the National Register of Historic Places. The architectural design features a grand stone entry flanked by brick columns on the first floor, wide bay windows, a circular leaded skylight, generous ornate plasterwork, and stained-glass windows. The upper floors have been converted to apartments for senior citizens, while the first-floor historic common areas are open to the public to tour. Open weekdays and weekends by appointment. Free to tour. (800) 879–1112 or (620) 232–3707.

Mined Land Wildlife Area. Several hundred water-filled former strip pits dot the Mined Land Wildlife Area, creating about 1,500 acres of public waters near the communities of West Mineral and Pittsburg. More than 200 lakes in the area are managed for fishing.

Lakes range in size up to fifty acres. Sport fish are abundant here, with largemouth bass, spotted bass, channel catfish, walleye, and a specially stocked lake trout being favorites of anglers.

Native grasses have been reintroduced here, along with a variety of wildlife. Several marshes have been constructed to attract ducks and geese, and a giant project has been launched to increase the number of geese in the area.

With its diversity of terrain and animal life, the Mined Land Reclamation Area is becoming popular with photographers and wildlife observers, as well as hunters. Quail, white-tailed deer, and wild turkey are found in abundance, as are raccoons, muskrats, bobcats, coyotes, and a herd of rather photogenic buffalo. Call for location and directions. (800) 879–1112, (620) 231–1212, or (620) 231–3173 (Department of Wildlife and Parks).

Pittsburg State University/Kansas Technology Center. Ford and Rouse Street, Pittsburg, KS 66762. Teaching, research, and service are the university's mission. To that end, its most significant project in terms of size and cost is its $27.7 million Kansas Technology Center. Covering twenty acres, the building is two football fields long and houses graphics and imaging technologies, technology studies, technical education, and engineering technology. The facility includes four lecture halls, numerous specialized laboratories, and staff offices. Pittsburg State University's arts programming includes a Visiting Writer's Series, the Southeast Kansas Symphony, an active theater season and two galleries, the University Gallery and the Harry Krug Gallery, that are open to the public on weekdays. The Performing Arts and Lectures Series (PALS) presents a series of events including workshops and residencies with artists like Robert Mirabel, the Count Basie Orchestra, and others. Aside from its fine arts programs, the university offers intercollegiate athletics, economic services, cooperative programs with school districts, and various special educational programming opportunities. Phone (620) 235–4305 for information on upcoming exhibitions. For more information on any PALS event: (620) 235–4795. For all other information: (620) 235–4122; www.pittstate.edu.

WHERE TO EAT

As the "Fried Chicken Capital of Southeast Kansas," Pittsburg is home to ethnic-influenced restaurants that serve fried chicken with German potato salad, coleslaw with garlic dressing, and peppers, tomatoes, and bread. This custom began in 1934, when Anne Pichler's husband was injured in the mines. Born near Budapest, the woman best known as Chicken Annie had a family to raise and started selling her fried chicken out of her home to make a living. Eventually Chicken Annie opened her restaurant, which became so famous that it began to draw competitors. In 1943 Mary Zerngast opened her fried chicken restaurant across the road from Chicken Annie's. Chicken Mary and Chicken Annie went head to head as the famous southeast Kansas chicken wars heated up. Today, these and other family-owned restaurants still compete for business as the fowl play continues. The chicken places open at 4:00 P.M. for dinner only on weekdays; those open on Sunday offer dinner from 11:00 A.M. to 8:00 P.M. They include the following:

Barto's Idle Hour. 201 South Santa Fe, Frontenac, KS 66763. Closed Sunday and Monday. $$; ☐. (620) 232-9834.

Chicken Annie's of Girard. K-5 east of Girard, Girard, KS 66743. Closed Monday and Tuesday. $$; ☐. (620) 724-4090.

Chicken Annie's Original. 1143 East 600th Avenue, Pittsburg, KS 66762. Closed Monday. $$; ☐. (620) 231-9460.

Gebhardt Chicken Dinners. 124 North 260th Street, Mulberry, KS 66756. Open Friday through Sunday. $$; ☐. (620) 764-3451.

Chicken Mary's. 1133 East 600th Avenue, Pittsburg, KS 66762. Closed Monday. $$; ☐. (620) 231-9510.

Pichler's Chicken Annie's®. 1271 South 220th Street, Pittsburg, KS 66762. Closed Monday. $$; ☐. (620) 232-9260.

OTHER RESTAURANTS OF INTEREST

Otto's Cafe. 711 North Broadway, Pittsburg, KS 66762. Built in 1945 as an annex to old Hotel Stilwell, this dining establishment is a throwback to the days when coffee shops were plentiful. Simple food, prepared well, is what you'll find here. Breakfast features everything from omelettes and waffles to French toast and biscuits and gravy. If you're in the mood for Otto's excellent version of fried chicken, you can have it for lunch or dinner. Leave room for homemade dessert. Open for breakfast, lunch, and early supper. Closed Sunday. $-$$; (no cards). (620) 231-6110.

Jim's Steak House. 1912 North Broadway, Pittsburg, KS 66762. Established in 1938, this third-generation family-owned and -operated restaurant has been in the same location for more than sixty years. Renowned in the area for its juicy steaks, the restaurant also offers chicken and seafood specialties. Jim's serves dinner only, starting at 4:00 P.M. Closed Sunday. $$–$$$; ☐. (620) 231-5770.

WHERE TO SHOP

Frontenac Bakery. 211 North Crawford, Frontenac, KS 66763. Established in 1900, this bakery has been passed down through five generations and still produces Italian breads and bread sticks that are famous in this part of the state. Closed Tuesday and Saturday. (620) 231-7908.

Pallucca & Son. 207 East McKay, Frontenac, KS 66763. This off-the-beaten-path find is a fun place to stop and shop. Opened in 1909, Pallucca's is family-owned and -operated and specializes in imported Italian foods. The meat department carries everything you need for making a great Italian sandwich, from large imported Italian hams to handmade Italian sausage. Fine pasta, dessert items, candies, and sauces from Italy line the shelves, along with American-made products. Open daily. (620) 231-7700.

WHERE TO STAY

The Old Miner's Guest House. 423 East 126 Highway, Pittsburg, KS 66762. This former coal camp house from the 1890s has been moved to the site overlooking a former strip pit that's now filled with water and hundreds of fish. A Flat John boat and paddleboat are available for your use. The two-bedroom home has a queen-size bed made from hundred-year-old barn beams. Next door is a 1940s milking barn that holds dried herbs and flowers grown on site. Antiques, candles, and bath salts are also for sale here. $; ☐. (620) 231-7733; www.apexcorp.com/~gplace/miner.

Southwest Day Trip 2

Ottawa, KS · Garnett, KS
Chanute, KS

Don't head out on this trip expecting blockbuster attractions. The towns listed here all have shady, tree-lined streets and historic old homes and buildings that have been lovingly preserved. In this part of Kansas, pharmacies are still called drugstores, and most of them have real soda fountains that serve limeades and lemonades made from fresh-squeezed fruit. Two of the biggest reasons to head this way are a unique bed-and-breakfast that is a collectors' extravaganza and a museum that is the only one of its kind in America.

OTTAWA, KS

From Kansas City head south on I–35 to Ottawa, where you'll find everything from flea-market merchandise and old-fashioned soda fountains to historic sites commemorating "Naked Voters."

Ottawa University, established in 1883, boasts architectural assets, as does the Franklin County Courthouse and the restored 200 block of the central business district, listed on the National Register of Historic Places.

Ottawa has plenty of shops that specialize in furniture, collectibles, primitives, and "junque." You may want to time your visit with Skunk Run Days, the second weekend in June. Or if you're more inclined to head for the water, you might want to visit the town on your way to Pomona or Melvern Reservoir.

Ottawa is one of many towns promoted by the Franklin County Historical Society. The organization puts out a number of self-guided tour brochures on the area, filled with information on historic sites of interest.

Now, about the "Naked Voters." This is a stop along the way on Franklin County Historical Society's Northeast Tour through Peoria, Wellsville, and other areas around Ottawa. This site commemorates forty-three free-state men who were so desperate to cast their ballots against slavery in 1858 that they skinny-dipped their way to the polls.

Granted, there's not much to see there now, but just imagine forty-three zealous voters fording three turbulent creeks in order to vote. Ponder, if you will, whether Americans today would go to such lengths. Would they strip off all their clothing, drop it on the bank, and plunge into a creek—just to enact a new law? Would they show up naked at the polls, letting their birthday suits drip dry in the open air? Of course not: They'd be arrested. Yet in 1858 the free-staters who made it to the polls defeated the pro-slavery issue by a "bare" minimum. A kind neighbor, who did not require that they dress for dinner, fed them before they returned home. For information: Franklin County Convention and Tourism Bureau, 109 East Second Street, P.O. Box 580, Ottawa, KS 66067; (785) 242–1411; www.idir.net/~fctv.

WHERE TO GO

Dietrich Cabin. South of the Ottawa Library in Ottawa's City Park (Fifth and Main Streets), Ottawa, KS 66067. The 1859 cabin is a memorial to a courageous couple who suffered hardships on the Kansas frontier. It has been moved from its original location to the park and is open to tour. Call for hours. Free. (785) 242–1232 or 242–1411.

Elizabeth "Grandma" Layton Exhibit. Wellsville City Library, 115 West Sixth Street, Wellsville, KS 66092. Elizabeth Layton was a remarkable artist whose work gained recognition in her later years. Having been through years of therapy, shock treatment, and drugs to find relief from depression, she tried drawing self-portraits to lift her emotional spirits. So effective was the relief that "Grandma" Layton went on to become a painter. Her work has been represented in

numerous galleries and museums around the country, including the Smithsonian's National Museum of American Art in Washington, D.C. Through her artwork Grandma Layton spoke out against racism, commercialism, and nuclear war. Free. Call for hours. (785) 883-2870.

Franklin County Courthouse. Third and Main Streets, Ottawa, KS 66067. Built in 1893 by noted architect George P. Washburn, the courthouse features a complex, steep-pitched hip roof with intersecting gables and four square corner towers. It has a four-sided clock, bell tower, and a statue of Justice that stands over the west gable. Tours are available from the Franklin County Historical Society. Free. (785) 242-1232.

Midland Railway Excursion Train. P.O. Box 412, Baldwin City, KS 66006. The Midland Railway is located just north of Ottawa on U.S. 59. It operates an authentic re-creation of an American local passenger train and makes a 7-mile round-trip through scenic farmland and woods, using early-twentieth-century vintage coaches. Open mid-May through October. Call for hours and reservations. Fee. (785) 371-3410; www.midland-ry.org.

Old Depot Museum. One block west of Main Street on Tecumseh Street, Ottawa, KS 66067. Operated by the Franklin County Historical Society, the two-story limestone building was constructed in 1888 as a depot for the Kansas City, Lawrence, and Southern Kansas Railway. Exhibits here include a model railroad and displays highlighting a number of Franklin County historical events. Fee. Call for hours. (785) 242-1250 or 242-1411.

Ottawa University. Tenth and Cedar Streets, Ottawa, KS 66067. Founded in 1865, the university is a four-year coeducational liberal arts college affiliated with the American Baptist Churches, USA. Tauy Jones Hall, one of the most prominent features on campus, is named for the first person to promote the university. (785) 242-5200; www.ottawa.edu.

WHERE TO SHOP

Ottawa Antique Mall and Restaurant. 202 Walnut, P.O. Box 133, Ottawa, KS 66606. Housed in a former soft-drink bottling plant, the mall features aisles of collectibles and furniture, plus lots of flea market–style merchandise. There is also a full-service restaurant and soda fountain. Closed Monday. (785) 242-1078.

WHERE TO EAT

Allegre Pharmacy, Soda Fountain, and Luncheonette. 304 South Main Street, Ottawa, KS 66067. You can get nostrums for your nose or grab a quick bite before you hit the road. The soda fountain itself isn't the old-fashioned kind, but you can still get creamy malts, shakes, and sundaes that will fill you up. Closed Sunday. $; ☐. (785) 242–3092.

J&D Family Pharmacy. 601 Main Street, Wellsville, KS 66092. Sodas, malts, limeades, freezes, and hand-dipped ice cream can be enjoyed at the pharmacy's old-fashioned soda fountain, complete with a wonderful wooden back bar featuring Art Nouveau stained glass. Closed Sunday. $; ☐. (785) 883–2462.

GARNETT, KS

From Ottawa head south on U.S. 59 to Garnett. This small community features three lakes, more than 1,000 acres of parks, a hiking/biking trail, an unusual bed-and-breakfast, and a small but interesting museum that displays works of regional artists and more. For more information: The Garnett Chamber of Commerce, 419 South Oak Street, Garnett, KS 66032; (785) 448–6767.

WHERE TO GO

Anderson County Courthouse. Garnett Town Square, Garnett, KS 66032. Designed by prominent architect George P. Washburn, the courthouse was dedicated in 1902 and is listed on the National Register of Historic Places. A classic example of Romanesque architecture, it features a restored courtroom with stained-glass windows. Open weekdays. Free. (785) 448–6767.

Cedar Valley Reservoir. 7.5 miles west of Garnett, on Kentucky Road, Garnett, KS 66032. The beautiful scenery here provides the perfect getaway, with floating docks, boat loading ramps, picnic areas, and wilderness and RV camping facilities. Free. Boating, fishing, and camping permits required. (785) 448–5496.

Crystal Lake, Veterans Memorial Park. South U.S. 59, Garnett, KS 66032. This small lake features a quiet, shady park, complete with ducks and geese for feeding. Bird-watching, picnicking, and fishing are favorite pastimes of residents. Trout season is January through March, when fishing is permitted and prizes are given. Free. Fishing and camping permits required. (785) 448-5496.

Lake Garnett. North Lake Road, Garnett, KS 66032. The lake offers recreational facilities that include a golf course, campsites, sporting clay range, swimming pool, and much more. Free. Boating, fishing, and camping permits required. (785) 448-5496.

Mary Bridget McAuliffe Walker Art Collection. Garnett Public Library, 125 West Fourth Avenue, Garnett, KS 66032. A rare collection of paintings, sculptures, prints, and drawings donated to Garnett by Maynard Walker features works by John Steuart Curry, Edouard Manet, and Jean Baptiste Corot. The conservators from Kansas City's Nelson-Atkins Museum of Art have restored many of the paintings. Docent tours are available by reservation. Free. Closed weekends. (785) 448-3388.

Prairie Spirit Rail Trail. Kansas Department of Wildlife and Parks, 419 South Oak Street, Garnett, KS 66032. This 33-mile trail passes through Garnett on what was once the Santa Fe Railroad right-of-way. It provides a picturesque hiking and biking excursion in and around the city. Motorized wheelchairs are welcome. Trail permits are not required inside city limits but are needed for youngsters under sixteen who venture outside town. Open daily during daylight hours. Free. & . (785) 448-6767; www.prairiespirit.org.

Santa Fe Depot. Main Street and Eighth Avenue, Garnett, KS 66032. Built during the depression years, this depot saw the passage of many trains until its closing in 1974. Beautifully restored in 1996, it now serves as a trailhead for users of the Prairie Spirit Rail Trail. The depot visitor center provides tourism information and has exhibits of railroad memorabilia on display, along with a wildflower garden. Free. & . (785) 448-5496.

WHERE TO SHOP

Goodies. 124 East Fourth Avenue, Garnett, KS 66032. This three-story building contains hard-to-find antiques and exquisite oak furniture, as well as a selection of keepsakes and crafts. Closed Monday. (785) 448-6712.

Sodas and Such. 122 East Fifth Avenue, Garnett, KS 66032. The old-fashioned soda fountain offers fresh limeades and ice-cream favorites. A variety of gifts can be found here, including Precious Moments figures, Russell Stover candies, perfumes, pottery, and stuffed animals. Closed Sunday. (785) 448–6122.

WHERE TO EAT

Maloan's. Fourth Avenue and Oak Street, Garnett, KS 66032. Housed in an 1883 building that was once a bank, the restaurant offers a fine-dining experience in a lovely setting that features high ceilings, oak furniture, and cloth-covered tables set with flowers. Flavorful prime rib, steaks, and shrimp are favorites. Open Monday through Friday from 11:00 A.M. to 1:30 P.M. and Friday and Saturday evenings from 5:00 to 9:00 P.M. Sunday brunch is served from 10:00 A.M. to 1:00 P.M. $$; ☐. (785) 448–2616.

WHERE TO STAY

The Kirk House. 145 West Fourth Avenue, Garnett, KS 66032–1313. This 12,000-square-foot, twenty-two-room home serves as a bed-and-breakfast *and* an art museum. Designed in 1913 by prominent architect George Washburn, the residence is an eclectic mix of paintings, antiques, pottery, furniture, and collectibles that owners Robert Logan and Robert Cugno have placed throughout the house. The two California transplants have accumulated so many quality furnishings and collectibles that their bed-and-breakfast has become a must-see attraction for anybody who loves studio pottery, paintings, George Stevens–designed furniture, and furnishings by Stickley, Heywood Wakefield, Roycroft, and Frank Lloyd Wright, Jr.

The home's elegant library reflects the work of great American and international artists. The kitchen pantry is stocked with an assortment of authentic Russell Wright dinnerware, upon which breakfast is served. The basement is a mini museum where American art pottery such as Rookwood and Roseville shares space with Mexican art, paintings, and pottery.

On the third floor, there is a delightful two-bedroom suite that features a ceiling decorated with 650 yards of handwoven fabric designed by Logan, a talented weaver whose rugs may be seen throughout the home. The suite overlooks an arbor and fishpond.

Breakfast features a variety of tempting dishes—everything from grilled salmon to scrambled eggs with garden-fresh herbs.

The Kirk House is open for tours as well as overnight stays mid-October through mid-May. Five tastefully appointed guest rooms can accommodate up to ten people. Leave children and pets at home. $$; (no cards). (785) 448-5813.

CHANUTE, KS

Close your eyes. Imagine, if you will, that you are in the middle of deepest Africa. All around you is the sound of jungle drums and pounding hooves of thousands of zebras and wildebeests. Well, open your eyes, get in your car, and head for Chanute, home of the Martin and Osa Johnson Safari Museum. Exhibits here showcase the life of two of the most extraordinary explorers, naturalists, and photographers of the twentieth century.

WHERE TO GO

Carlson Brothers Farm/Corn Maze. Rural Chanute, KS 66720. Six acres of this working grain farm have been turned into a corn maze. From July to October, when the corn is harvested, wander around through the twists and turns looking for a way out. When you do, take time to explore the antique farm equipment on display, or take a straighter path along some of the nature trails on the farm. Call for directions. Fee. (620) 431-1151.

Chanute Art Gallery. 17 North Lincoln, Chanute, KS 66720. The gallery provides a showcase for local area artists and Kansas Prairie Printmakers, such as Birger Sandzen and Charles Capps. Unique for a small town, the gallery has more than 1,000 square feet of exhibit space and includes a gift shop featuring handcrafted items and original art. Special exhibits change monthly. Closed Sunday. (620) 431-7807.

Chanute Office of Tourism. 101 South Lincoln Street, Chanute, KS 66720. You can get directions, information, and recommendations inside the center, which is itself a tourist attraction. It is located inside the historic Flat-Iron Building, constructed in 1907. The structure has a unique wedge-shaped design. Former tenants have included the Western Union Telegraph Company, two drug-stores, a tavern, and a confectionery. The renovated building is now home to the Chanute Office of Tourism and Main Street Chanute. Closed Saturday and Sunday. ♿ . (800) 735–5229 or (620) 431–5229; www.chanuteks.com.

The Martin and Osa Johnson Safari Museum. 111 North Lincoln Street, Chanute, KS 66720. The number-one museum in Kansas, this repository of rare artifacts and memorabilia offers a look at Africa in the early part of the twentieth century, when it was still a mysterious, dark continent. At that time Africa was confined to the machinations of movie moguls, who plied the public with yarns about Tarzan the Apeman and mega-monkeys like King Kong. Yet deep in the heart of Kansas, in the little town of Chanute, there is the ultimate documentation of wilderness and cultures that have long since vanished from the earth.

At one time the cannibals of Borneo and game-choked savannas of Africa represented an overwhelming diversity of life on this planet. The early work of Martin and Osa Johnson captured the first photographic records of remote and little-known regions of the world in the early decades of the twentieth century. The intrepid Kansas couple were explorers in the same mold as Sir Richard Burton and Stanley and Livingstone. Their revealing photography, field journals, detailed expedition reports, and extensive correspon-dence—spanning fifty years—are showcased inside displays at the Martin and Osa Johnson Safari Museum.

The tangled forests of Borneo, the Congo, and the Solomons are displayed in a treasure trove of wildlife motion pictures, thousands of still photos, and an assortment of artifacts brought back from the primitive regions they described in their best-selling books and articles. The couple made two expeditions to the South Seas, in 1917 and 1919, and later ventured to Borneo. Barely managing to escape with their lives, they filmed the exploits of a cannibal chief and his band of merry men, who were much more interested in sampling the tasty specimens from Kansas than posing for the camera.

The Johnsons' extended voyages to Africa, coupled with their South Seas films, brought them global fame, during which time the John-sons made *safari* and *simba* household words. To understand the couple's enormous popularity in the 1920s and 1930s, one has only to

look at their friends: Charlie Chaplin gave them a one-reel film to show to the South Seas cannibals, and the great Harry Houdini held a going-away party in the couple's honor. George Eastman, founder of Eastman Kodak, traveled with the Johnsons on occasion, financially supporting one of their trips and making sure the Johnsons were adequately supplied with Kodak products. Supported by private membership (famed naturalist George Schaller and his wife are Honorary Life Members), the museum is getting national attention.

The Martin and Osa Johnson exhibit is located inside the restored Santa Fe Train Depot, where it shares space with a magnificent collection of masks and artifacts touted by *African Arts Magazine* as "the finest West African collection between Chicago and California."

Dioramas portray African art and artifacts from Mali, horned crocodile headdresses and wood carvings from Nigeria, carved masks from Guinea, 14-foot-high Sirige masks held in place by mouthpieces worn by warriors, and much more, plus a 10,000-volume natural history library and research facility that is open to the public to enjoy.

Educational programs on Africa, including special shows for groups of handicapped or visually impaired visitors, are also available. Do not miss the museum's extraordinary gift shop, which is filled with imported art and handcrafted items that you won't see elsewhere, unless you plan to travel to Africa sometime. Open daily. &. Fee. (620) 431-2730; www.safarimuseum.com.

Walking/Driving Tours of Historic Chanute. c/o The Chanute Office Of Tourism, 101 South Lincoln Street, Chanute, KS 66720. There are twenty-four homes on the drive-by tour, and some are spectacular. The Greystone Estate (209 South Highland Street) was built in 1910 in the Italian Renaissance style. It features a red tile roof with dormers, redbrick walls, beveled and leaded glass in the main entrance, a carriage house, a garden house, reflecting pools, and a gazebo. Other homes in the area feature everything from Spanish-Mediterranean and Art Deco architecture to Queen Anne–Gothic Revival structures and "Painted Ladies." A self-guided tour brochure is available from the Chanute Office of Tourism. A second tour takes you through the history of twelve downtown businesses. (800) 735-5229 or (620) 431-5229; www.chanuteks.com.

WHERE TO EAT

Cardinal Drug Store. 103 East Main Street, Chanute, KS 66720. This old-fashioned drugstore is owned by Jim Chappell, who bought it in 1978. At the time, the soda fountain had been torn out to make more sales space. Chappell spent a lot of time looking for soda-fountain furniture and found an impressive array of furnishings that included a 1914 solid oak back bar complete with stained glass and enormous mirror, plus a 1937 marble fountain and equipment. Four high-seated chairs with arms and a 1908 solid brass cash register complete the illusion that you've just entered another era. Coca-Cola is made the old-fashioned way, using syrup and carbonated water. You can also get everything from sodas and sundaes to limeades and phosphates. The soda fountain is flanked by cabinets displaying old patent medicines, such as Lydia Pinkham's Blood Medicine, still in the original box. Dr. Miles' Heart Tonic and Regulator and a bottle of Scarless Liniment dating back to 1910 are among the curiosities. Closed Sunday. $; ☐. (620) 431-9150.

Dino's. 501 North Santa Fe, Chanute, KS 66720. This dining establishment serves steaks, seafood, and chicken dishes in a roadhouse ambience. Closed Sunday and Monday. $$; ☐. (620) 431-6223.

Elisa's Mexican Restaurant. 116 West Main Street, Chanute, KS 66720. The local ethnic cuisine of Chanute is best experienced at Elisa's, where the whole Navarez family is involved in making corn tortillas and other original Mexican dishes. Try the chimichangas! Elisa's is open for lunch and dinner but closes for a few hours in midafternoon. Closed on Sunday. $; ☐. (620) 431-4380.

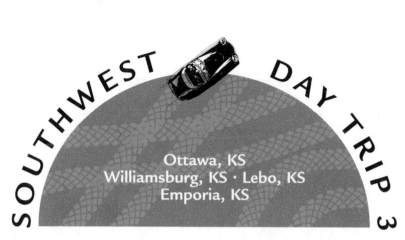

SOUTHWEST DAY TRIP 3

Ottawa, KS
Williamsburg, KS · Lebo, KS
Emporia, KS

This interesting Day Trip is one that hard-core foodies will like. It takes you to a truck stop, a barbecue joint, and an old-fashioned soda fountain where you can actually get a decent limeade.

Don't worry if you can't find the actual town of Lebo. You're basically looking for a big plateful of chicken-fried steak, which can be found at a sprawling truckers' paradise called Beto Junction—which is designated as being in Lebo but is actually off U.S. 75 at exit 155. There's nothing much to do in Williamsburg but eat spicy pork ribs, play pool, and listen to the jukebox at Guy and Mae's Tavern. Ottawa, on the other hand, has great soda fountains, an unusual bed-and-breakfast, historic homes and buildings, lovely nature trails, and more.

OTTAWA, KS

For this excursion head south on I–35 to Ottawa (See SOUTHWEST FROM KANSAS CITY, DAY TRIP 2).

WILLIAMSBURG, KS

South of Ottawa, on I–35, is the dot-on-the-map town of Williamsburg. Its sole claim to fame is Guy and Mae's Tavern, which is worth a trip if you like hearty ribs and tasty sandwiches of beef and ham.

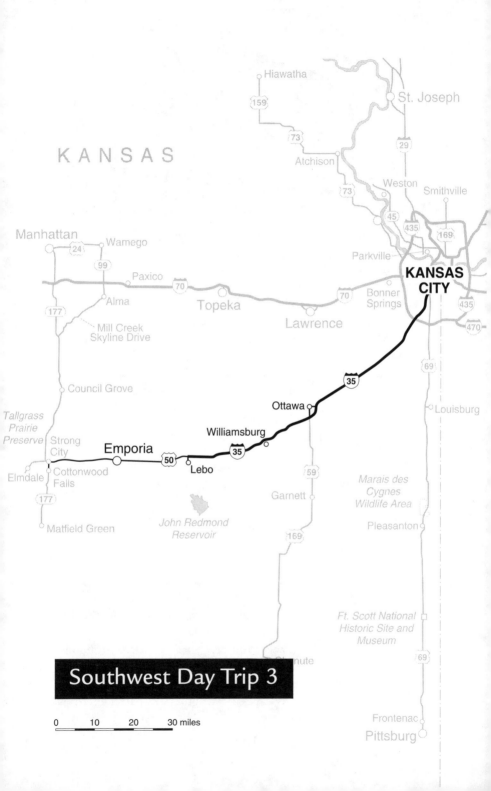

Southwest Day Trip 3

WHERE TO EAT

Guy and Mae's Tavern. Main Street, Williamsburg, KS 66095. There is no address for this unusual barbecue joint. It sits among some timeworn buildings on what appears to be the town's largest street. Inside you'll find thick sandwiches of lean beef and ham, plus hearty slabs of pork ribs served on butcher paper. The sweet and spicy sauce is served on the side; other side dishes include baked beans, coleslaw, and potato salad. Written up in regional and national magazines, the place offers an unusual ambience that features a jukebox, a pool table, and good food served at yesterday's prices. You can fill up here or pack some to go and keep heading south to Beto Junction for the rest of your movable feast. Closed Sunday and Monday. $-$$; (no cards). (785) 746-8830.

LEBO, KS

Fearless foodies will not shudder at the thought of downing enough cholesterol to plug a pipeline. You've had ribs, beef, and ham in Williamsburg, now head south on Interstate 35 to Lebo and Beto Junction, where you can fill up on "truck stop cuisine" and have an oil change at the same time. (Your car, that is).

WHERE TO GO

Beto Junction. I-35 and U.S. 75, Lebo, KS 66856. From Williamsburg keep heading south to U.S. 75 and exit 155. This sprawling truck stop takes its name from the first letters of four nearby cities: Burlington, Emporia, Topeka, and Ottawa. Food fans may want to make the trip just to chow down on trailblazer breakfasts that feature eggs with such meaty items as pork chops, chopped sirloin steak, ham, and Polish sausage. You can even have Beto Junction's fabulous chicken-fried steak with eggs, or order it for dinner.

Indeed, it is worth the drive just to savor the huge portions of this spectacular tenderized steak—dipped in a light, flaky batter and fried just right—nestled atop buttery, made-from-scratch mashed potatoes and crowned with country gravy. More than a meal, this is an all-you-can-eat experience. Catering to anybody on two wheels or more, the entire facility also includes a travel store that is great fun to browse through. If you're looking for a combination hair dryer/vacuum, you'll find it here, along with a wide range of Kansas gifts, greeting cards, and more. There's also a lube bay that specializes in vehicle repairs. Open daily. $$; ☐. (620) 256-6311.

EMPORIA, KS

Emporia touts itself as the "Front Porch to the Flint Hills," an area that makes up the largest unbroken tract of tallgrass prairie in the county. Certainly Emporia is a gateway that connects several highways leading to and from the Flint Hills region. Nine recreational lakes are located in and around Emporia, including John Redmond Reservoir and Melvern Lake. You can reach this historic town by following I–35 southwest from Lebo or by connecting with Emporia on U.S. 50 from Cottonwood Falls (see WEST FROM KANSAS CITY, DAY TRIP 5). You can also make a Flint Hills loop, taking Emporia north to Manhattan, Kansas (see WEST FROM KANSAS CITY, DAY TRIPS 4 AND 5).

Founded in 1857, Emporia has made a name for itself by being the home of the National Teachers Hall of Fame and birthplace of Pulitzer Prize–winning journalist William Allen White. White died in 1944, having achieved success and fame. President Franklin Delano Roosevelt eulogized him, saying that he "ennobled the profession of journalism."

Visitors who want to see the sites of the White family heritage can follow the signs bearing White's silhouette. Emporia is also home to Veterans Day and an All Veterans' Memorial. The now national celebration was introduced to Congress by Representative Ed Rees of Emporia in 1953, and President Eisenhower signed the bill into law in 1954. The All Veterans' Memorial was dedicated on May 26, 1991. For a complete rundown of many other things to see and do in

Emporia, plus self-guided-tour brochures of the Flint Hills, contact the Emporia County Convention and Visitors Bureau, 719 Commercial Street, P.O. Box 703, Emporia, KS 66801; (800) 279-3730 or (620) 342-1803; www.emporiakschamber.org.

WHERE TO GO

Emporia State University. 1200 Commercial Street, Emporia, KS 66801. Founded in 1863, the university was the state's first school for training teachers. Located on 200 acres, the campus offers special attractions of interest to tourists, such as the William Allen White Library. Manuscripts, correspondence, photographs, and other materials about the life and times of William Allen White can be found here. Free admission to all campus-related exhibits. &. (620) 341-5037; www.emporia.edu.

Emporia Zoo. South Commercial Street and Soden's Road, Emporia, KS 66801. This is one of the smallest accredited zoos in the country. It has an unusual assortment of birds, mammals, and reptiles, many of which are housed in natural habitats. The zoo also features exceptional botanical displays and spectacular holiday lights. Open daily. Free. &. (620) 342-6558.

Flint Hills National Wildlife Refuge. Fifteen miles southeast of Emporia, near Hartford. (Contact the refuge manager at 530 West Maple Street, P.O. Box 128, Hartford, KS 66854.) One of a system of 400 refuges administered by the U.S. Fish and Wildlife Service, the area is dedicated to the preservation and conservation of wildlife, primarily migratory waterfowl and bald eagles. Hiking, photography, boating, picnicking, camping, fishing, wild-food gathering, and hunting are allowed. Open daily. Free. (620) 392-5553; www.r6.fws.gov.

Lyon County Historical Museum. 118 East Sixth Avenue, Emporia, KS 66801. Located in the 1904 Carnegie Library Building, this is one of many sites in Emporia listed on the National Register of Historic Places. The building still contains its original leaded-glass windows, an ornate water fountain, beautiful oak woodwork, and other unique features. It houses artifacts and exhibits on a rotating schedule that help illustrate and interpret various phases of Kansas's Lyon County history and heritage. A great gift gallery specializes in items made by Kansas artisans. Closed Sunday and Monday. Free. &. (620) 342-0933.

National Teachers Hall of Fame. 1320 C of E Drive, Emporia, KS 66801. One of the city's premier attractions, the hall of fame nationally recognizes five teachers annually who have demonstrated a commitment to educating children from kindergarten through high school. The walls hold tributes to some of the best teachers in America, and there are galleries with cultural and artistic exhibits of general interest. Closed Sunday. Free. &. (800) 96-TEACH or (620) 342-5660; www.nthf.org.

Prairie Passage. Lyon County Fairgrounds, West U.S. 50 and Industrial Road, Emporia, KS 66801. Eight massive limestone sculptures celebrating Emporia's origins and history were designed by artist Richard Stauffer and produced by the 1992 Kansas Sculptors Association. The sculptures present a variety of images about the land, its forces, and its people. Open daily. Free. &. (800) 279-3730 or (620) 342-1803.

WHERE TO STAY

Seven Gables Bed and Breakfast Inn. 526 Exchange Street, Emporia, KS 66801. Built in 1893, this Victorian inn has three guest rooms, one of them in an upstairs turret. One room has a four-poster bed; another has a fireplace. A hot tub is also on the premises. Coffee, tea, and breakfast are served in a lovely outdoor courtyard, weather accommodating, with a fountain surrounded by antique roses. If you love the furnishings, you may wish to check out the owners' other business—an interior decorating company downtown called All the Things You Love. $; □. (620) 340-0783; www.allthe thingsyoulove.com/sg.

White Rose Inn. This elegant Victorian bed-and-breakfast features private suites with sitting rooms, Jacuzzis, and kitchen privileges. Guests arrive for afternoon tea and sumptuous treats and wake up the next day to the aroma of fresh-baked biscuits, coffee cakes, and muffins—or breakfast in bed for a special romantic treat. In-room massages, manicures, and pedicures can be arranged. $$; □. (316) 343-6336.

WHERE TO EAT

Diamond Creek Grille. 2702 West Fifteenth Avenue, Emporia, KS 66801. They bill themselves as offering good old Flint Hills hospitality, and you will love the rustic log-cabin setting. This is one of the only upscale places to eat in Emporia, but don't be frightened by the idea of high prices. Steaks and chicken Cordon Bleu, their specialties, are tasty and reasonably priced. $; ☐. (620) 340–0694.

KANSAS

Hiawatha

St. Joseph

159

73

29

Atchison

Weston
Smithville

73

45

435

169

Leavenworth

Manhattan

Wamego

24

Parkville

Konza
Prairie

99

Paxico

70

**KANSAS
CITY**

Alma

70

Bonner
Springs

435

177

Topeka

Lawrence

470

Mill Creek–
Skyline Drive

35

69

Council Grove

Ottawa

Louisburg

Tall
Grass
Prairie
Preserve

Strong
City

Williamsburg

35

Emporia

50

Lebo

Elmdale

Cottonwood
Falls

59

Marais des
Cygnes
Wildlife Area

177

Garnett

Matfield Green

John Redmond
Reservoir

169

Pleasanton

Ft. Scott National
Historic Site and
Museum

Chanute

69

0   10   20   30 miles

Frontenac

Pittsburg

West Day Trip 1

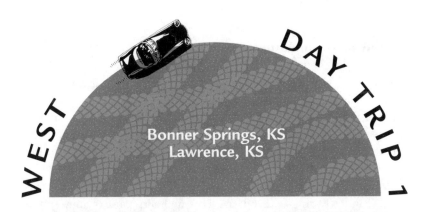

BONNER SPRINGS, KS

Bonner Springs is short drive west from Kansas City on I-70. It is home to Sandstone Amphitheatre and the renowned Renaissance Festival held here in fall. For information: City of Bonner Springs, 205 East Second Street, P.O. Box 38, Bonner Springs, KS 66012; (913) 422-1020; www.cometa/bonner.

WHERE TO GO

The National Agricultural Center and Hall of Fame. 630 Hall of Fame Drive (North 126th Street, northeast of I-70 at K-7), Bonner Springs, KS 66012. Visitors can view 30,000 historic agricultural museum exhibits at The National Farmers Memorials located on the premises. There are a turn-of-the-twentieth-century home and farm implements, a century-old railroad depot, a blacksmith shop, a one-room schoolhouse, and a mile-long nature trail with eighty-nine marked and identified specimens. Tour guides are available. Open daily. Fee. (913) 721-1075; www.aghalloffame.com.

Grinter House. 1429 South Seventy-eighth Street (Seventy-eighth Street and K-32), Kansas City, KS 66111. Located 8 miles east of Bonner Springs, this house stands on the site of the first ferry across the Kansas River. The two-story brick structure was built by Moses R. Grinter in 1857. Today it is a historic site and museum open to tour. Closed Monday. Free. (913) 299-0373.

Sandstone Amphitheatre. I–70 at the Bonner Springs exit; mailing address for special ticket arrangements: c/o 2310 West Seventy-fifth Street, Prairie Village, Kansas 66208. Sandstone is one of the Midwest's premier outdoor entertainment facilities. It offers a state-of-the-art sound system that caters to the biggest names in the music industry. Summer concerts feature everything from comedy and rock-and-roll to country and pop music. For special seating arrangements call (913) 384–8940; www.sandstonekc.com.

Wyandotte County Bonner Springs Park. 3488 West Drive (office), Bonner Springs, KS 66109. This 640-acre park is adjacent to The National Agricultural Center and Hall of Fame and features ball fields, tennis courts, shelter houses, a radio-controlled airplane flying field (permit required), and the Wyandotte County Museum. Open daily. Free. (913) 299–0550.

The Wyandotte County Historical Society and Museum. 631 North 126th Street, Wyandotte County Bonner Springs Park, Bonner Springs, KS 66012. The museum tells the history of Wyandotte County through exhibits that cover 350 million years of development, spanning a period from the Stone Age to today. Displays document the immigrant cultures who settled Kansas, from the native Kanza Indians to the pioneers who came from around the world to live and work in the area. Photographs and artifacts relating to Wyandotte County's industrial heritage and multicultural background can be found throughout the exhibit gallery and archives. Newspapers, county records, books, maps, and other materials offer a wealth of information for those interested in the early settlement of the state. Closed Monday. Free. (913) 721–1078.

WHERE TO STAY

Back in Thyme Guest House and Herb Garden. 1100 South 130th Street, Bonner Springs, KS 66012. This charming Victorian retreat features a hearty breakfast buffet in a sunny room overlooking the kitchen herb garden. The bed-and-breakfast offers four guest rooms, two with spacious private baths and one with a Jacuzzi and double vanity. Rates also include evening hors d'oeuvres and dessert. Young children can be accommodated if families wish to reserve the entire second floor. $$–$$$; ☐. (913) 422–5207.

LAWRENCE, KS

In 1863, when William Quantrill and his raiders burned Lawrence to the ground in the name of pro-slavery, who could know that the town would bounce back and become the foodie hangout and cultural mecca that it is today?

In 1999 Lawrence ranked among *The 100 Best Small Art Towns in America* by John Villani, and its university campus was written up as one of the nation's most beautiful campuses in *The Campus as a Work of Art*, by architect Thomas Gaine. With a long tradition of supporting the arts, the University of Kansas, or KU for short, offers one of the finest art museums in the Midwest, a theater that features twelve productions annually, and a School of Fine Arts that produces more than 400 events each year.

In addition, Rand McNally's *Places Rated Almanac* recognized Lawrence as having the most culture per capita in cities in America under 100,000 in population. The university's diverse student mix has brought innovation and energy to the unusually stable local economy. On a hill where pioneers once paused along the Oregon Trail, KU's limestone buildings play host to scholars who come to study and learn on the beautiful user-friendly campus.

Lawrence today offers plenty of attractions and a downtown filled with boutiques, galleries, and gourmet restaurants, yet it also has a history behind it worth learning.

It's hard to forget that Lawrence was Indian country for more than fifty years after the 1803 Louisiana Purchase. Kansas itself was a territory opened for settlement in 1854. During this time, there were problems with regard to the slavery issue. A bitter struggle ensued for territorial control. Lawrence had Yankee blood, and pro-slavery neighbors in Missouri found that hard to bear. When the town became a center for free-state activity, trouble soon brewed between the abolitionists and the pro-slavers. Quantrill's morning raid on August 21, 1863, left Lawrence a shambles, with hundreds reported dead or missing and homes and businesses destroyed.

When the Civil War ended, Lawrence's economy grew. The Kansas Pacific Railroad reached Lawrence in 1864, bringing new businesses and industry. In 1866 KU held its first session; Haskell Indian Nations University, now a registered National Historic Landmark, opened in 1884.

Today Lawrence, with its nineteenth-century Victorian homes and ornate downtown landmarks, has an identity all its own. You can discover more about Lawrence by contacting the Lawrence Convention and Visitors Bureau, 734 Vermont Street, Suite 101, Box 586, Lawrence, KS 66044; (888) LAWKANS or (785) 865-4499; www.visitlawrence.com.

WHERE TO GO

Clinton Lake. U.S. Army Corps of Engineers, 872 North 1402nd Road, Lawrence, KS 66049. Located 3 miles southwest of Lawrence, off Clinton Parkway (West Twenty-third Street), the lake provides 7,000 surface acres for boating, fishing, and swimming. Excellent opportunities for bicycling and for viewing wildlife abound here. There are more than 70 miles of hiking trails, plus camping and picnicking areas. The Clinton Lake Museum is open weekends during the summer and houses artifacts and exhibits on local history. Free. (785) 843-7665; www.kdwp.state.ks.us.

Haskell Indian Nations University. 155 Indian Avenue, Lawrence, KS 66046. This is one of the oldest educational institutions for Native Americans and Alaska Natives supported by the federal government. Founded in 1884, Haskell has evolved from an elementary school to a university offering a baccalaureate in elementary teacher education. Open only to members of federally recognized Indian nations, enrollment averages 800 students a semester. In the fall Haskell hosts an outdoor Indian Art Market in conjunction with Lawrence's annual Indian Arts Show. In the spring an outdoor powwow attracts hundreds of Native American and Alaska Native dancers and singers from across the United States. (785) 749-8404; www.haskell.edu.

Lawrence Arts Center. 200 West Ninth Street, Lawrence, KS 66044. Housed inside the 1904 Andrew Carnegie Library, the center opened its doors in 1975 to provide art education and classes and to support local artists. The center's Visual Arts Gallery showcases area works. Theatrical presentations are scheduled in the Performance Hall. Closed Sunday. Free. (785) 843-2787; www.lawrencearts center.com.

Old West Lawrence Historic District. From Sixth to Ninth Streets between Tennessee and Illinois Streets, Lawrence, KS 66044. The impressive nineteenth-century architecture here is listed on the National Register of Historic Places. Drive by the Plymouth Congregational Church, 925 Vermont Street, for a vision of spires, buttresses, and stained glass. (785) 865-4499; www.visitlawrence.com.

University of Kansas. Mount Oread Campus, P.O. Box 2173, Lawrence, KS 66045. The university is the only one in the nation with a Jayhawk mascot, a familiar image seen all over the campus and the city. The 1,000-acre campus is one of the prettiest in the country and features a pond called Potter Lake at the bottom of a grassy wooded knoll between the Campanile and Memorial Stadium. From the stop sign at the west end of Memorial Drive, you can turn left onto West Campus Road, where there are some sorority and fraternity houses. This leads to the Chi Omega Fountain. At the south side of the intersection is a large rock marking the site of many Oregon Trail campfires. If you go around the fountain, you'll wind up making a left turn onto Jawhawk Boulevard, the main drag of the campus. If school is in session, you'll need to stop and get a visitor's pass at the booth. Jayhawk Boulevard has some wonderful old buildings, including Strong Hall, Watson Library, and others. Detailed information and a map of the campus can be found at www.ukans.edu. Some stops on your itinerary might include these:

The Lied Center. Fifteenth and Iowa Streets, on the campus. This is the home for KU's Concert, Chamber Music, Broadway, and New Directions series. The $14.6 million multipurpose facility, which occupies a hillside on the highest ridge on campus, serves both the university and the Lawrence community. The lobbies here offer a magnificent view of the rolling hills and the Wakarusa Valley. The Lied Center provides a state-of-the-art setting for music, dance, theater, lectures, films, and convocations. Visitors are welcome to view the building during business hours, Monday through Friday. Tickets to events can be purchased at the box office. &. (785) 864-ARTS; www.lied.ku.edu.

Helen Foresman Spencer Museum of Art. Behind the Kansas Union on the KU campus, at 1301 Mississippi Street, Lawrence, KS 66045. This gem of a place houses one of the finest university art museums in the country. The facility is never boring; you can return each time and see something new. Eleven galleries offer changing exhibitions and art from the museum's collections that represent more than 4,000 years of world art history and include wonderful European and American paintings, sculpture, and photography. Japanese Edo-period painting and twentieth-century Chinese painting are of particular interest. The Spencer also affords art lovers a chance to experience touring exhibitions of remarkable works not found elsewhere in the area. &. Closed Monday. Free. (785) 864-4710; www.ukans.edu/~sma.

Museum of Anthropology. Spooner Hall on the KU campus, Lawrence, KS 66045. Drawings by famed Elizabeth Layton ("Grandma" Layton), beadwork artifacts from the Plains Indians, and more are part of the interesting exhibits here. The museum gift shop sells ethnic art from around the world. Open daily. Free. &. (785) 864-4245; www.ukans.edu/~kuma.

KU Natural History Museum. Dyche Hall, KU, Fourteenth Street and Jayhawk Boulevard, Lawrence, KS 66045. Listed on the National Register of Historic Places, the museum holds exhibits of Kansas and Great Plains animals and offers a historic panorama of North American plants and animals. On display are live bees, fish, snakes, and minerals. Open daily. Fee. &. (785) 864-4450; www.nhm.ukans.edu.

WHERE TO SHOP

Lawrence offers an exciting array of galleries, specialty and outlet shops, museums, and artists' studios. We can mention only a few in the space of this book. For a complete listing, contact the Lawrence Convention and Visitors Bureau, 734 Vermont Street, Suite 101, Box 586, Lawrence, KS 66044; (888) LAWKANS or (785) 865-4499.

The Bay Leaf. 725 Massachusetts Street, Lawrence, KS 66044. This interesting shop features the unusual and the essential in kitchen accessories and gifts for the home. It also offers a large variety of fresh-roasted gourmet coffees. Open daily. (785) 842-4544.

The Casbah. 803 Massachusetts Street, Lawrence, KS 66044. This eclectic boutique features a Third World atmosphere, replete with fertility dolls, Buddha statues, flowing cotton dresses, silver earrings, and other distinctive gifts. Open daily. (785) 843-5002.

Community Mercantile. 901 Iowa Street, Lawrence, KS 66044. "The Merc" has been serving the Lawrence community since 1974.

It is cooperatively owned and offers a full selection of organic and local produce in season. It has an extensive bulk department, with an excellent selection of coffees and teas, herbs, dairy products, and more. There are books and housewares, plus a meat department that features locally raised beef and poultry. Freshly baked goods, crafts by area artists, and a deli department round out the fare. Member benefits include special discounts and a monthly newsletter. Open daily. (785) 843-8544.

Lawrence Indian Arts Show. Haskell Indian Nations University, 155 Indian Avenue, Lawrence, KS 66046. American Indian art is highlighted with a juried competition presented in the fall by Haskell Indian Nations University, the KU Museum of Anthropology, and the Lawrence Arts Center. (785) 864-4245.

Farmers Market. 1000 block of Vermont Street, Lawrence, KS 66044. This is the largest and oldest farmers' market in the state. Local growers and farm producers offer products and produce ranging from fresh fruits and veggies to baked goods, herbs, and homemade condiments. Open Saturday morning and Tuesday and Thursday afternoon, May to November. (800) 888-LAWKANS or (785) 865-4499.

Phoenix Gallery. 919 Massachusetts Street, Lawrence, KS 66044. Works by local and regional artisans are represented here and include pottery, blown glass, jewelry, weaving, paintings, prints, and textiles. Open daily. (785) 843-0080.

The Raven Bookstore. 8 East Seventh Street, Lawrence, KS 66044. This bookstore specializes primarily in mysteries and hosts two mystery reading groups a month for customers. It also offers a British-import mystery section for many titles that are hard to find in this country. Fiction, history and regional studies, travel, nature, and other works of literature also fill the shelves. Open daily. (785) 749-3300.

Silver Works & More. 715 Massachusetts Street, Lawrence, KS 66044. This gallery sells gold and silver jewelry by local metalsmith Jim Connelly. It also offers crafts, claywork, textiles, handmade paper, studio glass, and designer-craftsman furniture. Closed Sunday. (785) 842-1460.

Tanger Factory Outlet Center. East Lawrence exit 204 off I-70, Lawrence, KS 66044. This brand-name manufacturers' outlet offers shoppers savings of 40 to 60 percent off regular retail prices on clothes, shoes, luggage, leather goods, books, accessories, housewares, and more. Coupon books are available. Open daily. (800) 4-TANGER or (785) 842-3341.

Waxman Candles. 609 Massachusetts Street, Lawrence, KS 66044. Situated at the northern end of Historic Downtown Lawrence, this unique shop produces handmade candles, including the one-of-a-kind "Silhouette," which has a backlit effect as it burns and is quite a showstopper. Three tons of candles wait to be sold here. A product catalog is also available. Open daily. (785) 843-8593.

WHERE TO EAT

Free State Brewing Co. 636 Massachusetts Street, Lawrence, KS 66044. This is the first brewery to operate in Kansas since the state passed a prohibition law more than a century ago. Located inside a renovated trolley barn, this combination brewery-restaurant produces a small variety of high-quality beer, using fresh, natural ingredients. The restaurant offers an interesting menu that includes everything from stir-fried veggies to fresh fish and steak. Brewery tours are offered Saturday at 2:00 P.M. Open daily. $-$$; ☐. (785) 843-4555.

La Prima Tazza. 638 Massachusetts Street, Lawrence, KS 66044. Bring some friends or settle down with a good book and enjoy espresso and gourmet coffees and desserts in a warm and friendly setting that is reminiscent of the coffeehouses of the 1960s. Open daily. $; ☐. (785) 832-CAFE.

Paisano's II. 2112 Southwest Twenty-fifth Street, Lawrence, KS 66044. Like its sister restaurant in Topeka, Kansas, this bistro serves excellent Italian-inspired food. Entrees range from veal and chicken dishes to pasta dishes redolent with delectable sauces. The portions are large and the prices reasonable. Open for lunch and dinner. Closed Sunday. $$; ☐. (785) 838-3500.

Panda Garden. 1500 West Sixth Street, Lawrence, KS 66044. The menu offerings at this popular Chinese restaurant include vegetarian and noodle dishes, along with seafood, pork, chicken, and beef items. Specialties are roasted duck cooked with fresh onion, ginger, and plum sauce; Hunan mussels in ginger, garlic, and oyster sauce; and other delights. Open daily; dim sum and sushi are served for Sunday lunch. $$; ☐. (785) 843-4312.

Paradise Cafe. 728 Massachusetts Street, Lawrence, KS 66044. This restaurant has served "good real food" since 1984. Breakfast includes steamed rice and veggies with homemade cornbread and blueberry buttermilk pancakes. Try a special-recipe garden burger or fresh salad niçoise for lunch. Dinner specials feature fresh seafood, steak, and chicken dishes. Vegetarian items are always available. Breads, baked goods, and desserts are made from scratch. The place is usually crowded, so be prepared to wait. Open daily. $$; ☐. (785) 842-5199.

Pachamama's. 2161 Quail Creek Drive, Lawrence, KS 66046. This restaurant features an international menu that changes monthly. The uniquely inspired cuisine features everything from fish to wild-game entrees. Open daily. $$–$$$; ☐. (785) 841-0990.

Plum Tree. 2620 Iowa Street, Lawrence, KS 66046. Make the drive to Lawrence just to dine at this restaurant. Here authentic Chinese cuisine is showcased in an extensive menu featuring more than eighty different dishes from all the provinces of China. There are Peking duck, Hunan shrimp, and many other old and new favorites. A complete American menu is also available. Banquet facilities are offered for up to one hundred people. Open daily. $$; ☐. (785) 841-6222.

Stone Canyon Pizza. 3801 West Sixth Street, Lawrence, KS 66044. The excellent gourmet pizza with crispy crust is just one reason to visit Kevin Heaton's downtown restaurant. The water landscaping, outdoor bar, and rotating menu of pasta specialties in this old warehouse building create a wonderful environment for family outings or big gatherings with friends. $; ☐. (785) 830-8500.

Sylas and Maddy's Homemade Ice Cream. 1014 Massachusetts Street, Lawrence, KS 66046. This is the place to come for banana splits, sundaes, malts, milk shakes, sodas, and homemade waffle cones filled to the brim with fantastically rich and creamy ice cream made on the premises. Choose from 130 rotating flavors that include Da Bomb (Oreos, chocolate chips, and cookie dough), prairie pumpkin nut, and pineapple cheesecake, or chocolate chip and peanut butter chocolate chip made with superior chunks of chocolate. Take a cooler so that you can pack a pint or a quart to go. Yum! Open daily. $; ☐. (785) 832-8323.

Teller's Restaurant. 746 Massachusetts Street, Lawrence, KS 66044. Located in a historic 1877 bank building, Teller's features Italian cuisine, including pasta, chicken, lamb, and wood-fired brick-oven pizza. A contemporary blend of works by Kansas artists Stan

Herd and Jon Havener complements original bank fixtures, such as the 20,000-pound safe door securing the rest rooms. Open daily. $$; ☐. (785) 843–4111.

Wheatfield's Bakery. 904 Vermont Street, Lawrence, KS 66044. This delightful place features fresh-baked breads made with Kansas wheat. Everything from traditional favorites like sourdough and raisin breads to cookies and truffles are made on the premises, along with soups, sandwiches, and stuffed pastries. Open daily for lunch and dinner; a full breakfast is served until 2:00 P.M. on Sunday and until 10:00 A.M. on weekdays. $–$$; ☐. (785) 841–5553.

WHERE TO STAY

Circle S Guest Ranch & Country Inn. 3325 Circle S Lane, Lawrence, KS 66044. This charming retreat has been continuously owned and operated through five generations since the late 1800s. The ranch spans more than 1,200 acres and includes more than 400 head of cattle. More than twenty ponds dot the surroundings and there is abundant wildlife. The inn itself was built to resemble a Kansas barn. Twelve spacious guest rooms offer private baths and views. Some feature claw-foot or whirlpool baths and fireplaces. Breakfast is served here from Sunday through Thursday. On Friday and Saturday a four-course dinner is included in the price of the room. Call for directions. $$$; ☐. (785) 843–4124.

The Eldridge Hotel. 700 Vermont Avenue, Lawrence, KS 66044. This downtown hotel is the only hotel in Lawrence listed as an official Historic Hotel of America. Completely destroyed during Quantrill's Raid in 1863, the structure was rebuilt and reopened as the current Eldridge Hotel in 1986. All forty-eight rooms are suites, and the hotel restaurant serves a great Sunday brunch. $$; ☐. (785) 749–5011 or (800) 527–0909; www.eldridgehotel.com.

Halcyon House Bed and Breakfast. 1000 Ohio Street, Lawrence, KS 66044. A century-old restored home, Halcyon House offers a living room, two patios, and a lovely glass-enclosed kitchen. Eight uniquely styled and furnished bedrooms include a master suite with a king-size bed and private bath and a suite with two double beds, private bath, and fireplace. A complete breakfast is served daily and features homemade muffins, omelettes, fresh fruit, and coffee. $$; ☐. (785) 841–0314.

TOPEKA, KS

Heading west on I–70, you'll reach Topeka, one of the largest cities on the historic Oregon Trail. The capital of Kansas, Topeka lies on rich, sandy river-bottom land where Indians lived for many years using the Kansas (Kaw) River for navigation. Each year Topeka celebrates its Native American heritage with the Shawnee Country Allied Tribes All Nations Powwow, held Labor Day weekend.

The Kaw River also drew to it three French Canadian brothers who started a ferry service across the river in 1842. They married three Kanza (Kansas) Indian sisters whose tribe had lived in the area for many years. Thus marked the beginnings of Topeka as a stopping point on the Oregon Trail. Years later one of the couples celebrated the election of their grandson, Charles Curtis, as vice president of the United States—the only U.S. vice president of Native American descent.

Topeka's proximity to the Oregon and Santa Fe Trails and the railroads played a key role in the city's development. The Atchison, Topeka, and Santa Fe Railroad, once headquartered here, is still one of the city's major employers.

Topeka has a rich abundance of attractions, including one of the most extensive rose gardens in the country, a tropical rain forest, an international raceway offering topflight motorsports events, and several interesting museums. With a host of citywide festivals, area attractions, and historic sites, Topeka is enjoying newfound popularity as a great place to live and visit. For more in-

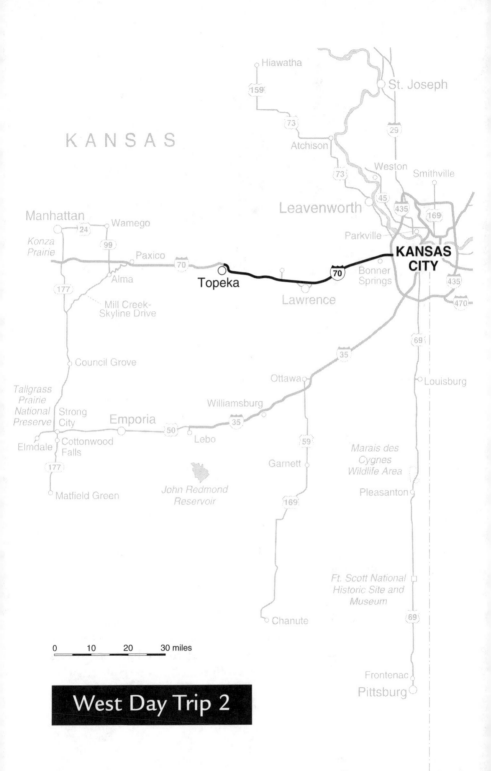

KANSAS

Hiawatha

St. Joseph

159

73

29

Atchison

Weston

Smithville

73

Leavenworth

45

435

169

Manhattan

Wamego

24

Parkville

KANSAS
CITY

Konza
Prairie

99

Paxico

70

Topeka

70

Bonner
Springs

435

Alma

Lawrence

470

177

Mill Creek-
Skyline Drive

69

35

Council Grove

Ottawa

Louisburg

Tallgrass
Prairie
National
Preserve

Strong
City

Emporia

50

Williamsburg

35

Lebo

59

Marais des
Cygnes
Wildlife Area

Elmdale

Cottonwood
Falls

Garnett

177

169

Pleasanton

Matfield Green

John Redmond
Reservoir

Ft. Scott National
Historic Site and
Museum

69

Chanute

0   10   20   30 miles

Frontenac

Pittsburg

West Day Trip 2

formation contact the Topeka Convention and Visitors Bureau, 1275 Southwest Topeka Boulevard, Topeka, KS 66612; (800) 235–1030 or (785) 234–1030; www.topekacvb.org.

WHERE TO GO

Binkley Gardens. c/o Topeka Beautification Association, 4536 Southwest Elevation Lane, Topeka, KS 66610. Every April visitors can see more than 35,000 tulips and 12,000 daffodils in this three-and-a-half-acre private garden, which features formal flower beds, informal gardens, woods, a formal pond, and a meandering stream. The garden has many flowering trees and more than twenty-five varieties of shrubs, along with hundreds of perennials. Exotic birds in aviaries also add to the colorful surroundings. Call for annual dates and times. Fee. (800) 235–1030 or (785) 478–4624.

Cedar Crest. Located off I–70 and Fairlawn Road, Topeka, KS 66606. The home has been the official residence of the Kansas governor since 1962. Built in 1928, this twelve-room French Norman–style home overlooks the Kansas River Valley. It was designed by W. D. Wight of Kansas City and was named for the numerous cedar trees on the property. The home is nestled on 244 acres that include hiking trails, fishing ponds, and nature areas open to the public. Public tours are offered on Monday between 1:00 and 4:00 P.M. Large groups of eight or more require reservations. Free. (785) 296–3636.

Combat Air Museum. P.O. Box 19142, Topeka, KS 66619. Head west on I–70 and stay on the turnpike until you reach exit 177 (southbound Topeka Boulevard). Watch for signs leading to the main entrance of Forbes Field and Hangar 602. Dedicated to restoring, preserving, and displaying aircraft and artifacts, this museum is the only one in the world to display operational aircraft from every armed conflict utilizing powered aircraft. Housed here are surveillance aircraft fighters, missiles, and other military pieces, dating from 1917. Visitors can walk through one of the early 1950 radar planes and browse through the many exhibits. Open daily. ♿ . Fee. (785) 862–3303.

Gage Park. 635 Southwest Gage Boulevard, Topeka, KS 66606. Topeka's 160-acre Gage Park features many attractions, including the following:

Carousel in the Park. The antique carousel was built around 1908 by New York's Herschell-Spillman Company. It was purchased by the city of Topeka in 1986 and totally restored for the public to enjoy and ride. Open daily in warm weather. Fee. (785) 368–3838.

Reinisch Rose Garden. This is one of the most extensive rose gardens in the country, with more than 350 varieties and 7,000 bushes. It is one of twenty-three test gardens in the nation for hybridizers and has one of the most complete displays of All-American Winners selected since 1940 on public view. Internationally famous for its beauty, the Reinisch Rose Garden was founded in 1931 and named after Topeka's first park superintendent. Today the roses grow in a lovely setting of rock gardens and pools. The red Topeka Rose stands majestically in the center of the garden. Blooming season normally is June through October; peak time, early June and mid-September. Open daily. Free. (785) 272–6150.

Topeka Zoological Park. Exhibits include the Tropical Rain Forest (see below) and "Gorilla Encounter," which allows visitors to view the creatures in an open environment from a glass-enclosed area. African lions, Japanese macaques, and Chinese muntjac deer are part of the displays. Warm weather makes the Water Bird Lagoon a pleasant place for bird-watching. There are many attractions to visit, including the Children's Zoo; it features a traditional red barn and a series of wooden corrals that create a farmlike setting for visitor-friendly animals. Check the Web at www.topekazoo.org.

Black Bear Woods. Opened in 1996, this is the first of several natural exhibits devoted to Kansas animals. A large wood ramp and deck provide viewing areas of the bears' home. There are a pool, tall trees for them to climb, natural berries to eat, and a large area for playing, sleeping, and just being bears.

The Tropical Rain Forest. Located inside Topeka Zoological Park, this re-creation of a South American ecosystem sprouted from the plains in 1974 and continues to flourish. On cold-weather days there's nothing like a warm and toasty rain forest to keep you warm. The damp, pungent smell mingles with the sweet odor of rare flowers and plants; coupled with the cries of exotic birds, the rain forest is a rare experience to savor. Housed in a 30-foot-high geodesic dome, 100 feet in diameter, the Tropical Rain Forest supports some of the rarest and most exotic plant and animal life in the world. This is a bird lover's paradise. The feathered creatures here are so lavishly colored that they look as though they have been dipped in richly textured paints. Many of the other inhabitants are so well camouflaged that most visitors miss them. Many are nocturnal and quite a few move freely about the dome, so be careful not to step on anybody's toes! Exhibits are open daily. ♿ . Fee. (785) 272-5821.

Heartland Park Topeka. 1805 Southwest Seventy-first Street, Topeka, KS 66619. Hailed as one of the finest motorsports facilities in North America, Heartland Park Topeka opened in 1989 as the only major, multimillion-dollar, multiuse motorsports complex to be built in this country in thirty years. The fastest quarter-mile elapsed time in the history of drag racing was set at the facility in 1990, when the late Gary Ormsby hurtled his Top Fuel dragster down the Heartland strip at an incredible 296 miles per hour.

All the state-of-the-art elements found here are designed with the spectator in mind, from the 2.5-mile road-race course to the 0.25-mile drag strip—one of the fastest in the world. The viewing berms afford spectators an excellent view of the Grand Prix road-race course, while the modern grandstands offer onlookers a look at the pit-stop action. Open for seasonal events. ♿ . Fee. (800) 43-RACES or (785) 862-4781; www.hpt.com.

Historic Ward-Meade Park. 124 Northwest Fillmore Street, Topeka, KS 66606. Old-fashioned fun can be had at this unusual city park. It features five and a half acres of living history that includes a restored 1870 Victorian mansion, a log cabin, a train depot, a one-room schoolhouse, a stone barn, a drugstore, and botanical gardens.

The Potwin Drug Store is worth seeing. A 1920s-style building was designed to house fixtures that were once part of Edelblute's Drug Store in Potwin, Kansas. There is a superb back bar and marble counter perfect for sipping sodas. On the second floor of the Potwin Drug Store, professional, medical, and dental offices appear as they would have a century ago. Also on the park premises is the Mulvane General Store, featuring yesteryear decor and gift items for sale.

Staffed by volunteers, the park offers special meals for groups and organizations. One of the most popular and original dinners is served at fireside tables in the Ward Cabin. The hearthside-cooked food includes ham or smoked turkey, sweet potatoes, Irish potatoes, spiced fruit, baked biscuits, and cookies; homemade ice cream is served as well. The family-style fare is offered from October 15 through March 15. Reservations are required. Historic Ward-Meade Park also features an elegant Victorian dinner, served buffet-style in the dining room of the mansion. You get a choice of entree, salad, and vegetable, plus homemade scones and ice cream for dessert. A minimum of twenty-five persons is required, as are reservations. Fee. Open daily. (785) 368-3888; www.topeka.org.

Kansas Museum of History. 6425 Southwest Sixth Street, Topeka, KS 66615. Located on the historic Oregon Trail, the museum holds one of the country's largest prairie collections of memorabilia and historic objects. In the permanent gallery, "Voices from the Heartland: A Kansas Legacy" tells the story of Kansas, from its first inhabitants to modern-day culture. The past comes alive through interactive video displays and exhibits that feature an 1866 log house; a Southern Cheyenne buffalo-hide tepee; a locomotive with coal, dining, and sleeping cars attached; and more. You can catch the pioneer spirit as you browse through special areas, such as a children's Discovery Place, where hands-on discovery is encouraged. Open daily. &. Free. (785) 272-8681; www.kshs.org.

Kansas State Capitol Building. Tenth and Jackson Streets, Topeka, KS 66612. In an election held in November 1861, Topeka was selected as the capital city of Kansas. It took thirty-seven years to finish the work on the State Capitol, which was finally completed in 1903. The grounds surrounding the building contain monuments of interest, including a statue of Abraham Lincoln located southeast of the capitol. In 1915 Robert Merrell Gage was just out of school and living with his parents when he completed the figure of Lincoln in the barn adjacent to his parents' home.

Southwest of the capitol is another monument by Gage, dedicated to the pioneer women of Kansas. A bronze replica of the Statue of Liberty, at the northwest section of Capitol Square, and a replica of the Liberty Bell, at the east side of Capitol Square, complete the grouping.

Inside the building, murals by John Steuart Curry and David Overmyer tell an unusual pioneer story. Check out the huge panel of a furious John Brown on the second floor. The dome has a great view, but you've got to climb to get there. The Governor's Office and both houses of the Kansas Legislature are worth noting. There are guided tours on weekdays. &. Free. (785) 296-3966; www.kshs.org.

Mulvane Art Museum. Washburn University, Seventeenth and Jewell Streets, Topeka, KS 66621. Built in 1922, this is the oldest visual-arts museum in the state. It offers changing exhibits from its permanent collection and focuses on contemporary art from the Mountain-Plains region. ♿ . Free. (785) 231–1010, ext. 1324; www.washburn.edu.

WHERE TO EAT

Topeka is filled with family restaurants and fast-food places. The official visitor's guide has a complete listing. Contact the Topeka Convention and Visitors Bureau, 1275 Southwest Topeka Boulevard, Topeka, KS 66612; (800) 235–1030 or (785) 234–1030. In the meantime here are some recommendations:

Annie's Place. Gage Shopping Center, 4014 Gage Center Drive, Topeka, KS 66604. This family-owned restaurant bakes its buns fresh daily, along with dinner rolls, cinnamon rolls, and desserts. The baker is visible through a "showroom" in the restaurant. Annie's also grinds prime beef to make its famous gourmet burgers. Don't forget to try the renowned "hot air fries," cooked without grease. Ask for a side order of chicken gravy, which is served with chunks of white-meat chicken. $$; ☐. (785) 273–0848.

"Grazie" the Italian Bistro. 435 South Kansas Avenue, Topeka, KS 66603. Located in the downtown area, this small, intimate restaurant is operated by the owners of Paisano's Ristorante (see below). Featured repasts include pasta dishes, aged steaks, and veal, complemented by a fine wine list. Open for lunch and dinner. Closed Sunday. $$–$$$; ☐. (785) 357–6545.

Paisano's Ristorante. Fleming Place, 4043 Southwest Tenth Street, Topeka, KS 66617. Like its Lawrence, Kansas, counterpart, Paisano's serves superior Italian food. Appetizers include tasty mushroom caps stuffed with sausage and baked in white wine cream sauce. Entrees include veal and chicken dishes, Pesce al Vino Bianco (lobster, shrimp, scallops, crab, and whitefish in a sage and garlic cream sauce), and penne primavera (penne pasta sautéed in extra-virgin olive oil, garlic, and fresh basil sauce, then tossed with vegetables and topped with crumbled Gorgonzola cheese). The portions are large and the prices reasonable. Early-bird lunch special: Entrees are half-price before 11:30 A.M. Open daily for lunch and dinner. $$; ☐. (785) 838–3500.

The Plantation Steak House. 6646 North Topeka Boulevard, Topeka, KS 66617. In business for more than thirty years, the restaurant puts out a good steak at a reasonable price. $$; ☐. Closed Sunday. (785) 246-9797.

WHERE TO STAY

The official visitor's guide to Topeka lists everything from good motel chains to bed-and-breakfasts. For information contact Topeka Convention and Visitors Bureau, 1275 Southwest Topeka Boulevard, Topeka, KS 66612; (800) 235-1030 or (785) 234-1030; www.topekacvb.org.

Brickyard Barn Inn. 4020 Northwest Twenty-fifth Street, Topeka, KS 66618. This 1927 dairy barn has been converted into an elegant country inn with an inviting pool. A good choice for business travel and romantic getaways, the Brickyard Barn Inn features a full or continental breakfast served in relaxing surroundings. As a "private party facility," it is also available for corporate entertaining, weddings, luncheons, cocktail parties, and dinners. $$-$$$; ☐. (785) 235-0057; www.cjnetworks.com/~um002me.

The Elderberry. 1035 Southwest Fillmore Street, Topeka, KS 66604. This restored 1887 Queen Anne home is located 6 blocks from the State Capitol in the central Holiday Park area. Beveled-glass windows, oak woodwork, pocket doors, and triple-sheeted beds add to this elegant home's comfort and hospitality. You have the option of enjoying a full or continental breakfast in one of the home's two guest rooms or of joining other guests in the lovely dining area and being served on antique Flow Blue china and Depression glass. $$; (no cards). (785) 235-6309; www.kbba.com/elderberry.

Fieldstone Bed and Breakfast and Vineyard. 7049 East 149th Street, Overbrook, KS 66524. Located south and east of Topeka off U.S. 56, this unusual establishment is situated on 200 acres of land that includes a vineyard, a catfish-stocked pond, and an orchard. Guests stay in a renovated turn-of-the-twentieth-century limestone home replete with antiques and family heirlooms. The home can accommodate from eight to ten guests and features a spectacular top-floor room that comes equipped with a pool table, a wet bar, and a bath that offers a hot tub, a steam room, and a shower. A full country breakfast includes farm-fresh eggs, asparagus in spring, and assorted fresh fruits in season. Honeymoon packages and group/family-reunion rates are available. $$-$$$; □. (785) 665-7643.

St. Gregory Suites. Seventh and Harrison Streets, Topeka, KS 66612. Don't let the exterior fool you; the interior is first-class. Located 1 block from the State Capitol, this small, intimate hotel has all the upscale amenities for modest prices. The suites feature plush couches and queen-size beds, gilt-edged mirrors, collectibles, glass-topped coffee tables, walk-in closets, and kitchenettes with refrigerators and stoves. A continental breakfast is served in a parlorlike setting. Business machines, laundry facilities, and extended-stay discounts are also available. $$; □. (800) 337-4109 or (785) 233-8347.

Senate Luxury Suites. 900 Southwest Tyler Street, Topeka, KS 66612. As intimate as a bed-and-breakfast and as grand as a first-class hotel, the Senate Luxury Suites appeals to business and leisure travelers alike, with fifty-two elegantly furnished suites. Guests are treated to a complimentary breakfast and are invited to relax in the lower lounge while enjoying the nightly manager's cocktail reception. $$-$$$; □. (800) 488-3188 or (785) 333-5050.

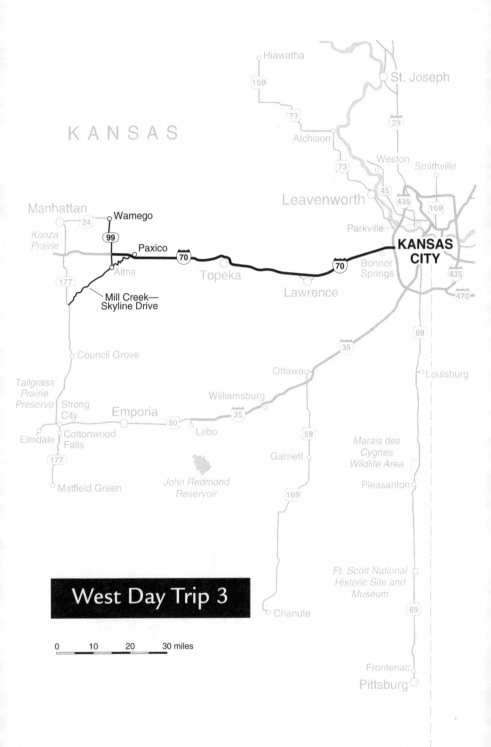

KANSAS

Hiawatha

St. Joseph

159

73

Atchison

29

73

Weston

Smithville

Leavenworth

45

435

169

Manhattan

Wamego

24

Parkville

Konza
Prairie

99

Paxico

70

**KANSAS
CITY**

Alma

70

Bonner
Springs

435

177

Topeka

Lawrence

470

Mill Creek—
Skyline Drive

69

Council Grove

35

Louisburg

Ottawa

Tallgrass
Prairie
Preserve

Williamsburg

Strong
City

Emporia

50

35

59

Elmdale

Cottonwood
Falls

Lebo

Marais des
Cygnes
Wildlife Area

177

Garnett

Matfield Green

John Redmond
Reservoir

169

Pleasanton

Ft. Scott National
Historic Site and
Museum

West Day Trip 3

Chanute

69

0   10   20   30 miles

Frontenac

Pittsburg

PAXICO, KS

Drive west on I–70 to Paxico. Exit 333 leads to the Fields of Fair Winery, adjacent to the interstate, and exit 335 takes you into town.

WHERE TO SHOP

Fields of Fair Winery. I–70 at exit 333, Rural Route 1, Box 19, Paxico, KS 66526. The first licensed winery in Kansas, Fields of Fair cultivates several varieties of Kansas wines. The winery offers tours, a tasting area, gourmet food items, wine accessories, and a deli. Free (fee for wine and food). (800) 732–1984 or (785) 636–5560; www.fieldsoffairwinery.com.

   Mill Creek Antiques. 107 Newbury, Box 156, Paxico, KS 66526. This shop sells beautiful wood and coal heating stoves along with antiques and collectibles. It specializes in the restoration of authentic stoves, which are cleaned, repaired, and recast, if needed. The nickel parts are replated or buffed until they gleam. Once restored to their original beauty, the stoves become one-of-a-kind works of art, as well as a practical and economical means of generating warmth and beauty for your home. (785) 636–5520.

MILL CREEK–SKYLINE DRIVE, KS

From Paxico head south to Alma along Mill Creek–Skyline Drive, which you can pick up outside of town. Look for signs or ask for directions. The scene is miles of rolling hills and prairie under a sweeping sky. Native bluestem prairie grass follows vast stretches of virgin land in a seemingly endless vista. At times the expanse is so immense that one can see the curve of the earth. Sky and land merge as one. It takes the breath away.

Where is this? Surely not Kansas. It's supposed to be flat. It shouldn't look like New Mexico or Montana. But it does, along Mill Creek–Skyline Drive. The drive is clearly marked, and the byway takes you past land covered with stone fences. A historical marker tells you that the 1867 law abolishing open range provided payment to landowners for building and maintaining the venerable stone fences that still stand today. The only sound is your car as it hums along the road, and if you stop along the way and sit quietly, you can almost feel the 1800s surround you: the buffalo, the Indians, the pioneers—they were here, and it's hard to tell where the past stops and the present begins.

WAMEGO, KS

Head north on K–99 to Wamego. A small community of 4,000 persons, the town is located on the Vermillion River, where Louis Vieux, a Potawatomie Indian, operated the first ferry along the Oregon Trail. Wamego is also the birthplace of Walter P. Chrysler, who built the car named after him. The annual Tulip Festival, held in April at the city park, offers a beautiful floral display, along with entertainment and food. For information: Wamego Area Chamber of Commerce, P.O. Box 34, Wamego, KS 66547; (785) 456-7849; www. wamego.org.

WHERE TO GO

The Columbian Theatre Museum and Art Center. 521 Lincoln Avenue, P.O. Box 72, Wamego, KS 66547. In 1994 a $1.8 million renovation restored the luster and elegance to this century-old theater. Rare 1893 murals, the only remaining set of decorative art from the 1893 Chicago World's Fair, grace the walls of the 250-seat theater, which features a guest-artist series, musical concerts, drama and dance productions, educational programs, and regional art exhibits. Docent-guided tours are available by appointment. A performing arts schedule is available. Fee (for events). (800) 899–1893 or (785) 456–2029.

Dutch Mill. Wamego Area Chamber of Commerce, P.O. Box 34, Wamego, KS 66547. This is Kansas's only authentic operating stone Dutch mill. Built in 1879 and listed on the National Register of Historic Places, the mill overlooks the beautiful city park—a perfect place for picnicking. The mill grinds wheat to flour while you watch, and you can purchase products to take back home. (785) 456–2040 or 456–9119.

WHERE TO EAT

Friendship House. 507 Ash Street, Wamego, KS 66547. The bakery items sold here use stone-ground flour from the Dutch Mill and are made from scratch each day along with tasty sandwiches, homemade soups, breads, and pastries that include cookies, muffins, and sweet rolls. Weekly menu items include bread pudding, fresh-baked pie (Friday), and honey wheat *bierocks,* unique hamburger and cabbage pocket sandwiches. Work by local artists and crafters is also on display and for sale. $; □. (785) 456–9616.

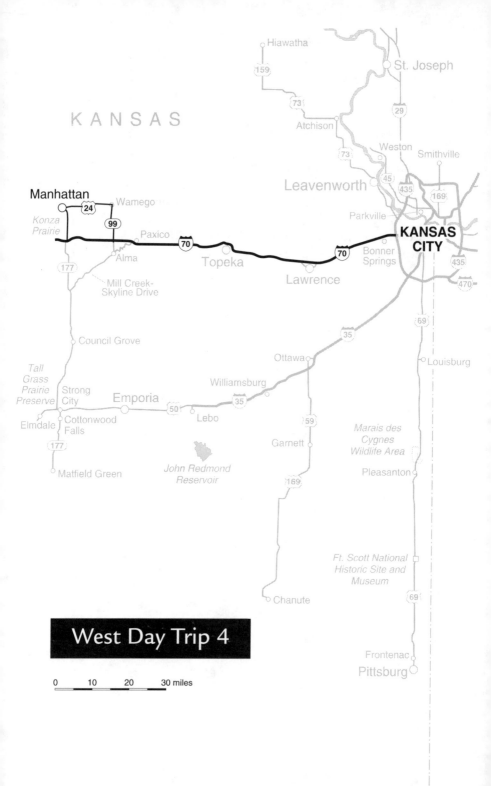

KANSAS

Hiawatha

St. Joseph

159

73

29

Atchison

Weston

Smithville

73

435

Leavenworth

45

169

Manhattan

24

Wamego

99

Parkville

KANSAS CITY

Konza Prairie

Paxico

70

70

435

Alma

Topeka

Bonner Springs

177

Lawrence

470

Mill Creek-
Skyline Drive

Council Grove

35

69

Ottawa

Louisburg

Tall Grass Prairie Preserve

Williamsburg

Strong City

Emporia

50

35

Elmdale

Cottonwood Falls

Lebo

59

177

Garnett

Marais des Cygnes Wildlife Area

Matfield Green

John Redmond Reservoir

Pleasanton

169

Ft. Scott National Historic Site and Museum

69

Chanute

Frontenac

Pittsburg

West Day Trip 4

0   10   20   30 miles

Manhattan, KS

MANHATTAN, KS

Touting itself as the "Little Apple®," Manhattan is located in the heart of the scenic Flint Hills—the last large preserve of native tall-grass prairie in America. From Wamego, Manhattan is only a short drive west on U.S. 24. This thriving college town isn't a destination for tourists looking for whopper-size attractions—and that is part of its charm. Like the prairie itself, Manhattan has a lot to offer, but you have to look for it.

Kansas State University and the KSU Wildcat football team are located here, and home games are held on "Wildcat Weekends," drawing thousands of fans who converge on the city to participate in numerous events and activities that are part of the fun.

The university also boasts scientific research that is on the cutting edge of agricultural technology. Thanks to new techniques instituted here, KSU has produced great-tasting hormone- and antibiotic-free beef, poultry, pork, bread, pasta, pastry, milk, eggs, and ice cream.

Manhattan is a pretty place to visit. The streets are filled with lovely homes and venerable shade trees that offer respite on a hot Kansas day. Just a short drive from here is the Konza Prairie, a Nature Conservancy Preserve that features a pristine and beautiful landscape with a hiking trail open to the public. Manhattan is also the starting point for one of the most gorgeous scenic drives in America, according to *National Geographic's Guide to Scenic Highways and Byways*.

You'll want to spend more than a day here, so it's fortunate that the city has plenty of good restaurants, shops, and places to stay. For more information on what to see and do in the area, call the Manhattan Visitor Information Line at (800) 528–4748. For a free *Manhattan Visitors Guide,* contact the Manhattan Convention and Visitors Bureau, 501 Poyntz Avenue, Manhattan, KS 66502; (800) 759–0134; www.manhattan.org.

WHERE TO GO

Fort Riley. Museum Division, DPTM, P.O. Box 2160, Fort Riley, KS 66442–0160. Located 10 miles west of Manhattan, the grounds of historic Fort Riley hold colorful exhibits that showcase the history of the Great Plains. The beautifully restored Custer House stands as the only set of surviving officers' quarters from the fort's early history. Built in 1855 of native limestone, the quarters are nearly identical to the house that George Armstrong Custer and his wife occupied while residing at the fort. The Custer House also depicts military and family life on the western frontier during the Indian wars.

The U.S. Cavalry and First Infantry Division Museums are housed in separate buildings on the Main Post. The U.S. Cavalry Museum, located in Building 205 on Custer Avenue, houses displays that chronicle the years of the American mounted horse soldier from the Revolutionary War to 1950. Adjacent to the U.S. Cavalry Museum, the First Infantry Division Museum offers the history of this decorated division in life-size dioramas that portray the trenches and battlefields of both World War I and World War II, as well as the jungles of Vietnam and the sands of Desert Storm. Buffalo are still kept in a nearby corral as a further reminder of the history of America before fast-food franchises and tract housing bulldozed away much of the tallgrass prairie. Open daily. Free. (785) 239–3032; www.riley.army.mil.

Kansas State University. The 668-acre campus is located throughout Manhattan. Academically, KSU ranks first nationally among state universities in its numbers of Rhodes, Marshall, Truman, and Goldwater scholars. Founded in 1863, KSU has a number of internationally recognized programs that attract teachers and students from around the globe. Its College of Agriculture offers the only worldwide programs in grain, milling, baking, and feed science and management. Its College of Architecture, Planning, and Design, where all programs are professionally accredited, is one of only five public, comprehensive design schools in the nation.

The College of Veterinary Medicine is internationally recognized as a center for the study of livestock diseases. It has a top-notch veterinary medicine program and hospital—complete with emergency rooms for both large and small animals—that is considered to be one of the finest in the country. (It's not unusual to find a trio of doctors simultaneously performing eye surgery on a cat, leg surgery on a llama, and something you don't want to know about on a cow.) Ongoing cancer research and numerous projects with NASA have enhanced its educational reputation. In addition, the university is drawing attention for its excellent hotel and restaurant management business programs.

As far as cutting-edge research goes, the Department of Animal Sciences and Industry has invented a new steam process to kill those nasty bacteria that thrive on uncooked meat and has also created a way to produce hormone- and antibiotic-free dairy products. (785) 532-6592; www.ksu.edu.

KSU's campus holds several attractions, including the following:

Aggieville. Located on the southeast edge of the KSU campus. This full-service shopping area is a center for student activity and is the oldest shopping center of its kind in Kansas (see also Where to Shop).

Marianna Kistler Beach Museum of Art. 701 Beach Lane, KSU Campus, Manhattan, KS 66501. This beautiful and unique building holds the university's art collection. The museum promotes appreciation of the fine arts through exhibitions of works by popular regional artists and through various educational and outreach programs. It also offers displays held in conjunction with other museums of art around the country. As a Lending Affiliate for the National Gallery of Art in Washington, D.C., the museum enables teachers to borrow educational resource materials developed by the National Gallery. Closed Monday. ♿ . Free. (785) 532-7718.

Call Hall. Dairy and Poultry Science Building, Claflin and Mid-Campus Road, across from the Bob Dole Center on campus (see Where to Eat).

Milford Lake. Four miles northwest of Junction City, c/o Milford State Park, 8811 State Park Road, Milford, KS 66514. Kansas's largest reservoir is one of the state's most productive for anglers. Walleye, crappie, smallmouth bass, and wiper—a hybrid between white and striped bass—abound in the lake waters. Wipers are a "fighting fish" that are relatively new to the area. Weighing six to eight pounds, they join up with white bass and cruise together in the early summer to the main part of Milford to search for their favorite food of shad. According to experts, that's the time the wipers and white bass are easy to catch. With more than 16,000 surface acres and 163 miles of shoreline, there are plenty of fish around for the eating. Milford Lake and its surrounding 21,000 acres make up one of Kansas's prime outdoor habitats, and the body of water is one of the more scenic lakes in the area.

The Milford Nature Center/Fish Hatchery is located at the base of Milford Dam and offers displays and exhibits that explore the surrounding natural area. Free. (785) 238-3014.

Sunset Zoo. 2333 Oak Street, Manhattan, KS 66502. From I-70 take exit 303 into Manhattan to Fort Riley Boulevard; take this east to Westwood and turn north onto Westwood and then left onto Oak Street. The fifty-six-acre zoo may be small, but it is one of the most romantic zoos in the Midwest. That's because love is always in bloom here and lots of animals grow up healthy thanks to the zoo's excellent breeding program. There are thirteen endangered species in the zoo, including snow leopards and red pandas that have managed to thrive in captivity.

Other zoos, including the famed San Diego Zoo, send their animals here for breeding purposes because of the zoo's spectacular success rate at producing healthy zoo babies. The medical care for animals is unique. With KSU's renowned veterinary medical school and exotic medicine program available at all times, two KSU vets are employed by the zoo to monitor and care for the animals and their offspring. Most of the keepers and docents are pre-veterinary-med students, a factor that also helps to maintain the high standard of animal care and exhibition. Sunset Zoo has the only traveling Zoomobile program in the state and offers a lineup of special events annually, including festivals on both Memorial Day weekend and Labor Day. Open daily. ぐ. Fee. (785) 587-APES.

Tuttle Creek Lake. Kansas Department of Wildlife and Parks, Tuttle Creek, 5020-B Tuttle Creek Boulevard, Manhattan, KS 66502. Fifteen miles north of I-70 on K-177 and framed by the Flint Hills, the reservoir is one of the region's largest. The 14,000-acre lake is surrounded by 104 miles of irregular, wooded shoreline, and its wildlife, water, and climate make it a good spot for outdoor recreation. White bass, crappie, channel catfish, and spawn fishing draw anglers, who come in spring and summer to drop a line in any of the numerous sites around the lake that are available for fishing. Other activities include boating, waterskiing, swimming, hunting, picnicking, camping, and other outdoor sports. Pontoon and fishing boat rentals, fishing supplies, fuel, boat-slip rentals, and concessions are available at the marina. Dinner cruises aboard a houseboat are offered for small groups. Free (user fees and permits charged in certain areas). (785) 539-7941; www.kdwp.state.ks.us.

WHERE TO SHOP

Aggieville. Southeast of the KSU campus, Manhattan, KS 66502. The first shopping center in Kansas is named for the former KSU Aggies. Today it is a pre- and postgame host to Wildcat sporting events. Aggieville offers more than one hundred businesses that feature shopping, dining, dancing, and nightlife, all within walking distance of KSU and concentrated in a little over 4 blocks. Everything from barbecue to women's clothing can be found here. Part of the fun is trying out the food, which ranges from cappuccino and croissants to Cajun jambalaya and gumbo. (785) 776-8050; www.aggieville.org.

Manhattan Town Center. 100 Manhattan Town Center, Manhattan, KS 66502. This regional mall in the heart of downtown Manhattan offers an assortment of fine stores, specialty shops, restaurants, and services. Anchored by Dillard's, Sears, and J. C. Penney, it offers one-stop shopping if you're in a hurry to find what you're looking for. Open daily. (785) 539-9207.

WHERE TO EAT

Although Manhattan touts itself as being the "Little Apple®," it might also be called the "City of Ice Cream." The town has two excellent creameries located within the city limits that are worth the drive.

Call Hall. Dairy and Poultry Science Building, Claflin and Mid-Campus Road, across from the Bob Dole Center on the KSU campus, Manhattan, KS 66502. Although the locals know about it, newcomers seldom realize that a place like this could actually exist outside a health food store. Thanks to the scientific laboratories in the Dairy and Poultry Science Building, all the superb-tasting milk, butter, cheese, and ice cream comes straight from the cow to your mouth, hormone-free with no antibiotics. The pure and natural ice cream is made fresh weekly and contains 12 percent butterfat (the special vanilla ice cream has 16 percent butterfat—which is to swoon from). There are forty flavors of ice cream that change daily, and each one is better than the one before it. You could spend an entire day snarfing down sundaes, sodas, malts, and shakes, but then you would be waddling rather than walking back to your car. You might want to bring a cooler and plenty of ice to take back some of the terrific cheese and butter sold here. Open daily. $; (no cards). (785) 532-1292.

Gold Fork. 1724 Anderson, Manhattan, KS 66502. Breakfast here can be a portabello mushroom omelette with fresh spinach and cheddar. If you prefer lunch or dinner, there are nearly 200 items on a sizable menu that offers everything from Oriental chicken salad and chicken dinners to baby back ribs and Black Angus fillets. The desserts are not to be missed. $-$$; □. (785) 776-5909.

Harry's Uptown Supper Club. 418 Poyntz, Manhattan, KS 66502. Turn-of-the-twentieth-century elegance, complete with wing-back chairs, crystal chandeliers, and cloth-covered tables, highlights the ambience at this establishment. The wine list is extensive, and the menu features hand-cut Kansas choice beef, fresh seafood, chicken, and pasta. The raspberry cheesecake is delightful and so is the apple pie. $$-$$$; □. (785) 537-1300.

Hibachi Hut. 608 North Twelfth Street, Manhattan, KS 66502. The Cajun-inspired menu offers everything from boudin (rice and pork Cajun sausage), red beans and rice, jambalaya, and bayou catfish served with jambalaya on the side. The Cajun Feast includes gumbo to red beans and rice, and choice of blackened catfish fillet or top sirloin, served with cornbread, plus homemade bread pudding with whiskey sauce. $-$$; □. (785) 539-9393.

Little Apple Brewing Company. 1110 Westloop Shopping Center, Manhattan, KS 66502. Refreshing handcrafted brews and certified Angus beef steaks are the claim to fame at this friendly restaurant and pub that caters to football lovers. $-$$; □. (785) 539-5500.

WHERE TO STAY

Manhattan has several good hotels, motels, and bed-and-breakfasts from which to choose. For a complete rundown call (800) 759-0134. In the meantime here are a couple of recommendations:

Guest Haus Bed and Breakfast. 1724 Sheffield Circle, Manhattan, KS 66503. A Flint Hills view, a fishpond, and a cedar-lined walking path are part of the amenities here. A continental breakfast is offered with your choice of room. $$; (no cards). (785) 776-6543 after 4:00 P.M.; www.kbba.com/guesthaus.

Morning Star. 617 Houston Street, Manhattan, KS 66502. Within just blocks of the KSU campus, Morning Star features large windows and an expansive front porch for watching the comings and goings around town or spending some quality time with Ginger and Lucy, the two resident Boston terriers. Each of the five guest rooms is a corner room with private bath and in-room whirlpool. Are you familiar with Greek omelettes? If not, you'll be delighted when breakfast is served. No children. $$; ☐. (785) 587-9703; www.morningstaronthepark.com.

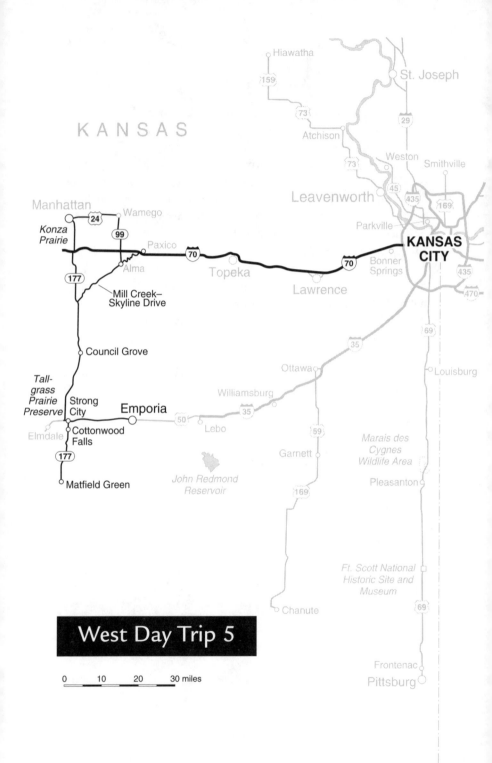

KANSAS

Hiawatha

St. Joseph

159

73

Atchison

29

Weston

Smithville

73

Leavenworth

45

435

169

Manhattan

Wamego

24

Konza
Prairie

99

Parkville

KANSAS
CITY

Paxico

70

Alma

Topeka

70

Bonner
Springs

435

177

Lawrence

470

Mill Creek–
Skyline Drive

Council Grove

69

35

Ottawa

Louisburg

Tall-
grass
Prairie
Preserve

Strong
City

Emporia

Williamsburg

35

Elmdale

Cottonwood
Falls

50

Lebo

59

Marais des
Cygnes
Wildlife Area

177

Garnett

Matfield Green

John Redmond
Reservoir

169

Pleasanton

Ft. Scott National
Historic Site and
Museum

69

Chanute

West Day Trip 5

0   10   20   30 miles

Frontenac

Pittsburg

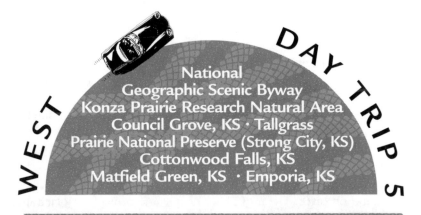

WEST · DAY TRIP 5

National
Geographic Scenic Byway
Konza Prairie Research Natural Area
Council Grove, KS · Tallgrass
Prairie National Preserve (Strong City, KS)
Cottonwood Falls, KS
Matfield Green, KS · Emporia, KS

NATIONAL GEOGRAPHIC SCENIC BYWAY

If you're feeling stressed out, burned-out, or just plain bummed out, then get in your car and head west on I-70 in the direction of the National Geographic Scenic Byway (Kansas K-177) and the Kansas Flint Hills. Named one of 200 scenic drives in the nation, and the only one in Kansas, by *National Geographic's Guide to Scenic Highways and Byways,* K-177 runs for 84 miles meandering from Manhattan to Cassoday, through a region of rounded limestone hills covered with bluestem prairie. Along the way you'll reach the eastern segment of the Konza Prairie Research Natural Area, and from there you can visit the Tallgrass Prairie Preserve, Kansas's first national park. Keep on traveling south and you'll come to the bed-and-breakfast country of Council Grove and Cottonwood Falls as well as a 5,000-acre retreat in Matfield Green.

KONZA PRAIRIE RESEARCH NATURAL AREA

Just south of Manhattan, the **Konza Prairie Research Natural Area** is easily viewed from adjacent highways. K-177 parallels the eastern segment of the preserve, and I-70 runs along most of its southern border. To reach the Konza Prairie entrance from K–177, drive to the east end of the Kansas River Bridge and turn onto Mc-Dowell Creek Road (County Road 901S). The entrance is about 6 miles down the road on the left. (From I–70 take exit 307 and drive northeast on McDowell Creek Road. The entrance is approximately 5 miles on your right.)

Owned by the Nature Conservancy and managed by Kansas State University for the purpose of scientific study of this natural ecosystem, the Konza Prairie is the most intensively studied grassland on earth. The number of people and projects involved in the support and study of the Konza Prairie has not been duplicated elsewhere. This scenic area, named for the Kanza Indians who once roamed here, covers more than 8,600 acres of unplowed, uncultivated land filled with 70 species of dominant grasses and more than 500 species of wildflowers, shrubs, and trees.

The bison herd that lives here is part of a scientific effort to study the effect of these native grazers upon the grasslands. Fire, along with innumerable animals who grazed here, shaped the landscape, and it is here at Konza that the effects of both are being investigated.

Most of the Konza Prairie Research Natural Area is closed to the public. However, a self-guided nature trail is open daily and trail maps are available at the front gate.

The Fall Visitors Day, offered every other year, is filled with special tours and presentations. Tour guides are available with advance reservations. Pack your binoculars, since deer and hawk sightings are a common occurrence. Open from dawn to dusk year-round. Free. (785) 587-0441; www.konza.ksu.edu.

COUNCIL GROVE, KS

Council Grove can be reached by heading south from Manhattan on scenic K–177 or by taking the equally pretty Mill Creek–Skyline Drive from Alma to K–177 and going south from there. By now your eyes must be used to the gentle, undulating countryside around you, so it should come as no surprise that Council Grove is smack in the middle of Kansas's native grassland, known as the Flint Hills.

The historic town of Council Grove got its name from a negoti-ated treaty between U.S. commissioners and the Osage Indian chiefs in 1825, an agreement that granted whites safe passage along the Santa Fe Trail.

A camping and meeting place for explorers, soldiers, traders, and Native Americans, Council Grove offered ample water, grass, and abundant wood that made it a rendezvous point for wagon trains heading west.

John Fremont's expedition of 1845 and Colonel A. W. Doniphan's troops bound for Mexico in 1846 camped on this site. In 1849 the Overland Mail was established with the supply headquarters at Council Grove, followed the next year by monthly coach service.

Council Grove today offers a quaint shopping district, restau-rants, and lodging. The second weekend in June, it hosts Wah-Shun-Gah Days, a major festival with a parade, Indian powwow, rafting, and arts-and-crafts fair.

The historic town offers an informative self-guided walking-tour brochure, filled with historic things to see that include the wheel ruts left by the wagon trains heading west; the Custer Elm, where George Armstrong Custer camped prior to his Little Big Horn en-counter; and the Council Oak, named for the treaty signed beneath the tree by the Osage Indians and the U.S. commissioners.

For group tours contact the Council Grove Visitors Bureau, 212 West Main Street, Council Grove, KS 66846; (800) 732-9211 or (620) 767-5882; www.councilgrove.com.

WHERE TO GO

Flint Hills Tours. c/o Council Grove Convention and Visitors Bu-reau, 212 West Main Street, Council Grove, KS 66846. This four-county consortium promotes travel throughout the region and offers tours to Council Grove, Emporia, Cottonwood Falls, and other places of interest. All excursions travel through the Flint Hills—the largest unbroken tract of tallgrass prairie left in North America. Draped in bluestem grasses and colorful wildflowers during warm weather, the Flint Hills are an ancient reminder of our planet's ecological history. The surface of the Flint Hills is composed of limestone sediment and thin layers of chert (commonly known as flint) that were deposited by inland seas more than 200 million years ago.

Centuries of erosion formed the rugged, high escarpments found in Chase County and the gently rolling landforms around Council Grove. Woodland Indians once roamed the area, and archaeological digs at Eldorado and Council Grove have unearthed many prehistoric campsites.

The early settlers in the area found that a combination of farming and ranching was not only possible in this region but often necessary for survival. Today's successful farmer-stockman must also use the rich bottomland soil for growing crops such as wheat, soybeans, corn, milo, and alfalfa, while employing the upland prairie, with its wonderful native grasses, for grazing cattle.

Kansas has produced nine world-champion rodeo cowboys, and six of them have lived in the region. The Flint Hills Rodeo, one of the oldest consecutively held rodeos in Kansas, occurs annually the first weekend in June, in Strong City. The event is included in tour packages offered by Flint Hills Tours, Inc., which also features a "Santa Fe Trail" excursion that travels from Emporia to Council Grove, the main rendezvous on the trail. From here the trip heads to Cottonwood Falls and Strong City, traversing miles of grazing land, where prairie grasses and wildflowers thrive.

Cottonwood Falls offers attractions such as the Chase County Courthouse, the oldest courthouse still in use west of the Mississippi. It was completed in 1873. Entered on the National Register of Historic Places in 1971, the 113-foot structure is constructed of hand-cut native limestone and was built in the Louis XIII French Renaissance architectural style.

Visitors can also tour the Chase County Historical Museum, which holds a collection of artifacts that interpret the history of the county. The museum also has interesting memorabilia relating to the 1931 Knute Rockne plane crash that occurred 10 miles south of Cottonwood Falls and claimed the life of the famed Notre Dame football coach.

The Flint Hills Tours through German-Mennonite country is another experience to savor. The German-speaking Mennonites who settled the region in the 1870s have left a rich legacy behind. Stops include a private farm on the Gnadenau Trail, where the wheel ruts left by the immigrant wagons en route to Hillsboro and Goessel can still be seen. (800) 732–9211 or (620) 767–5882.

WHERE TO SHOP

Trowbridge Classics. 113 West Main Street, Council Grove, KS 66846. You aren't likely to find another person wearing the same dress you've bought at this unusual women's clothing boutique that offers accessories, purses, and jewelry to go with your one-of-a-kind find. (620) 767–6992.

The Apothecary Shops. 115–119 West Main Street, Council Grove, KS 66846. The Canopy, Aldrich Apothecary, and Santa Fe T-Shirt Shop constitute a grouping of stores that feature a pharmacy, a boutique, and one of the last remaining soda fountains in Kansas. The soda fountain was installed in the 1920s and is marked by distinctive tile that adorns the fountain front, an original back bar, and a brass foot rail. In addition to cherry phosphates, sodas, sundaes, and shakes, you can order a cup of gourmet coffee or some frozen yogurt to go.

The adjacent full-line pharmacy opened in 1892 and has been refurbished with a nostalgic charm highlighted by a restored pressed-tin ceiling and antique fixtures. The soda fountain and pharmacy are connected with the Santa Fe T-shirt shop, which specializes in T-shirts, gifts, and collectibles such as Precious Moments and Snowbabies. (800) 499–9747 or (620) 767–6731.

WHERE TO EAT

Hays House 1857 Restaurant and Tavern. 112 West Main Street, Council Grove, KS 66846. This National Historic Landmark was built in 1857 by Seth Hays, great-grandson of Daniel Boone and cousin of Kit Carson. As the oldest continuously operated restaurant west of the Mississippi, the tavern is an attraction on the Santa Fe National Historic Trail tour. In its early days it was host to theatricals, court proceedings, mail distribution, and church services, as well as serving good food to all.

Now a comfortable stop for modern-day travelers, the Hays House offers delicious foods served in a relaxed atmosphere. Specialties include aged Kansas beef, homemade breads, and desserts. The Victorian-inspired second floor houses the Hays Tavern, which offers a fully stocked bar in the evening. The restaurant also features several private dining rooms. Closed Monday. $$; ☐. (620) 767–5911.

WHERE TO STAY

The Cottage House Hotel/Motel. 25 North Neosho Street, Council Grove, KS 66846. This restored Victorian hotel is on the National Register of Historic Places and has been serving travelers for more than a century. It features modern comforts in nostalgic surroundings and offers a relaxing atmosphere, with gazebo-style porches, a sauna, and period furnishings. Each of the twenty-six rooms in the main hotel has a distinctive style. Stained glass and a brass-and-iron bed are featured in the bridal chamber. A continental breakfast is served each morning. $$; ☐. (800) 727-7903 or (620) 767-6828.

The Flint Hills Bed and Breakfast. 613 West Main Street, Council Grove, KS 66846. This quaint lodging, with its original yellow pine and oak woodwork, hardwood floors, and antique-appointed accommodations, offers guest rooms with private baths and a two-room suite with private bath and queen-size beds. You can relax on one of the home's two large porches or stroll through Council Grove's historic downtown, just 2 blocks away. A full country breakfast is served daily. $$; ☐. (620) 767-6655.

TALLGRASS PRAIRIE NATIONAL PRESERVE (STRONG CITY, KS)

This unique cooperative between the National Park Trust and the National Park Service is 2 miles north of Strong City (on Route 1) and contains 10,894 acres of tallgrass prairie, which is leased to the National Park Service. Expansive rolling hills and wide-open vistas greet you as you experience the beauty of this quiet land. From April 10 through October 31, a 7-mile bus tour is available to take you through the area. The natural prairie cycle of climate, fire, and animal grazing has sustained this beautiful land, where nearly 400 species of plants, 150 kinds of birds, 31 species of mammals, and reptiles and amphibians reside.

Also at the preserve is the Z-Bar/Spring Hill Ranch, home of the original owner, Stephen F. Jones. The eleven-room structure, built with hand-cut native limestone, is characteristic of the Second Empire style of nineteenth-century architecture. Also on the premises is a massive three-story barn and Lower Fox Creek School, a one-room schoolhouse located on a nearby hilltop. Brochures are available for self-guided tours. Docent tours are given hourly between April 10 and October 31. Fee. For information: Tallgrass Prairie National Preserve. c/o National Park Trust, Route 1, Box 14, Strong City, KS 66869. (620) 273-8494.

WHERE TO STAY

Clover Cliff Ranch. Rural Route 1, Box 30-1, Elmdale, KS 66850. Bring your own horse along to ride the trail that runs along this 4,000-acre working cattle ranch located east of Strong City, off U.S. 50. Hiking, fishing, and general all-purpose relaxing are other amenities found at the ranch, which is listed on the National Register of Historic Places. The main house offers four guest rooms, two with private baths. There are also adjacent guest houses that are truly "homes away from home." The larger one features two bedrooms, a loft area with twin beds, a sitting room, two baths, kitchen facilities, a fireplace, and a television. The smaller guest house has two bedrooms, a sleeper sofa, one bath, kitchen facilities, a fireplace, and a television. Breakfast is served in the main house. Meetings, receptions, luncheons, or a tour and tea can also be scheduled. $$-$$$; (no cards). (800) 457-7406 or (620) 273-6698; www.clovercliff.com.

COTTONWOOD FALLS, KS

The oldest settlement in Chase County, the tiny hamlet of Cottonwood Falls is located in the center of the picturesque Flint Hills. The best time to visit the area is spring, fall, or early summer, rather than during a hot summer scorcher. Don't be fooled by appearances; there are plenty of things to see and do around the town, provided you know where to go. Cottonwood Falls also boasts a renowned country inn that is definitely worth the drive. For information on Cottonwood Falls: Chase County Chamber of Commerce, 318 Broadway, Cottonwood Falls, KS 66845; (800) 431-6344.

WHERE TO GO

Chase County Courthouse. Broadway and Pearl Streets, Cottonwood Falls, KS 66845. Built in 1872 of native limestone, the courthouse is an impressive structure. Listed on the National Register of Historic Places, it remains the oldest courthouse in continual use in Kansas. Each year more than 6,000 visitors from around the country visit the structure, marveling at the architectural design, stonework, and spiral staircase. Guided tours of the courthouse can be arranged in advance. Fee. For information: The Chase County Chamber of Commerce, 318 Broadway, Cottonwood Falls, KS 66845; (800) 431-6344.

Chase County Historical Society Museum. 301 Broadway, Cottonwood Falls, KS 66845. The museum holds historic memorabilia and artifacts of the area, including information about the demise of Knute Rockne, the famous Notre Dame coach who was killed when his airplane crashed in heavy fog near here in 1931. Donation requested. Closed Monday and Thursday. (620) 273-8500.

WHERE TO SHOP

Fiber Factory. 209 Broadway, Cottonwood Falls, KS 66845. Watch century-old looms in operation. Customers can make their own rope on an original old-time rope machine. You can purchase handwoven rugs, placemats, blankets, and scarves to take home. Open daily. (620) 273-8686.

Flint Hills Gallery. 321 Broadway, Cottonwood Falls, KS 66845. The gallery features the paintings of Chase County artists, along with custom-made spurs, knives, belt buckles, and hat racks. The shop also sells jewelry, Indian baskets, drums, and stained glass. Closed Sunday. (620) 273-6454.

Jim Bell & Son. 322 Broadway, Cottonwood Falls, KS 66845. If you're looking for a unique shopping experience, try this place. The restored building was opened in 1927 as a retail store for real cowboys. It still supplies any piece of custom-made tack the working cowboy needs, plus there's a boot and saddle repair shop located in the store's basement in case you decide to gallop into town on your horse. Even nonworking cowboys and cowgirls can find the latest styles in western and casual wear for the entire family, from boots and hats to outdoor wear, hunting apparel, and more. Open daily. (620) 273-6381.

WHERE TO EAT

Emma Chase Cafe. 317 Broadway, Cottonwood Falls, KS 66845. The restaurant serves delightful sandwiches, entrees, ice cream, and desserts in a laid-back setting. Hours vary. Call before you go. Closed Monday. $; (no cards). (620) 273-6020.

    Grand Central Hotel and Grill. 215 Broadway, Cottonwood Falls, KS 66845. Looking for a little espresso, Asti Spumante, champagne, or Carmel Valley sauvignon blanc to perk up your day? What better place to find it than smack in the middle of a vast midwestern plain.

    Located in the center of the Flint Hills, along the one and only main thoroughfare of town, this restaurant specializes in Sterling Silver, a line of Certified Premium USDA Choice steaks so terrific that you'll think you've died and gone to Kansas.

    Entrees are served with salad, choice of potato or vegetable, and fresh bread and butter. Dessert can be Grand Central cheesecake topped with cherries or almond amaretto or homemade bread pudding with New Orleans bourbon sauce. The full-service restaurant offers lunch and dinner to the public and an elegant continental breakfast daily to hotel guests. Closed Sunday. $$-$$$; □. (800) 951-6763.

WHERE TO STAY

Grand Central Hotel and Grill. 215 Broadway, Cottonwood Falls, KS 66845. Definitely not your little roadside prairie motel, the Grand Central Hotel and Grill is a must-stop on your way through Kansas. The AAA four-diamond hotel and restaurant opened in 1884 and reopened in 1995; the hotel has been restored beyond its original elegance. Located 2 miles from the Tallgrass Prairie National Preserve and 1 block west of scenic K-177, the Grand Central offers ten beautifully appointed rooms, all designed with a western flair. Its full-service restaurant offers lunch and dinner to the public and an elegant continental breakfast daily to hotel guests.

    For starters there are queen- and king-size beds draped with

Egyptian cotton duvets and sheets purchased in Paris. Plush VIP robes, Jacuzzi showers, full concierge service, complimentary continental breakfast, and meeting rooms for private dining and corporate retreats are offered. A very nice handicapped-accessible room on the first floor has its own outdoor porch. The hotel is happy to provide guests with a variety of outdoor experiences that include nature hiking, horseback riding, and fishing.

Another unusual offering is the "Prairie Drifter"—the hotel's 1958 wheat truck takes you on a 16-mile trip through the prairie, a trek ending with a sunset that stretches over the horizon with no man-made obstructions to mar the view. $$$; □. (800) 951-6763 or (620) 273-8381; www.grandcentralhotel.com.

MATFIELD GREEN, KS

From Cottonwood Falls, head south on K-177 to Matfield Green, where the main thing to do is rest, relax, and renew yourself at a sprawling retreat called The Homestead Ranch.

WHERE TO STAY

The Homestead Ranch. R.R. 1, Box 32, Matfield Green, KS 66862. This 4,000-acre working cattle ranch offers a great setting for exploring new skills and appreciating life in the slow lane.

Five weeks out of the summer, the ranch is filled with children learning the realities of riding, horse care, and ranch life. They feed chickens, clean horse stalls, and spend about six hours a day on horseback. The highlight of a week's camping experience is the night spent in an authentic Conestoga wagon out on the Santa Fe Trail. Kids cook over an open fire and are encouraged, often unsuccessfully, to gather buffalo chips and cow pies for fuel.

Women's retreats feature ranch chores such as hay stacking and fence building, but you can also spend your time fishing or soaking in a hot tub. The bunkhouse sleeps up to twelve persons. The Homestead Ranch serves as a site for meetings and conferences as well as a nice getaway for individuals who want to take a break from the high-

tech world. $$$; (no cards). ♿. (620) 753-3415; www.guest
ranches.com/homestead.

EMPORIA, KS

From Matfield Green you can retrace your route back to Cotton-
wood Falls or Strong City and head east to I-35 and Emporia, or pick
up I-35 at entrance points north or south of Matfield Green.
(See SOUTHWEST FROM KANSAS CITY, DAY TRIP 3.)

Leavenworth, KS
Atchison, KS
Hiawatha, KS

LEAVENWORTH, KS

Located off U.S. 73, Leavenworth contains an amazing amount of memorabilia and history. As the "First City of Kansas," Leavenworth was at the forefront of the transportation revolution. From boat to wagon to railroad, the town led the way in opening the vast resources of America. The new transportation-themed Leavenworth Landing Park, located adjacent to the Missouri River, features exhibits that portray the town's part in forging a path through the American West.

All along the Overland Trails, U.S. Cavalry fortifications such as Fort Leavenworth sprang up to defend western settlement. Between 1838 and 1845 a military road was constructed through the Indian Territory to connect Fort Leavenworth in Kansas and Fort Gibson in Oklahoma. Throughout the years the road was traveled by soldiers, immigrants, Indians, outlaws, and traders.

Today the old military road no longer exists, but modern U.S. 69 and other connecting pathways located near its original route have been designated the Frontier Military Scenic Byway. Fort Leavenworth and Fort Scott, two of the remaining historic Kansas forts lying along that route, are open to tour today.

Established by Colonel Henry Leavenworth in 1827, Fort Leavenworth was a cantonment to protect wagon trains headed west and to help maintain peace with the Native Americans. Leavenworth was also the starting point for exploration parties. When travel to California began in the 1840s, thousands of prairie schooners passed through the posts. Supplies to support the wagons flowed upriver in great quantities. The freight firm of Russell, Majors, and Waddell supplied 4,000 ox teams that hauled sixteen million pounds of freight annually by wagon train.

By 1857 Leavenworth, with a population of nearly 5,000, had survived a disastrous fire to greet Abraham Lincoln as he gave his fifth address in the territory on December 3, 1859.

During the pre–Civil War strife, Leavenworth suffered, but unlike other towns that were ruined by the war, Leavenworth curiously experienced growth. The railroads grew, as did schools and businesses. Like Weston and St. Joseph, Leavenworth also saw steamboat and river traffic, and by 1883 it was well on its way to becoming the leading city in the West.

But expansion came too rapidly for the town, and eventually the bubble burst. Leavenworth did not become the capital of Kansas as everyone had predicted. Instead, it has remained the seat of Leavenworth County.

Yet Leavenworth has had its share of the famous and infamous. In 1895 the Fort Leavenworth Military Prison was transferred to the Department of Justice, and Congress authorized 1,000 acres of military reservation for a penitentiary.

The U.S. Penitentiary at Leavenworth was completed in 1906 and has housed infamous criminals within its walls, including Al Capone, "Machine Gun" Kelly, and Robert Stroud, the "Birdman of Alcatraz."

Leavenworth has a long list of good guys, too. Civil War General William T. Sherman practiced law here, and restaurateur Fred Harvey built his magnificent home on one of the tree-shaded streets. William F. "Buffalo Bill" Cody, army scout and showman, came to Leavenworth in 1853 when he was ten years old. Working for J. B. "Wild Bill" Hickok, he helped outfit trains with supplies for the Overland Stage Company. Cody married a Missouri bride and settled down in Leavenworth, employed as a scout for the Kansas Cavalry.

Leavenworth's U.S. Army Command and General Staff College, on the post, educated such famous students as Douglas MacArthur, George Marshall, Black Jack Pershing, Dwight Eisenhower, and Colin Powell.

To learn more about Leavenworth's history, you can visit its museums and monuments. A drive on scenic U.S. 73 past St. Mary's College, established in 1858, will take you there. Or if you are coming from Weston, it's a short drive south down K-45 and a jog west on K-92 into town.

The Leavenworth Area Convention and Visitors Bureau, 518 Shawnee Street, P.O. Box 44, Leavenworth, KS 66048, can supply you with brochures, self-guided-tour booklets, and other information on the city. (800) 844-4114 or (913) 682-4113; www.lvarea.com.

WHERE TO GO

Berlin Wall Monument. On the grounds of Fort Leavenworth, Fort Leavenworth, KS 66027. Get directions from the Visitor Information Center located just inside the fort's main gate on Grant Avenue. Three sections of the destroyed Berlin Wall were donated to Fort Leavenworth because of the worldwide influence of the U.S. Army Command and General Staff College. The design of the memorial expresses three themes: a "falling position," representing the crumbling of the wall; a horizontal position depicting the wall's destruction, and a vertical position that symbolizes democracy. Open daily. Free. (800) 844-4114.

Chapel of the Veterans. Dwight D. Eisenhower VA Medical Center, U.S. 73, Leavenworth, KS 66027. The stained glass here will take your breath away. Constructed in 1893, the Chapel of Veterans was included in 1921's *Ripley's Believe It or Not,* which stated that this was the only chapel in the world where Catholic and Protestant services could be held simultaneously under one roof.

Combined Arms Center & Fort Leavenworth. Seventh and Metropolitan Streets, Fort Leavenworth, KS 66027. Established in 1827, this is the oldest military installation in continuous service west of the Mississippi River. In the early part of the nineteenth century, it played an important role for settlers and wagon trains heading west. Generals George Custer, William Sherman, Robert E. Lee, Douglas MacArthur, Dwight D. Eisenhower, George S. Patton, Omar Bradley, "Stormin' Norman" Schwarzkopf, and Colin Powell were stationed here. Today it is home to the Combined Arms Center, the Command and General Staff College, and the U.S. Disciplinary Barracks. A self-guided-tour booklet is available in the

Frontier Army Museum Gift Shop on the premises. Visitors are welcome to drive through the fort year-round. (913) 684–5604; www.leav.army.mil. The following on-site places are of note:

Buffalo Soldier Monument. Grant Avenue and the south bank of Smith Lake, Fort Leavenworth, KS 66027. This monument, dedicated July 25, 1992, honors the African-American soldiers who served in the Ninth and Tenth Cavalry Regiments from 1866 until the armed services were integrated following World War II. Open daily. &. Free. (913) 684–5604.

The Frontier Army Museum. Off Reynolds Avenue, Fort Leavenworth, KS 66027. The museum blends the history of Fort Leavenworth with that of the Frontier Army from 1817 to 1917. The outstanding exhibits graphically relate the history of the U.S. Army and its role in western expansion. The carriage used by Abraham Lincoln on his visit to Kansas in December 1859 is displayed here. A special story hour about pioneer life is offered to elementary school children by appointment. Open daily. &. Free. (913) 684–5604.

Rookery. 12–14 Sumner Place, Fort Leavenworth, KS 66027. This was the temporary home of the first territorial governor of Kansas and is the oldest continuously occupied house in the state, built in 1834. A National Historic Landmark, it once housed First Lieutenant Douglas MacArthur, who lived here as a bachelor officer. The Rookery is not open to tour. (913) 684–5604.

Fort Leavenworth National Cemetery. On the post, Fort Leavenworth, KS 66027. More than 20,000 veterans representing every war since 1812 are buried here. The large monument near the flagpole marks the grave of Colonel Henry Leavenworth, for whom the fort and the city of Leavenworth are named. Captain Thomas West Custer, brother of General George A. Custer, is buried here beside other officers of the Seventh Cavalry who died at Little Bighorn. Open daily. &. Free. (913) 684–5604.

First City Museum. 734 Delaware Street, Leavenworth, KS 66048. Here you can find a collection of early frontier memorabilia and artifacts, including buggies and cutters that were manufactured in Leavenworth. The museum houses a 1913 C. W. Parker carousel, possibly the oldest primitive carousel in the country. Closed Sunday through Wednesday. Donations. (800) 844–4114 or (913) 682–1866.

Fred Harvey Residence. Seventh and Olive Streets, Leavenworth, KS 66048. In the early days of railroading, passengers on the Santa

Fe stopped at Fred Harvey restaurants for good food. The Harvey waitresses were the subject of a movie (*The Harvey Girls*), and Fred Harvey, founder of the chain, made a fortune. He lived here in the nineteenth century until his death in 1901. The building now houses the city and county offices. The home is not open to tour at present, but will soon be the National Fred Harvey Museum. (800) 844-4114 or (913) 682-4113.

Leavenworth Landing Park. Missouri River and Esplanade, Leavenworth, KS 66048. This transportation-themed park is decorated with sculptures depicting different modes of transportation throughout Leavenworth's history. The Paddle Wheel Plaza is reminiscent of the actual riverboat landing located in this same area. The Roundhouse Plaza uses inlaid paving stones depicting the railroad roundhouse that was located at the eastern end of the downtown area. Another unique feature is a raised four-state map constructed of terrazzo and brass; it locates the rivers, trails, and railroads that were an important part of Kansas's history. Open daily. ♿. Free. (913) 651-2132.

Performing Arts Center. 500 Delaware Street, Leavenworth, KS 66048. This 1938 theater is an interesting example of American Art Deco architecture. Now on the National Register of Historic Places, the structure was donated to the city by Durwood, Inc., and today hosts live performances by Leavenworth's River City Community Players. Call for a schedule of upcoming performances. (913) 682-4113.

Riverfront Community and Convention Center. 123 South Esplanade, Leavenworth, KS 66048. The totally renovated and expanded 1888 Union Pacific Train Depot, now called the Riverfront Convention and Community Center, is located on the banks of the picturesque Missouri River in the heart of historic downtown Leavenworth. The multipurpose complex provides attractive, well-equipped meeting rooms, with on-site recreational opportunities and banquet service by the Harvey Girls upon request. Open daily. ♿. Free (fee charged to tour or use the facility). (800) 844-4114 or (913) 651-2132.

Carroll Mansion. 1128 Fifth Avenue, Leavenworth, KS 66048. More than a museum, this elegant 1867 Victorian home is a masterpiece of elaborately carved woodwork and stained-glass windows. You can feel the style and spirit of the age as you travel through this sixteen-room mansion. The parlor contains fine Sevres, Dresden, and Early American porcelain, Steuben glass, and lovely furniture. Elsewhere in the museum you'll see antiques from Leavenworth homes, some of them brought up the river by steamer in the past.

In the kitchen, along with the pitcher pump and woodstove, is a copper sink, a refinement of the period. The bathroom contains a lead tub that supplied both hot and cold water and a shower-bath, newfangled oddities that were probably among the first in the West. Old quilts and hand-loomed coverlets are displayed in the bedrooms, and a child's room contains a collection of antique toys. The museum is maintained by the Leavenworth County Historical Society and is a must for nostalgia lovers. Open daily. Fee. Group tours can be arranged by calling (800) 844-4114 or (913) 682-7759.

WHERE TO EAT

The Corner Pharmacy. Fifth and Delaware Streets, Leavenworth, KS 66048. The pharmacy has been around since 1871, and its old-fashioned soda fountain and lunch counter are a throwback to the days when you could get good food and medicine all in one trip. Breakfast and lunch are served at the Victorian-style soda fountain, which comes complete with mahogany bentwood swivel stools and a mirrored back bar. The shakes, malts, and sodas are served in glass containers with the cans from the mixer alongside. The Corner also features homemade chili and an assortment of sandwiches, plus terrific fresh-squeezed limeades and homemade lemonades. Closed Sunday. $; ☐. (913) 682-1602.

High Noon Saloon. 206 Choctaw Street, Leavenworth, KS 66048. Housed in the old 1858 Great Western Manufacturing Company Building, the restaurant features good barbecue and the Frontier Prairie Brewing Company. Closed Sunday. $$; ☐. (913) 682-4876.

Homer's Drive Inn. 1320 South Fourth Street, Leavenworth, KS 66048. In business for more than sixty years, Homer's began its longtime tradition serving nickel mugs of root beer back in 1931. Since then it's become renowned for its burgers—especially the bacon cheeseburger, served with a side of fries and freshly made coleslaw. Open daily. $; (no cards). (913) 682-3034.

Mama Mia's. 402 South Second Street, Leavenworth, KS 66048. Enjoy a lovely landscaped backyard with garden pool while you wait during the summer months. The menu features Italian dishes and hand-cut steaks. Open Tuesday through Friday for lunch and Tuesday through Saturday for dinner. $$; ☐. (913) 682–2131.

The Oasis Cafe. 604 Cherokee Street, Leavenworth, KS 66048. The Mediterranean cuisine served here features a wide selection of beef, lamb, chicken, veal, and seafood dishes. Open for lunch Tuesday through Thursday; dinner is offered Tuesday through Saturday. $$; ☐. (913) 722–0888.

Skyview Restaurant. 504 Grand, Leavenworth, KS 66048. This restaurant is located inside a restored 1892 home and is widely known for its gracious dining in a Victorian atmosphere. Open for dinner only; closed Sunday, Monday, and Tuesday. $$; ☐. (913) 682–2653.

The Tea Room. 505 Delaware Street, Leavenworth, KS 66048. This quaint restaurant is located within the Leavenworth Antique Mall in the historic riverfront downtown area. It features homemade desserts and a variety of entrees, often prepared by guest chefs. When the local River City Community Players have a production at the Performing Arts Center across the street, the Tea Room offers a dinner-theater package. Open Monday through Saturday for lunch. $$; ☐. (913) 682–0777.

WHERE TO STAY

The Prairie Queen Bed and Breakfast. 221 Arch Street, Leavenworth, KS 66048. Named in honor of a Missouri riverboat that stopped in Leavenworth, this 1868 home has been restored to elegance. It features three bedrooms with king-size beds and private baths, and a full breakfast, afternoon tea, and evening snack of your choice. $$; ☐. (913) 758–1959; www.prairiequeen.com.

ATCHISON, KS

A picturesque drive north on U.S. 73 from Leavenworth takes you past green rolling hills and valleys that lead to Atchison. During the mid-nineteenth century, Atchison was an important center of overland freighting. In 1859 the Atchison, Topeka, Santa Fe Railway Company was founded here. A renovated 1880s-era freight depot now houses the Santa Fe Depot Visitors Center, historical museum, and gift shop.

Atchison is filled with history, museums, antiques and specialty shops, and magnificent nineteenth-century mansions, many of which are located on the beautiful Missouri River bluffs. A walking-and-driving-tour brochure is available from the Atchison Chamber of Commerce, Santa Fe Depot Visitors Center, 200 South Tenth Street, P.O. Box 126, Atchison, KS 66002. Guided tours for groups of fifteen or more are available with advance notice. (800) 234–1854 or (913) 367–2427; www.atchison.org.

WHERE TO GO

Amelia Earhart Birthplace Museum. 223 North Terrace Street, Atchison, KS 66002. This historic home, where Amelia Earhart was born in 1897, is listed on the National Register of Historic Places. Interpretive displays, newspaper and magazine clippings, and family belongings tell the story of the legendary aviatrix. Open daily May through October, afternoons and by appointment from November through April. ♿ . Fee. (913) 367–4217.

Amelia Earhart Earthwork. Warnock Lake, Atchison, KS 66002. This one-acre portrait of Amelia Earhart is on a hillside near Warnock Lake. It comprises live plantings, stone, and other natural materials. It is the first perpetual crop artwork created by famed Kansas artist Stan Herd and was designed to commemorate Earhart's one-hundredth birthday. A nearby viewing deck offers a good look at the earthwork and photographic displays that illustrate how the artist created his unusual portrait. Free. (800) 234–1854 or (913) 367–2427.

Atchison Trolley. 200 South Tenth Street, Atchison, KS 66002. The trolley offers hour-long tours of the city and its historic sites and attractions. Special themed tours are offered for fall, Halloween, and Christmas. Open May, June, July, and August. Dates vary. Fee. (913) 367–2427.

Benedictine College. 1020 North Second Street, Atchison, KS 66002. The college has been rated by *US News & World Report* as one of the best liberal arts colleges in the nation. Founded more than 135 years ago by the joint Catholic communities of Mount St. Scholastica and St. Benedict's Abbey, the entire Second Street complex is listed on the National Register of Historic Places. Visitors can tour the campus, which is located above a river bluff affording a breathtaking autumn view. Tours are given through prior arrangement and are free. (913) 367–5340; www.benedictine.edu.

Atchinson Heritage Conference Center. 710 South Ninth Street, Atchison, KS 66002. The conference center is located on the spacious grounds and peaceful setting of Mount St. Scholastica. Minutes away from the heart of Atchison, it provides dormitory accommodations, meeting rooms, and catering facilities for business seminars and religious retreats. Fee. (913) 367–1162; www.atchison heritage.com.

Muchnic Art Gallery. 704 North Fourth Street, Atchison, KS 66002. Monthly displays by regional artists are exhibited amid elegant furnishings of one of Atchison's most spectacular Victorian mansions. The interior features rich woodwork, fine hand-tooled leather, brilliant stained-glass windows, and elaborate fireplaces. Open Saturday and Sunday afternoons and 10:00 A.M. to 5:00 P.M. on Wednesday. Free (fee for tour groups). (913) 367–4278; www.atchison-art.org.

International Forest of Friendship. South of Atchison on K–7 near Warnock Lake. Trees from all fifty states and thirty countries grow here. Spend a pleasant afternoon walking along a path engraved with the names of famous aviators, and spend a minute or two reflecting at a memorial for the astronauts who died aboard the Space Shuttle *Challenger*. There's no charge here, but donations are welcome. (913) 367–2427.

WHERE TO SHOP

Ball Brothers Gift Shop. 504 Commercial Street, Atchison, KS 66002. An old-fashioned lunch counter with a soda fountain is the centerpiece on the main floor of this always-busy drugstore. Downstairs is a gift shop specializing in housewares, Atchison souvenirs, and Precious Moments collectibles. Closed Sunday. (913) 367–0332.

Nell Hill's. 501 Commercial Street, Atchison, KS 66002. This large, upscale store specializes in furniture, prints, pictures, and home accessories. Closed Sunday. (913) 367–1086; www.nellhills.com.

"Once Again" Antiques and Books. 507 Commercial Street, Atchison, KS 66002. A nice selection of antiques and oak furniture, as well as hardback and paperback books, can be found here. Closed Sunday. (913) 367-0056.

WHERE TO EAT

Marigold Bakery and Cafe. 715 Commercial Street, Atchison, KS 66002. This European-style cafe serves fresh-baked breads and breakfast goods. Lunches feature specialty sandwiches, soups, and salads, along with homemade pies, cakes, and cookies. Closed Sunday and Monday. $; □. (913) 367-3858.

The River House Restaurant. 101 Commercial Street, Atchison, KS 66002. American fare is served in an open, airy atmosphere amid the charm of a restored 1870 building that was the former headquarters and business hotel of the Atchison & Nebraska Railroad. Open daily. $$; □. (913) 367-3330.

WHERE TO STAY

Glick Mansion Bed and Breakfast. 503 North Second Street, Atchison, KS 66002. Listed on the National Register of Historic Places, the mansion was built in 1873 and named after its owner, Governor George Washington Glick. In 1913 the home underwent renovation by Kansas City's most innovative architect, Louis Curtiss, who converted it from a Victorian-style structure to a Tudor Revival manor. Guest rooms feature private baths and queen-size beds. A full breakfast is served in the spacious dining room. $$-$$$; □. (913) 367-9110.

St. Martin's Bed and Breakfast. 324 Santa Fe Street, Atchison, KS 66002. Built in 1948, this yellow two-story B&B's five individually decorated rooms have canopied beds, claw-foot tubs, and antiques. It's a great getaway for adults but not for kids under age ten. $$; □. (913) 367-4964; www.stmartinsbandb.com.

HIAWATHA, KS

A "grave situation" awaits you in the tiny town of Hiawatha, Kansas. It's a "Ripley's Believe It or Not" kind of thing, and if you want to know more, head north on U.S. 73 from Atchison to U.S. 159 and on to Hiawatha, or if you're coming from St. Joseph, take U.S. 36 West to one of the most unusual monuments to love you'll ever see.

WHERE TO GO

The Davis Memorial. Mount Hope Cemetery, Hiawatha, KS 66434. From Horton take U.S. 159/73 north to Hiawatha. Or if you're coming from St. Joseph, take U.S. 36 West. It's worth the drive to see one of the most unusual monuments ever built. Each year thousands of people come to see the tomb and sign their names on the guest register mounted at the site of this strange rendering of love and loss.

When Sarah Davis of Hiawatha died in 1930, her husband, John M. Davis, perpetuated her memory by building a memorial that contains eleven life-size figures depicting the couple at various stages of their married life.

Davis spent a whopping sum of $500,000 to have the imported marble and granite figures carved by Italian craftsmen. He died penniless in a county home for the aged in 1947. A statue of Sarah, complete with angel wings, was positioned over the vault in which his coffin was placed, and her body rests in the crypt next to his. Atop that stone slab is a kneeling statue of Davis.

Although Davis's death and funeral were written up in *Life* magazine, few people attended the service. Only one man, Horace England, the tombstone salesman, seemed genuinely concerned by Davis's passing. Open daily. Free. No phone.

Gus's Restaurant. 604 Oregon Street, Hiawatha, KS 66434. Here you'll find a basic country-style interior and an open kitchen area, so you'll have the opportunity to talk with Gus or the other cooks as they prepare hot beef sandwiches or pork tenderloin with a Greek flair, courtesy of Gus. $; (no cards). (785) 742-4533.

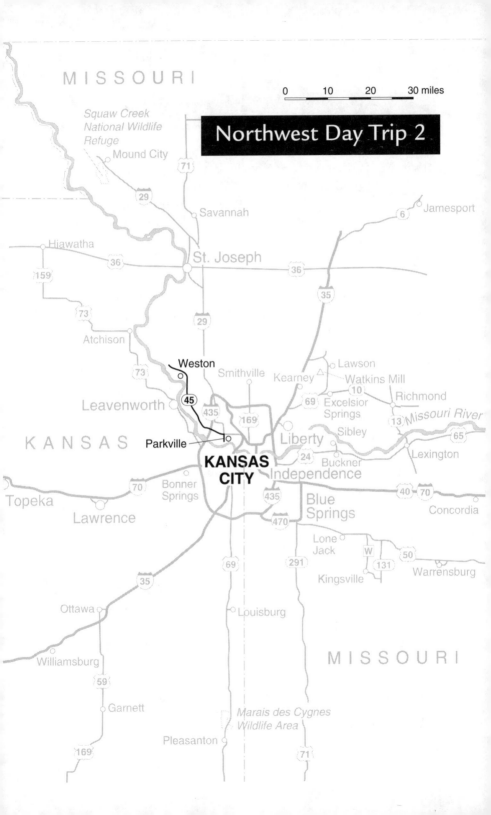

PARKVILLE, MO

The land for the town of Parkville was purchased in 1840 by Colonel George S. Park, a veteran of Sam Houston's cavalry who recognized the value of riverfront land for steamboat trade. As trade and commerce grew along the river, so did Parkville.

Despite floods and train derailments, the town of Parkville is not only alive and well, it's thriving. There isn't a single vacancy in its downtown shops, which combine specialty items with antiques, crafts, books, clothing, home furnishings, and art.

Park University, formerly Park College, was founded in 1875 and sits high on a bluff overlooking the town. It has always been an integral part of city activities, frequently opening its facilities to the community.

Getting to Parkville from Kansas City is easy. It's northwest of the city on M–45 and is also accessible by Interstates 435, 70, and 35. The town's amenities include English Landing Park, a short block from downtown. It offers a walking trail by the river, picnic facilities, basketball goals, a volleyball court, and the unique Waddell A-Frame Bridge, listed on the National Register of Historic Places. Parkville also boasts an unusual nature sanctuary that makes for a pleasant retreat.

The city has a festival atmosphere year-round. There's a Parkville Jazz and Fine Arts River Jam in June and Christmas on the River in December. Information on Parkville, as well as a walking-tour brochure, can be obtained from the Main Street Parkville Association,

207 Main Street, Suite B, Parkville, MO 64152, (816) 505-2227, or the Parkville Chamber of Commerce, 1201 East Street, Parkville, MO, 64152; (816) 587-2700; www.parkvillemo.com.

WHERE TO GO

Parkville Mini Golf. 7 Mill Street, Parkville, MO 64152. This challenging eighteen-hole miniature golf course is great for families with children. There is room for private parties and birthday groups. Located on the bluff overlooking downtown Parkville, the course offers an unbeatable view of the town below and a clubhouse that houses a full-service snack bar and video game entertainment. Hours change seasonally. Fee. (816) 505-9555.

Parkville Nature Sanctuary. Main entrance behind Parkville City Hall, 1201 East Street, Parkville, MO 64152. Featuring more than 110 acres of natural fields, woodlands, ponds, and small waterfalls, the sanctuary makes a wonderful getaway from the stress of the city. The volunteer staff offers guided nature hikes and special events. Open daily. Free. ও . (816) 741-7676; www.parkvillemo.com.

Park University. 8700 Northwest River Park Drive, Parkville, MO 64152. The university has a unique and contrasting campus that boasts buildings listed on the National Register of Historic Places. A variety of educational offerings is available to the public. Free tours are given Monday through Friday. Be sure to visit the underground library and classrooms. ও . (816) 741-2000; ext. 6211; www.park.edu.

WHERE TO SHOP

Angela & Company. 112 Main Street, Parkville, MO 64152. This interesting shop offers a wide variety of items, including safari-inspired pillows, trunks, animals, and other home accessories. Closed Monday. (816) 741-9675.

Garden Goddess. 5 Main Street, Parkville, MO 64152. This gallery for the home and garden features unique handcrafted work. Designs by Heather McCartney (former Beatle Paul McCartney's daughter) include tabletop ceramics, picture frames, candles, throws, and pillows. Closed Monday. Hours vary seasonally. (816) 505-0225.

Home Embellishments. 102 Main Street, Parkville, MO 64152. This shop provides contemporary local art for your home, from knobs and pulls to whimsical yard accessories. Closed Monday. (816)505-1022.

9 Lives. 103 Main Street, Parkville, MO 64152. "Reincarnated" furniture is given another life here. It's cleaned, repaired, and sold good as new. Also featured are unusual furnishings from the '30s through the '70s. Closed Monday. (816) 741-4448.

Northland Exposure Artists Cooperative Gallery. 130 South Main Street, Parkville, MO 64152. If you're looking for one-of-a-kind finds, check out this unusual gallery located in English Landing. The latest addition to Parkville's bustling arts community, Northland Exposure Gallery is owned and operated by fifty regional artists from a two-state area. Inside you'll find exceptional silver and glass jewelry designs and exciting works in watercolor, acrylic, oil, mixed media, pottery, and handcrafted paper. Closed Monday. (816) 746-6300.

Parkville Coffee & Fudge. 113 Main Street, Parkville, MO 64152. This upscale shop specializes in packaged wines and wine accessories and gourmet coffee, locally roasted and flavored in-house. The store features a full espresso bar with cookies, biscotti, and muffins, Missouri River Bottom Fudge, gift items, and more. Closed Monday. (816) 587-4200.

River's Bend Gallery. 106½ Main Street, Parkville, MO 64152. The climb up just a few steps to the second gallery is worth the effort for the wonderful collection of fine art, decoratives, and wearable art that Kristy and Rick McKibben have assembled from artists around the country. The gallery is bright and spacious and filled with creative work that reflects that spirit. $$; ☐. (816) 587-8070; www. kmcink@kcnet.com.

Yikes. 105 Main Street, Parkville, MO 64152. The Soho-inspired collection of fashion-forward women's clothing, jewelry, and gift items in this boutique appeals to youthful buyers looking for something different. Handmade soaps, handbags, hair accessories, and imported body products from France are also offered. Closed Monday. (816) 505-1654.

WHERE TO EAT

A Cherry on Top. 10 Main Street, Parkville, MO 64152. This cafe and ice cream shop serves breakfast, lunch, and snacks throughout the day and is a great gathering spot for locals. The festive decor will tell you why kids like it for birthday parties. Call for hours. $; (no cards). (816) 505-2788.

Cafe des Amis. 112½ Main Street, Parkville, MO 64152. Fine French cuisine is the latest arrival on the food scene of Parkville in the upper level of a building built in 1844. The restaurant is building a reputation for delicious crepes, but daily specials run the gamut of everything delectable from the French. $$; ☐. (816) 587-3844.

PaPa Frank's. 2 East Street, Parkville, MO 64152. Missing from the Parkville dining scene since the Great Flood of '93, PaPa Frank's original Italian cuisine has returned in a bigger setting that also includes the future site of the River Heritage Frontier Museum. Everything is great here, but the lasagna is what keeps the crowd returning. $-$$; ☐. (816) 587-7272.

Stone Canyon Pizza Co. 15 Main Street, Parkville, MO 64152. Appetizers, pizza, pasta, salads, and sandwiches are served at this popular Parkville establishment. Clowns and magicians entertain kids on Friday night. Open for lunch and dinner. $; ☐. (816) 746-8686.

The Power Plant Brewery. 2 Main Street, Parkville, MO 64152. Owned by the same people who operate the River Market Brewing Company in Kansas City, this popular eatery is housed in the former Park College Power Plant, built in 1918. It features a variety of soups, salads, sandwiches, and entrees along with handcrafted beers. $-$$; ☐. (816) 746-5051.

WHERE TO STAY

Down to Earth Lifestyles Bed and Breakfast. 12500 Northwest Crooked Road, Parkville, MO 64152. Opened in 1982, this lovely modern home was built as a bed-and-breakfast. It features an indoor heated swimming pool and eighty-six acres complete with farm animals and ponds for fishing. Four guest rooms with private baths can accommodate couples and families with children. Guests are treated to country breakfasts made to order. Saturday and Sunday brunch is offered, depending on the number of guests, and often includes a meat dish, potatoes, egg casserole, fruit bowl, and whatever else the owner feels like fixing. Ask about the special honeymoon package. $$; (no cards). (816) 891-1018; www.bbon line.com/mo.

WESTON, MO

Taking M–45 out of Parkville leads you to Weston in a matter of minutes. Weston is one of the oldest and most picturesque river towns in Missouri. Founded in 1837, Weston still preserves its antebellum homes, which rest peacefully on hillsides and bluffs that once overlooked the Missouri River. It seems that the Missouri, mighty fickle lady that she is, decided to change her course after the Flood of 1884, which left Weston drained of its bustling potential as a river town, with the river diverted to a channel 2 miles away.

Weston's many antiques shops contain a treasure trove of goodies. Everything from country primitives, antique dolls, and Depression glass to European furniture and country crafts can be found along Main Street. A brochure listing many of the places to visit is available from the Weston Development Company, 502 Main Street, P.O. Box 53, Historic Weston, MO 64098; (816) 640–2909; www.ci.weston.mo.us. Call ahead; many businesses are closed on Monday. Weston telephone numbers listed with a 640 exchange are toll-free from Kansas City.

WHERE TO GO

New Deal Tobacco Warehouses, Inc. Highways 45 and P, Weston, MO 64098. Weston's brown gold attracts countless visitors to the only tobacco market west of the Mississippi River. Six million pounds of burley tobacco cross the floors of the two Weston warehouses annually. Open daily from early November through late January or by appointment. Free. (816) 386–2226.

Pirtle's Weston Vineyards Winery. 502 Spring Street, Weston, MO 64098. Housed in a former church, this winery has vineyards in northern Platte County. Wine and cheese tastings are available for groups. Mead (honey wine) is a specialty here. On the premises is a wine garden where you can sip wine and enjoy sausage, cheese, Tuscan loaves, and fruit. Open daily. (816) 640–5728.

Price-Loyles Home. 718 Spring Street, Weston, MO 64098. Robert E. Lee's and Daniel Boone's descendants occupied this lovely Federal-style home from 1864 to 1989. Original family furnishings, including children's and Civil War memorabilia, are part of what you'll see here. Open by appointment. Fee. (816) 640–2383.

Red Barn Farm. 163000 Wilkerson Road, Weston, MO 64098. Get the kids and yourself into life on a real working farm. Turkeys, geese, and chickens roam the property along with goats, pigs, and cows in pens. Take a hayride through corn and soybean fields, or pick apples and pumpkins during the autumn months. Pick strawberries in May and June. There's a small gift shop in the big red barn. The farm is open daily April through December or by appointment. Fee. (816) 386–5437.

Snow Creek, Inc. Snow Creek Drive, Weston, MO 64098. Five miles north of Weston on M–45, Kansas City's own downhill ski area includes intermediate trails, chairlifts, and beginner areas with rope tows. A day lodge features a cafeteria-style restaurant, a lounge, ski rentals, a ski school, and ticket sales. Open daily and at night from mid-December through March, depending on the weather. Fee. (816) 640–2200; www.peakresorts.com; Snow Report Line: (816) 589–SNOW (toll-free from Kansas City).

Weston Historical Museum. 601 Main Street, Weston, MO 64098. Founded in 1960, the museum offers displays depicting life in Platte County from prehistoric days through World War II. Exhibits include household items, tools, glassware, china, furniture, historic documents, and other items. Mini tours can be arranged by reservation. Open afternoons; closed Monday and mid-December through mid-March. Free. (816) 386–2977 or 640–2650.

WHERE TO SHOP

Einstein's Toy Emporium. 411 Main Street, Weston, MO 64098. This fun, hands-on store features classic toys, wooden trains, and educational products for kids of all ages. Closed Monday. (816) 640–2393.

McCormick Distilling Company Country Store. 420 Main Street, Weston, MO 64098. Founded in 1856, McCormick Distilling Company is best known for being the oldest continuously active distillery still operating on its original site. The store sells McCormick products and other Weston memorabilia. Closed Monday. (816) 640–3149.

Missouri Bluffs Boutique and Gallery. 512 Main Street, Weston, MO 64098. Clothes hounds looking for something nobody else has will love this place. The gallery section showcases Missouri and Kansas art, and the boutique is one of the best places in Missouri to find uncommon clothes, jewelry, and accessories. You'll find a variety of styles here, from Native American, Asian, and African to vintage-inspired, contemporary, and locally made natural fiber garments. Like most other customers, you may wind up spending a lot of time trying on various ensembles and playing with the unusual baubles, so tell your significant other to bring along reading material while you shop. Closed Monday. (816) 640–2770.

Weston Brewing Company. 504 Welt Street, Weston, MO 64098. Established in 1842 by German immigrant John Georgian, the Weston Brewing Company was touted as the "oldest brewery west of the Hudson River." The Royal Brewery, as it was then called, sponsored the first Kansas City Royals baseball team in the early 1900s, and in its heyday the Weston Royal label was well known throughout the Midwest and even in Europe. In the early 1900s the brewery produced 20,000 barrels annually, introducing a Royal Pilsner label advertised as "the beer that made Milwaukee jealous."

The new Weston Brewing Company opened in 1997. It's located next to the original stone walls of the Royal Brewery. Visitors can tour the operation and see yesteryear's photographs and memorabilia on display in the tasting room. A short video is shown, explaining the brewery's history and the current microbrewing process. Tours are offered on weekends, and customers have an opportunity to sample fine lagers and ales made the way they did it in the nineteenth century. Closed Monday. (816) 640–5245.

The Youngblood Gallery. 415 Main Street, Weston, MO 64098. This gallery offers a wide variety of accessories for the home, including hand-painted pottery, antique reproduction furniture, willow furniture, brass and pewter, home fragrances, and an interesting art collection. Closed Monday. (816) 640–2996.

WHERE TO EAT

America Bowman Restaurant. Short and Welt Streets, Weston, MO 64098. This is the place to find a fine home-cooked lunch and dinner, served in a pre–Civil War setting. Inside this restaurant is Pat O'Malley's Pub. It was patterned after Granary Tavern in Limerick, Ireland. Closed Monday. $$; ☐. (816) 640–5235.

Avalon Cafe. The restaurant is located inside an 1847 antebellum home and features Continental cuisine prepared by French-trained chefs and co-owners. Choose from beef tenderloin in Missouri bourbon sauce to American lamb chops in burgundy butter. Desserts are excellent. Closed Monday. $$; ☐. (816) 640–2835.

The Vineyards. 505 Spring Street, Weston, MO 64098. Local wines are served up in this 1845 antebellum structure, together with lamb, duck, beef tenderloin, and other house specialties. Closed Monday. $$–$$$; ☐. (816) 640–5588.

Weston Cafe. 407 Main Street, Weston, MO 64098. A full-service menu is offered, with homemade desserts and weekend buffets. Open daily. $–$$; ☐. (816) 640–5558.

WHERE TO STAY

Benner House Bed and Breakfast. 645 Main Street, Weston, MO 64098. This beautiful Victorian home, overlooking downtown Weston, offers four guest rooms with two private baths. A main parlor, a sitting room, and a wraparound front porch are available for relaxing. $$; ☐. (816) 640–2616; www.bbim.org/bennerhouse.

The Hatchery. 618 Short Street, Weston, MO 64098. This 1845 antebellum bed-and-breakfast has four guest rooms with queen-size beds, gas-burning fireplaces, and private baths. A large outside garden is available for teas and weddings. $$–$$$; ☐. (816) 640–5700.

The Inn at Weston Landing. 526 Welt Street, Box 97, Weston, MO 64098. Located at the end of a block lined with pre–Civil War homes, the inn offers deluxe accommodations with the ambience of a mid-nineteenth-century Irish cottage. A high-pitched roof, low-set dormers, and gables define Celtic and rural British Isles influences. A full authentic Celtic breakfast features rashers, kippers, trifle cakes, and bramble jelly. An 1842 Irish pub is a favorite for private parties. $$; ☐. (816) 640–5788.

The Lemon Tree Bed and Breakfast. 407 Washington Street, Weston, MO 64098. Guests stay in an antebellum-era cottage with three guest rooms that feature adjoining private baths. Breakfast is held in the adjacent three-story Victorian home, separated from the cottage by multilevel decks, a koi pond, a swimming pool, and a spa. Guests are free to use all amenities. Fresh coffee and homemade muffins are delivered to your room in the morning, followed by a sumptuous breakfast served in the dining room or poolside. $$–$$$; ☐. (816) 386–5367.

ST. JOSEPH, MO

Located north on I-29, St. Joseph has the look and feel of a town that played a key role in American history. You can pick up pieces of the past by strolling down streets lined with elegant mansions and restored buildings that were built at a time when raising hemp and selling supplies to wagon trains made fortunes.

Founded in 1826 by Joseph Robidoux as a fur-trading post located in the Blacksnake Hills along the Missouri River, the town later became the starting point for settlers heading west over the Oregon Trail. In 1843 the community was named St. Joseph in honor of Robidoux's patron saint. Five years later gold was discovered in California, and in 1849 more than 20,000 forty-niners migrated through St. Joseph, buying food and supplies to sustain them on their journey.

Steamboats made this an important river town, but with the coming of the railroad in 1859 St. Joseph became the farthest point west to be reached by rail. Trains eventually eclipsed steamboats as the prevailing mode of transportation, but still a fast mail service was needed to the West Coast. Thousands of people turned out to watch the first run of the Pony Express on April 3, 1860. But the effort was too expensive and was abandoned, leaving the mail to the rails.

St. Joseph's Golden Age began in 1875, after the Civil War. During this time many commanding buildings were erected. The Victorian years made fortunes for many that would last several generations.

MISSOURI

Squaw Creek
National Wildlife
Refuge

Mound City

Conception

71

29

Savannah

St. Joseph

Hiawatha

36

36

159

35

73

Atchison

Weston

Smithville

Lawson

Watkins Mill

29

Kearney

10

Leavenworth

45

69

Excelsior
Springs

Richmond

43

169

13 Missouri Riv

Parkville

Liberty

Sibley

65

KANSAS

24

Lexington

Buckner

KANSAS
CITY

Independence

70

Bonner
Springs

435

Blue
Springs

40 70

Topeka

Concord

Lawrence

470

Lone
Jack

W

50

35

69

291

131

Warrensbur

Kingsville

Ottawa

Louisburg

MISSOURI

Williamsburg

59

Garnett

Marais des Cygnes

Northwest Day Trip 3

71

Jamespor

6

Many of the luxurious dwellings still stand and are on the National Register of Historic Places.

Several annual events in St. Joseph remain quite popular. These include the Pony Express-Jesse James Weekend in April, the Apple Blossom Parade and Festival in May, and Trails West in mid-August. For more information on events and attractions, contact the St. Joseph Convention and Visitors Bureau, 109 South Fourth Street, P.O. Box 445, St. Joseph, MO 64502; (800) 785-0360 or (816) 233-6688; www.stjomo.com.

WHERE TO GO

Albrecht-Kemper Museum of Art. 2818 Frederick Boulevard, St. Joseph, MO 64506. The museum holds one of the finest and most comprehensive collections of eighteenth-, nineteenth-, and twentieth-century American art in the Midwest. Included here are works by Thomas Hart Benton, Albert Bierstadt, George Caleb Bingham, George Catlin, and others. Since 1966 the museum has been housed in a 1935 Georgian-style mansion designed by architects Edward Buehler Delk and Eugene Meyer for William Albrecht, founder of the Western Tablet Company. For guided tours call in advance. Lunch is served on Wednesday. Closed Monday. &. Fee. (816) 233-7003; www.albrecht-kemper.org.

Creverling's Antique and Tour House. 1125 Charles Street, St. Joseph, MO 64501. This thirty-room Romanesque mansion was built in 1880 and contains beautiful woodwork and antique furnishings. Many of the collectibles on display inside the home are for sale. Open by appointment. Fee. (816) 232-9298.

Society of Memories Doll Museum. 1115 South Twelfth Street, St. Joseph, MO 64503. Doll collectors will find happiness in this collection of more than 600 dolls, ranging from 1840s "covered wagon dolls" to Barbies and Cabbage Patch Kids. Tours are available. Open Tuesday through Sunday or by appointment. Fee. (816) 233-1420.

Glore Psychiatric Museum. 3406 Frederick Street, St. Joseph, MO 64506. The permanent display covers 400 years of psychiatric history and includes exhibits such as the Bath of Surprise, O'Halloran's Swing, the Tranquilizer Chair, and the Hollow Wheel. There are also displays from St. Joseph State Hospital's history. Open daily. &. Free. (816) 387-2310; www.gloremuseum.org.

The Hall Street Historic District. North on Sixth Street to Hall Street, St. Joseph, MO 64503. Built during St. Joseph's Golden Age, the Hall Street mansions are on the National Register of Historic Places. The elegant homes display the fine designs inherent in nineteenth-century architecture. Stained-glass windows, towers, turrets, and trim make the area a showplace. Some of the homes here feature bed-and-breakfast accommodations. For more information on self-guided walking tours, contact the St. Joseph Convention & Visitors Bureau, 109 South Fourth Street, P.O. Box 445, St. Joseph, MO 64502; (800) 785-0360 or (816) 233-6688; www.stjomo.com.

Ice House Dinner Theatre. 103 West Francis Street, St. Joseph, MO 64501. Feast on an elegantly served dinner in the charming atmosphere of a century-old boiler room and enjoy an amusing performance by acclaimed local and regional actors. Open weekends. Fee. (816) 233-0676.

Jesse James Home Museum. Twelfth and Penn Streets, St. Joseph, MO 64502. The outlaw Jesse James was only thirty-four when he was killed by Bob Ford, a member of the former James Gang. James was living in the house with his wife and two children, under the assumed name of Tom Howard. Ford shot him from behind while he stood on a chair to straighten a picture. The bullet passed through his head and entered the wall. Visitors today can still see the bullet hole. Exhibits include artifacts obtained from the outlaw's grave when he was exhumed in 1995 for DNA tests, which showed a 99.7 percent certainty that it was Jesse James who was killed in his home on April 3, 1882. Open daily. Fee. (816) 232-8206; www.stjoseph.net/museum.

Patee House Museum National Historic Landmark. Twelfth and Penn Streets, St. Joseph, MO 64502. Opened in 1858 by John Patee, this was a luxurious hotel built at a cost of $180,000, a substantial sum for that era. It contained 140 guest rooms. Later it served as headquarters for the Pony Express. Exhibits feature a restored 1860 Pony Express headquarters, a replica of the first railway mail car invented for the Pony Express, and other Pony Express memorabilia. Railroad displays include an 1860 Hannibal and St. Joseph locomotive.

The 1854 Buffalo Saloon on the premises serves soft drinks. Also on the grounds is the Japanese Tea House Ice Cream Parlor. As St. Joseph's only Oriental teahouse in its own Japanese garden, it features ice cream, sodas, sundaes, malts, floats, and fortune cookies. Open daily. Fee. (816) 232–8206; www.stjoseph.net/museum.

Penn Street Square. Twelfth and Penn Streets, St. Joseph, MO 64503. Located in the heart of the city's historic museum area, Penn Street Square offers more than 20,000 square feet of antiques, crafts, art, and handmade items for sale. (816) 232–4626; www.stjomo.com.

Pony Express Museum. 914 Penn Street, St. Joseph, MO 64502. On April 3, 1860, a lone rider on horseback left from this stable to begin his famous historic ride. Now on the National Register of Historic Places, the Pony Express National Memorial features state-of-the-art exhibits that tell the dramatic story of the creation and operation of the Pony Express. Visitors can take a walk along the 70-foot diorama of the Pony Express Trail. Among the many hands-on displays is the *mochila* (mailbag), which can be changed from one saddle to another. Visitors can also pump water from the original stable well. Open daily; closed holidays. ঌ. Fee. (816) 279–5059 or (800) 530–5930; www.ponyexpress.org.

St. Jo Frontier Casino. 777 Winners Circle at Riverfront Park, St. Joseph, MO 64501. Take your pick of blackjack, craps, video poker, Caribbean stud poker, and other venues for spending your money on this riverboat. A buffet is featured daily, with brunch served on Sunday. Open daily. ঌ. Fee to play the games. (800) 888–2946 or (816) 279–7577; www.stjocasino.com.

St. Joseph Museum. 1100 Charles Street, St. Joseph, MO 64501. This 1879 Gothic-style mansion turned museum was copied after a castle on the Rhine and decorated later by the famed Tiffany Company of New York. The 5,000-piece Native American ethnographic collection is the largest in Missouri and represents more than 300 North American tribes. Items in the collection range from Pomo feather baskets to Haida copper masks. There are also local and natural history exhibits of interest. Open daily. Fee. (816) 232–8471; www.stjosephmuseum.org.

WHERE TO SHOP

Russell Stover Candy Outlet. 3839 Frederick Street, St. Joseph, MO 64506. An array of candy, chocolate, holiday treats, and special bulk items is available here at outlet prices. Open daily. (816) 232–3391.

Stetson Factory Outlet Store. 3601 South Leonard Road, St. Joseph, MO 64507. Abraham Lincoln was the nation's president when John B. Stetson made his first western fur-felt hat. The company still makes a wide selection of world-famous western felt, straw, and dress hats at direct-from-the-manufacturer prices. Closed Sunday. (816) 233-3286.

WHERE TO EAT

Barbosa's Castillo. 906 Sylvanie Street, St. Joseph, MO 64501. Located inside a family-owned 1891 mansion, Barbosa's offers authentic home-style Mexican food and good service in a pleasant atmosphere. Open for lunch and dinner daily. $; ☐. (816) 233-4970.

The Old Hoof and Horn Steakhouse. 429 Illinois Street, St. Joseph, MO 64507. Located in the heart of the Stockyards, this venerable restaurant has been serving good prime rib, steaks, and seafood for more than a century. $$; ☐. (816) 238-0742.

Sunset Grill and Speedliner Lounge. 4012 River Road, St. Joseph, MO 64505. Enjoy watching sunset on the river at this casually elegant establishment, which specializes in mesquite-grilled beef, poultry, and seafood. The restaurant has a good reputation for its catfish and prime rib and offers a nice selection of wine and imported beer. Open for lunch and dinner daily. $$; ☐. (816) 364-6500.

WHERE TO STAY

Harding House Bed and Breakfast. 219 North Twentieth Street, St. Joseph, MO 64501. This bed-and-breakfast is housed inside a gracious turn-of-the-twentieth-century home. It features a full breakfast and four guest rooms. $$; ☐. (816) 232-7020.

River Towne Resort. 4012 River Road, St. Joseph, MO 64505. Located on the Missouri River, these beautifully decorated and furnished riverfront cottages feature kitchenettes, spacious living areas, and patio areas with tables and chairs. Some cabins have Jacuzzi tubs and fireplaces. The resort's office is located at the Sunset Grill Restaurant and Speedliner Lounge (see Where to Eat). $$-$$$; ☐. (816) 364-6500.

Shakespeare Chateau Bed and Breakfast. 809 Hall Street, St. Joseph, MO 64506. Located in the heart of the Hall Street Historic

District, this Queen Anne mansion features an ornately carved wooden entryway, more than forty stained-glass windows, and heavily carved fireplaces. Each of the eight themed guest rooms comes with private bath; some feature Jacuzzis and hot tubs. A common room with television, mini refrigerator, coffeemaker, fax, and telephone is available for guests. A full gourmet breakfast is served. $$$; ☐. (816) 232-2667 or (888) 414-4944; www.shakespearechateau.com.

SAVANNAH, MO

From St. Joseph, head north on I-29 to U.S. 71 and Savannah. There's not much to do in town; the real reason to come here, if you are an animal lover, is to see how hundreds of injured or unwanted birds and raptors, dogs, cats, cougars, and other creatures are being saved and cared for by the owners of M'shoogy's. Who knows? Maybe you'll even find a nice, healthy neutered pet to take home.

WHERE TO GO

M'shoogy's Famous Emergency Animal Rescue World Headquarters. 11519 State Route C, Savannah, MO 64485. You don't have to be crazy to be "M'shoogy's," but you do have to love animals. Nestled on twenty-two acres of hilly country, M'shoogy's is a little over an hour from downtown Kansas City and is north of St. Joseph, on U.S. 71. More than 750 dogs, cats, and other assorted creatures are kept at this roadside haven, which is the largest no-kill animal shelter in the country. M'shoogy's compassionate owners, Gary and Lisa Silverglat, group all of the dogs by temperament in well-maintained outdoor runs. Each animal gets its turn to play in a large fenced area that surrounds a pond. About 3,000 of M'shoogy's residents are adopted out each year, which evens the odds that they're going to live much happier lives. M'shoogy's is also a Federal Migratory Rehabilitation Center and is now trying to restore injured birds to the wild.

To get there from St. Joseph, take U.S. 71 toward Savannah. Once you're in town, take a right at the Texaco station (Highway E). Take a left on Highway C and go down to the bottom of the hill. It's best to call for exact directions. Open daily. (816) 324–5824; www. critterconnections.com.

CONCEPTION, MO

Conception can be reached from Kansas City by taking I–29 north to U.S. 71, or from Savannah go north on U.S. 71 toward Maryville. Just before you reach Maryville, turn east on State Highway M. You'll see a sign for Conception Abbey. Drive on for 7 miles until you see the sign for Highway AH. Go left here and follow the road for 6 miles. Take a right on Highway VV and drive up two small hills to the abbey. Park in front of the church and walk to the guest entrance to the right. You can always call for further directions before you go. (660) 944–3100.

WHERE TO GO

Conception Abbey. P.O. Box 501, Conception, MO 64433. Individual and group retreats are offered at this Benedictine monastery, founded in 1873. Located just south of Maryville off U.S. 71, the monastery is an architectural masterpiece designed in the Romanesque style. Also on the premises is Conception Seminary College, a four-year seminary established in 1886.

Conception Abbey was dedicated in 1891 and was designated a Minor Basilica on its fiftieth anniversary by Pope Pius XII, becoming the fifth Minor Basilica in the country. The Basilica of the Immaculate Conception is breathtaking in design and, for those of any faith, represents a place to sit and contemplate.

The abbey has continued for years to open its doors to the public, inviting people in from the cold and often stressful environment around them. Many come here on weekend retreats to sit or walk the grounds in quiet meditation. The basilica is open each day to "pilgrims" for prayer and meditation and serves as a house of prayer for people of all faiths who enter its impressive wooden doors. It is open to the public during prayer services, including the evening vesper services, when the joyful and spirited harmony of the monks' voices becomes a welcome respite from the cacophony of the world.

Since hospitality is one of the defining characteristics of the Benedictine order, you can drop by any day for lunch at the abbey. The modestly priced, wholesome, and simple meal is served promptly at 12:35 P.M. and includes a salad, two main dishes, vegetable, dessert, and home-baked bread. Sunday dinner is also served here, at 11:30 A.M.

Lodging rates are also inexpensive. The abbey is not a resort, so don't expect fancy rooms and amenities. Do expect shared baths, long walks, beautiful sunsets, and plenty of fresh air.

If you have time, you might want to visit the gift shop, where you can buy unique cards and gifts from the abbey's Printery House. You can also write for the monastery's holiday catalogs, which feature everything from religious art and Terra Sancta gifts to El Salvador folk art and icons. Art from the Holy Land, carved by artists from around the city of Bethlehem, porcelain and hand-carved nativity scenes, and limited offerings of gold-plated and polished bronze jewelry are also offered. Open daily. Fee for overnight accommodations and meals. (660) 944-3100.

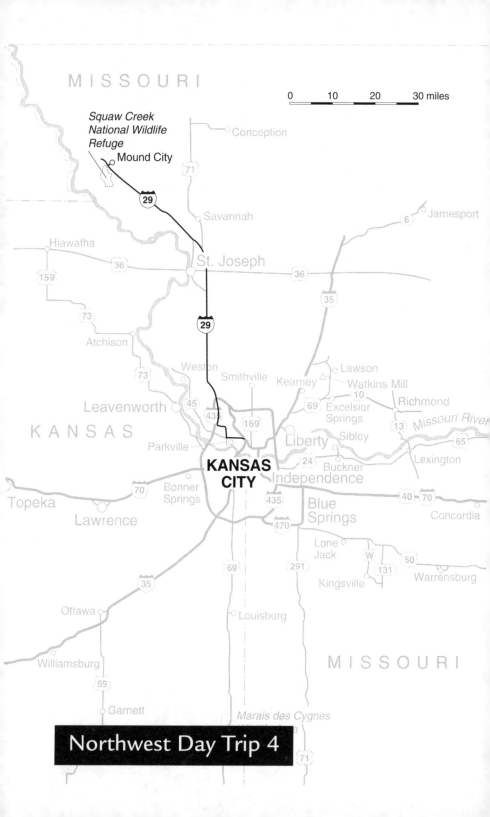

MISSOURI

0   10   20   30 miles

Squaw Creek National Wildlife Refuge
Mound City

(71)

(29)

Conception

Jamesport
(6)

Savannah

Hiawatha

(36)   St. Joseph   (36)

(159)

(35)

(73)

Atchison

(29)

Weston   Smithville   Kearney   Lawson
Watkins Mill   (10)
(69)   Excelsior   Richmond
Springs

Leavenworth   (45)
(435)   (169)   (13)   Missouri River

K A N S A S   Liberty   Sibley   (65)

Parkville   (24)   Buckner   Lexington

KANSAS CITY   Independence

Bonner   (40)━(70)
(70)   Springs   (435)

Topeka   Blue   Concordia
Springs
Lawrence   (470)

Lone   (50)
Jack   (W)   (131)
(35)   (69)   (291)   Warrensburg
Kingsville

Ottawa   Louisburg

Williamsburg

(59)   MISSOURI

Garnett   *Marais des Cygnes*

Northwest Day Trip 4

(71)

SQUAW CREEK NATIONAL WILDLIFE REFUGE (MOUND CITY, MO)

Squaw Creek National Wildlife Refuge is part of the National Wildlife Refuge System, administered by the U.S. Fish and Wildlife Service. Established in 1935, it provides more than 7,000 acres of man-made marshes where waterfowl and other creatures can find food, water, and shelter. The refuge is located 5 miles south of Mound City, a town that gets its name from the loess mounds that bound Squaw Creek to the east. The loess bluffs are a rare geologic formation of wind-deposited soil from the past glacial period. The stuff is crumbly and falls apart in your fingers.

You can reach the refuge by taking I-29 North to exit 79, then onto U.S. 159. Follow U.S. 159 West for 2½ miles and it will take you in front of the refuge headquarters. The drive is about 90 miles and takes around two hours.

Birding is good year-round, although fall and spring are the most spectacular times. White pelicans are present during September and April. In November and December the refuge offers visitors a special treat when bald eagles migrate to the area. During winter Squaw Creek is said to have one of the highest concentration of eagles in the United States, and eagle counts on the refuge have soared beyond 300 in the past.

The refuge holds an annual Eagle Days the first full weekend in

December, from 9:00 A.M. to 4:00 P.M. The event includes a live eagle program, special viewing sites, an auto tour, handouts, and various other programs—every hour on the hour. Open-house weekends are held in spring and fall and center on the bird migrations.

If you are making your first visit to Squaw Creek, you may want to ask some questions at the refuge headquarters, where you'll also find brochures about area wildlife. The refuge itself is open year-round from sunrise to sunset. Poaching has forced stricter adherence to the refuge's opening and closing hours. If you're found on the refuge after closing time, you risk receiving a stiff fine for trespassing.

After leaving the headquarters, take the bridge directly in front of it to the first observation tower you see, then turn left. An auto-tour route completes a 10-mile loop going through a variety of habitats. Follow the road around to Eagle Overlook, which is clearly marked on a sign. This is a split of land that extends into Eagle Pool, where you can mingle with the birds firsthand.

In warm weather look for red-tailed hawks, ring-necked pheasants, sandpipers, ring-billed gulls, terns, and owls. Fall and spring migrations often bring close to 200,000 snow geese, 100,000 ducks, and millions of blackbirds. Be sure to bring along a pair of binoculars to search for eagles, which perch along rows of high trees that border the water.

Mammals are more difficult to see than birds because of their nocturnal habits and the dense habitats they choose. But if you are patient and interested enough to wait and watch, you might observe white-tailed deer, opossums, raccoons, and coyotes along the roads. You don't have to be a Boy Scout to detect the presence of mammals; just look for their tracks in the snow, dust, or mud.

Hunting and camping aren't allowed. Bring your own snacks, especially energy foods and a thermos of something warm to drink on a cold day. The refuge temperature is about 10 degrees colder than it is in Kansas City and there's a wind-chill factor, so wear a sweater, plus a parka, hat, gloves, and boots in winter.

The refuge headquarters is open on weekends in spring from mid-March through the first weekend in May; in fall, from mid-October through the first full weekend in December. Free. (660) 442-3187; www.refuges.fws.gov.

WHERE TO EAT

Camp Rulo River Club. P.O. Box 237, Rulo, Nebraska 68431 (16 miles west of Squaw Creek on U.S. 159). As you cross the bridge over the Missouri River into Rulo, you'll catch a sign to your left that says CAMP RULO RIVER CLUB. Situated on the banks of the Missouri, this place offers catfish and country music. Chicken and steak dinners are also offered at moderate prices. Weekends are the liveliest. $$; □. (402) 245-4096.

Quackers Bar and Grill. 1012 State Street, Mound City, MO 64470. With a name like Quackers, the place has got to be low-key, casual, and filled with birding motifs. It's all of that, plus a great place for pizza, burgers, and tenderloin sandwiches any day of the week except Sunday. $; □. (660) 442-5502.

WHERE TO STAY

Big Lake State Park Resort. Eleven miles northeast of Mound City, Missouri, on M-111 and M-159, Bigelow, MO 64425. Located on a natural oxbow lake, this lovely state park offers cabins with fireplaces, a meeting room, a dining room, and motel rooms and suites with kitchenettes. The resort is closed the end of November through the last weekend in April. $$; □. (660) 442-5432; www.dnr.state.mo.us/dsp.

Historic Hugh Montgomery House Bed and Breakfast. 410 East Sixth Street, Mound City, MO 64470. Banker Hugh Montgomery built this beautiful Victorian home in 1881. Present owners Darla and Rick Saxton welcome you to enjoy one of the five bedrooms with antiques, Jacuzzis, and a snack tray with candy and soft drinks. In the morning the Saxtons provide a lovely continental breakfast. $$; □. (660) 442-5634; www.bbonline.com/mo/hhmh.

Regional
Information

Clay County Visitors Bureau 24-Hour Family Fun Line. (816) 792-7691.

Excelsior Springs Chamber of Commerce, 101 East Broadway, Excelsior Springs, MO 64024; (816) 630-6161; www.exsmo.com.

Jamesport Chamber of Commerce, P.O. Box 17, Jamesport, MO 64648; (660) 684-6682; www.jamesport-mo.com.

Liberty Chamber of Commerce, 9 South Leonard Street, Liberty, MO 64068; (816) 781-5200; www.ci.liberty.mo.us/.

Richmond Chamber of Commerce, 107 North Thorton, Richmond, MO 64085; (816) 776-6917; www.richmondmissouri.com.

Smithville Lake, Jerry L. Litton Visitor Center, 16311 Highway DD (south end of dam), P.O. Box 428, Smithville, MO 64089; (816) 532-0174; www.nwk.usace.army.mil/smithville.

Arrow Rock Merchants Association, P.O. Box 147–B, Arrow Rock, MO 65320; (660) 837-3335; www.arrowrock.org.

Boonville Chamber of Commerce, Katy Depot, Spring and First Streets, Boonville, MO 65233; (660) 882-2721; www.mo-river.net.

City of Independence Tourism Department, 111 East Maple Street, Independence, MO 64050; (816) 325-7111; www.ci. independence.mo.

Columbia Convention and Visitors Bureau, 300 South Providence, Columbia, MO 65205; (800) 652-0987 or (573) 875-1231; www.visitcolumbiamo.com.

Concordia Chamber of Commerce, 702 South Main Street, Concordia, MO 64020; (660) 463-2454; www.concordiamo.com.

The Friends of Rocheport, 501 Third Street, Rocheport, MO 65279; (573) 698-3207 or 698-3210; www.rocheport.com.

Hermann Tourism Group, 306 Market Street, P.O. Box 104, Hermann, MO 65041; (800) 932-8687; www.hermann.com.

Jefferson City Convention and Visitors Bureau, 213 Adams, P.O. Box 776, Jefferson City, MO 65102; (800) 769-4183 or (573) 634-3616; www.jeffersoncity.org.

Kingdom of Callaway Chamber of Commerce, 409 Court Street, Fulton, MO 65251; (800) 257-3554; www.callawaychamber.com.

Lexington Tourism Bureau, P.O. Box 132, Lexington, MO 64067; (660) 259-4711; www.historiclexington.com.

New Franklin Chamber of Commerce, 130 East Broadway, New Franklin, MO 65274; (660) 848-2288.

Sedalia Chamber of Commerce, 600 East Third Street, Sedalia, MO 65301; (800) 827-5295; www.visitsedaliamo.com.

Santa Fe Trail Growers Association, Route 1, Box 131-P, Waverly, MO 64096; (660) 252-0730.

Warrensburg Chamber of Commerce, 100 South Holden Street, Warrensburg, MO 64093; (877) OLD-DRUM or (660) 747-3168; www.warrensburgmo.com.

SOUTHEAST FROM KANSAS CITY

Lake of the Ozarks Convention and Visitor Bureau, P.O. Box 827, Osage Beach, MO 65065; (800) 386-5253; www.funlakes.com.

SOUTH FROM KANSAS CITY

Carthage Chamber of Commerce, 107 East Third Street, Carthage, MO 64836; (417) 358-2373; www.carthagenow.com.

SOUTHWEST FROM KANSAS CITY

Chanute Office of Tourism, 101 South Lincoln Street, Chanute, KS 66720; (800) 735-5229 or (620) 431-5229; www.chanuteks.com.

Crawford County Convention and Visitors Bureau, 117 West Fourth Street, P.O. Box 1115, Pittsburg, KS 66762; (800) 879-1112 or (620) 231-1212; www.morningsun.net/cvb.

Emporia Convention and Visitors Bureau, 719 Commercial Street, P.O. Box 703, Emporia, KS 66801; (800) 279-3730 or (620) 342-1803; www.emporiakschamber.org.

Fort Scott Chamber of Commerce, P.O. Box 205, Fort Scott, KS 66701; (800) 245-FORT; www.fortscott.com.

Franklin County Convention and Tourism Bureau, 109 East Second Street, P.O. Box 580, Ottawa, KS 66067; (785) 242-1411; www.idir.net\~fctv.

The Garnett Area Chamber of Commerce, 419 South Oak Street, Garnett, KS 66032; (785) 448-6767.

The Kansas Department of Wildlife and Parks, 14639 West Ninety-fifth Street, Lenexa, KS 66215; (913) 894-9113; www.kdwp.ks.state.us.

WEST FROM KANSAS CITY

Chase County Chamber of Commerce, 318 Broadway, Cottonwood Falls, KS 66845; (800) 431-6344.

City of Bonner Springs, 205 East Second Street, P.O. Box 38, Bonner Springs, KS 66012; (913) 422-1020.

Council Grove Visitors Bureau, 212 West Main Street, Council Grove, KS 66846; (800) 732-9211 or (620) 767-5882; www.councilgrove.com.

Lawrence Convention and Visitors Bureau, 785 Vermont Street, Suite 101, Box 586, Lawrence, KS 66044; (888)-LAWKANS or (785) 865-4499; www.visitlawrence.com.

Manhattan Convention and Visitors Bureau, 501 Poyntz Avenue, Manhattan, KS 66502; (800) 759-0134; www.manhattan.org.

Topeka Convention and Visitors Bureau, 1275 Southwest Topeka Boulevard, Topeka, KS 66612; (800) 235-1030 or (785) 234-1030; www.topekacvb.org.

Wamego Area Chamber of Commerce, P.O. Box 34, Wamego, KS 66547; (785) 456-7849; www.wamego.org.

NORTHWEST FROM KANSAS CITY

Atchison Chamber of Commerce, Santa Fe Depot Visitors Center, 200 South Tenth Street, P.O. Box 126, Atchison, KS 66002; (800) 234-1854 or (913) 367-2427; www.atchison.org.

Leavenworth Convention and Visitors Bureau, 518 Shawnee Street, P.O. Box 44, Leavenworth, KS 66048; (800) 844-4114 or (913) 682-4113; www.lvarea.com.

Main Street Parkville Association, 207 Main Street, Suite B, Parkville, MO 64152; (816) 505-2227.

Parkville Chamber of Commerce, 1201 East Street, Parkville, MO 64152; (816) 587-2700; www.parkvillemo.com.

St. Joseph Convention and Visitors Bureau, 109 South Fourth Street, P.O. Box 445, St. Joseph, MO 64502; (800) 785-0360 or (816) 233-6688; www.stjomo.com.

Weston Development Company, 502 Main Street, P.O. Box 53, Historic Weston, MO 64098; (816) 640-2909; www.ci.weston.mo.us.

Festivals and Celebrations

FEBRUARY

Step Back in Time Winter Festival, Jamesport, MO. Held the first week of February, the festival offers an open house, as well as arts-and-crafts demonstrations. (816) 684-6682; www.jamesport-mo.com.

MARCH

Wurstfest, Hermann, MO. Gourmet sausage makers compete at this annual mid-March event, where visitors get to sample sausages and buy them to take back home. (800) 932-8687; www.hermannmo.com.

APRIL

Big Muddy Folk Festival, Boonville, MO. This two-day event in early April features workshops and folk music performed by regional artists. (660) 882-2721; www.mo-river.net.

Dogwood Music Festival, Camdenton, MO. This annual mid-April rite of spring near the Lake of the Ozarks features a flat-pickin' music competition, arts and crafts, bluegrass music, art exhibits, and more. (800) 769-1004; www.camdentonchamber.com.

Pony Express–Jesse James Days, St. Joseph, MO. Relive the excitement of the Old West at this annual event, held the first weekend in April; it celebrates the beginning of the Pony Express and the end of the life of Jesse James. (800) 785-0360; www.stjomo.com.

Spring Homes Tour, Carthage, MO. The mid-April homes tour features some of the finest and most spectacular homes in Missouri. (417) 358-2373; www.carthagenow.com.

Tulip Festival, Wamego, KS. Held the third Saturday and Sunday of April in the city park, the event features beautiful floral displays, along with entertainment and food. (785) 456-7849; www.wamego.org.

Tulip Time at the Binkley Gardens, Topeka, KS. Three and a half acres of tulips, daffodils, and flowering trees come abloom for nine days in mid-April at this private garden where the owners open their doors to flower lovers everywhere. Contact the Topeka Convention and Visitors Bureau for exact dates. (800) 235-1030; www.topeka.org.

MAY

AAUW Square Fair, Town Square, Garnett, KS. Held the Saturday before Mother's Day, the event brings in more than one hundred crafters and artists. Ethnic cuisine, music, entertainment, rides, and a children's art area make this fun for the whole family. (785) 448-6767.

Apple Blossom Festival and Parade, St. Joseph, MO. The town celebrates the rite of spring the first weekend in May with concerts, craft booths, and other outdoor events. (800) 785-0360; www.stjomo.com.

Arrow Rock Annual Antique Show, Arrow Rock, MO. Antiques galore can be found at this event, held the third weekend in May. (816) 837-3470; www.arrowrock.org.

Civil War Reenactment, Carthage, MO. The reenactment of the 1861 Battle of Carthage, the first strategic battle of the Civil War, is held in mid-May at the Battle of Carthage State Historic Site. (417) 358-2373; wwwcarthagenow.com.

Fort Leavenworth Homes Tour and Frontier Army Encampment, Fort Leavenworth, KS. The first Saturday in May, many of Leavenworth's historic homes are open to tour. During the event, you can also witness living history interpretations of frontier Army life. (800) 444-4114; www.lvarea.com.

Gatsby Festival, Excelsior Springs, MO. An invitation-only art show exhibit, live entertainment, golf, parade, and more are part of this fun event, held the second weekend in May. (816) 630-6161; www.exmo.com.

May Day Festival, Jamesport, MO. The early May event features a craft show, carriage and buggy rides, and more. (816) 684-6682; www.jamesport-mo.com.

Maifest. Hermann, MO. German food, music, dancing, wine, and museum tours are part of the fun at this mid-May event. (800) 932-8687; www.hermannmo.com.

Memorial Day Weekend Salute to Veterans Parade and Air Show, Columbia, MO. More than one hundred floats, veterans' reunion groups, bands, military vehicles, and organizations participate. The air show features more than fifty military aircraft from World War I to the present, on the tarmac and flying. Other activities include high-flying performance jets and the U.S. Army Golden Knights Parachute Team in action. (573) 443-2651; www.visit columbiamo.com.

Mushroom Festival, Richmond, MO. The first weekend in May, Richmond celebrates its bounty of morel mushrooms with a celebration that includes a parade, plenty of food and craft booths, a model train show, a carnival, beer garden, and other activities. (816) 776-6916; www.richmondmissouri.com.

Spring Knap-In, Sibley, MO. Fort Osage offers a glimpse of days past as visitors witness the art of making arrowheads and tools from flint, a time-honored Native American tradition. (816) 650-5737; www.historicfortosage.com.

Spring on the Square, Liberty, MO. The early May event brings in visitors who can join in the festivities, which feature arts and crafts, entertainment, and more. (816) 781-5200; www.ci.liberty.mo.us/.

Topeka Jazz Festival, Topeka, KS. The last weekend in May more than two dozen nationally and internationally known musicians come to the Topeka Performing Arts Center to jam for thirty hours of the world's finest straight-ahead jazz. (785) 234-2787; www.topekacvb.org.

JUNE

Art in the Park, Columbia, MO. Mid-Missouri's largest fine-arts fair is held the first weekend in June and features fine arts and crafts, entertainment, and children's art activities. (573) 443-8838; www.visit columbiamo.com.

Country Stampede, Manhattan, KS. The hottest music and camping festival in Kansas is held every June and includes top country music stars, food, crafts, and camping under the stars. The summer event features special seating arrangements for handicapped individuals and festival-style lawn-chair seating for general admission. Entertainers in prior years have included Reba McEntire,

Tanya Tucker, and Tracy Lawrence. Fee. (800) 795-8091.

Downtown Twilight Festival, Columbia, MO. Every Thursday evening of the month there are free performances of local artists, musicians, clowns, and children's activities in the downtown area. (573) 442-6816; www.visitcolumbiamo.com.

Good Ol' Days, Fort Scott, KS. Fun, food, entertainment, and more can be had at this annual celebration, held the first weekend in June. (800) 245-FORT; www.fortscott.com.

Flint Hills Rodeo, Strong City, KS. The oldest consecutively run professional rodeo in Kansas brings in top cowboys and cowgirls from throughout the Midwest, who compete for more than $50,000 in prizes. A cowboy dance is held afterward on the covered dance floor near the arena. There's also a rodeo parade that follows a 2-mile route through downtown Cottonwood Falls and Strong City. The rodeo grounds are located on U.S. 50 at Strong City. (316) 273-6480 or (316) 273-6932.

Heritage Days, Lexington, MO. A parade, carnival, live music, and more highlight this mid-June celebration. (660) 259-3082; www.historiclexington.com.

Kingdom Days, Fulton, MO. This three-day festival is held at the end of the month. It's based on a Civil War confrontation between a Union general and the local militia. There are numerous reenactments, crafts, entertainment, children's activities, and more. (800) 257-3554; www.callawaychamber.com.

Parkville Jazz & Fine Arts River Jam, Parkville, MO. This popular two-day event is held the third Friday and Saturday in June in riverfront English Landing Park. There's jazz performed by nationally acclaimed musicians, plus a fine-arts exhibition that showcases regional talent in a juried competition. The festival has won the Missouri Main Street Best Promotional Event Award. (816) 505-2227; www.parkvillemo.com.

Scott Joplin Ragtime Festival, Sedalia, MO. Held the first week in June, this is the only classical ragtime festival in the world commemorating the noted composer's work. It brings musicians and visitors from around the globe to the birthplace of ragtime. Food, crafts, and free performances on the Maple Leaf Club grounds are part of the fun. (660) 826-2271; www.visitsedaliamo.com.

Skunk Run Days, Ottawa, KS. The second weekend in June, Ottawa holds a festival touting a quilt show, tours, and an arts-and-crafts fair. (785) 242-1411; www.idir.net\~fetv.

Wah-Shun-Gah Days, Council Grove, KS. On the third weekend in June the city hosts Wah-Shun-Gah Days, a major festival, with a parade, Native American powwow, rafting, and an arts-and-crafts fair. (800) 732-9211 or (620) 767-5882; www.councilgrove.com.

JULY

Amelia Earhart Festival, Atchison, KS. This annual festival, held in late July, honors the life and achievements of Atchison's favorite native daughter on her birthday. (800) 234-1854; www.atchison.org.

Fiesta Mexicana Week, Topeka, KS. The weeklong mid-July festival features authentic Mexican foods, crafts, and entertainment that celebrate Topeka's Hispanic culture. (800) 235-1030; www.topekacvb.org.

Fireworks Celebrations, Osage Beach, MO. Annual fireworks displays are presented by Tan-Tar-A (800-826-8272) and the Lodge of Four Seasons (800-843-5253).

Flint Hills Rodeo, Strong City, KS. The annual event features cowboy teams from Kansas and surrounding states, who compete in sanctioned events that are similar to real ranch activities. Everything from saddle bronc riding and team doctoring to team branding, team penning, and a wild horse race might be on the list of activities. (316) 273-6740 or 273-8472.

Fourth of July Celebration, Wamego, KS. The town hosts one of the largest parades in the state at this time of year, complete with a car show, tours of the venerable Columbian Theatre, a carnival, and fireworks. (785) 456-7849; www.wamego.org.

Fort Osage Independence Day, Sibley, MO. During this July 4 celebration visitors get to enjoy "speechifyin'," merrymaking, and fun at the historic fort. (816) 650-5737; www.historicfortosage.com.

Kansas River Valley Art Fair, Topeka, KS. Situated in Gage Park, the fair is held the last weekend in July and features 120 artists from all over the country showing works that range from oils and watercolors to pottery and sculpture. Music, stilt walkers, mimes, and jugglers are some of the other surprises in store. (785) 368-3888; www.topeka.org.

Kaw Valley Rodeo and Riley County Fair, Manhattan, KS. The last week in July, Manhattan hosts this world-class pro rodeo event, complete with broncs, bulls, cowboys, clowns, barrel racers, and sky-divers. (785) 537-6350; www.manhattan.org.

Missouri State Powwow, Sedalia, MO. This authentic intertribal gathering held in mid-July features three days of Native American cul-ture, food, dancing, and arts and crafts, including silver jewelry, furs, pottery, and paintings. (800) 827-5295; www.visitsedaliamo.com.

Missouri Town 1855 Independence Day, Fleming Park, Blue Springs, MO. This traditional July 4 celebration is part of this nineteenth-century living history park. Interpreters in period attire will offer activities such as children's games, flag raising, firing of the anvil, black powder demonstrations, and more. (816) 795-8200, ext. 1260; www.co.jackson.mo.us.

Platte County Fair, Tracy, MO. The oldest continuously running fair west of the Mississippi, the fair is nearly 140 years old and is held the third weekend in July. Live music, a carnival, fiddle and talent contests, a demolition derby, mud marathon, and more are featured. (816) 431-3247; www.plattecofair.com.

Sunflower State Games, Lawrence, KS. More than 10,000 ama-teur Kansas athletes compete in twenty-five sports over two week-ends in late July. (785) 842-7774; www.sunflowergames.org.

AUGUST

Great Stone Hill Grape Stomp, Hermann, MO. On the second Saturday in August, stomp to the music for fun and charity at this event where stompers are judged on the amount of juice produced and on "stomping style," which showcases unusual costumes and stomping techniques. Cash prizes are awarded to the winners of the "Grand Stomp-Off" competition. There's also a benefit silent auction of items donated by area businesses. (800) 932-8687; www.hermannmo.com.

Gus Macker 3-on-3 Basketball Tournament, Jefferson City, MO. Join the summertime fun in downtown Jefferson City the third weekend in August as hundreds of teams compete in America's largest 3-on-3 basketball program. (573) 634-3616; www.jeffersoncity.org.

Missouri River Festival of the Arts, Boonville, MO. Symphony, ballet, vocal, jazz, and big-band music are highlights of this per-forming arts festival, held the second week of August. (660) 882-2721;

www.mo-river.net.

Missouri State Fair, Sedalia, MO. Eleven days of shows, exhibits, and competitions draw nearly 400,000 people every year to this popular event. (800) 422–FAIR; www.mostatefair.com.

Trails West, St. Joseph, MO. More than 150 years of history are condensed into three days of fun and excitement on the third weekend in August. Top-name entertainers, musicians, artists, and crafters are part of the fun. (800) 785–0360; www.stjoearts.org.

U.S. Cellular Balloon Classic, Columbia, MO. This event, held the last weekend of August, benefits the Ronald McDonald House. Balloon launches in the evening, fly-ins, refreshments, music, and children's activities are part of the fun, weather permitting. (573) 474–1141.

SEPTEMBER

American Indian Heritage Weekend, Fort Scott, KS. On the last weekend of September, Fort Scott invites visitors to join in the re-creation of the region's historic past. (800) 245–FORT; www.fortscott.com.

Annual Ciderfest, Louisburg Cider Mill, Louisburg, KS. The last week in September and first week in October, the apple season gets under way with this yearly festival of food, fun, and entertainment. (913) 837–5202; www.cidermill.com.

Annual Fall Festival and Crafts Fair, Jefferson City, MO. This is the largest festival and crafts fair in mid-Missouri. (573) 634–2824; www.jeffersoncity.org.

Annual Lawrence Indian Arts Show, Lawrence, KS. Held in September and October, the cultural event features Native American artwork. A juried show and sale is open to the public and remains on exhibit through both months. A two-day outdoor Indian Market, held at Haskell Indian Nations University in September, features works from more than 155 Native American artists from across the country. This celebration of art tradition is a family event that features dancing, food, artist demonstrations, and hands-on children's activities. (785) 864–4245; www.visitlawrence.com.

Apple Jubilee, Waverly, MO. The mid-September jubilee includes apple judging, entertainment, music, contests, and plenty of family fun. Free tours of Waverly and area fruit markets and packing houses are available. Organized groups are welcome by appointment. (660) 493-2616.

Boone County Heritage Festival, Columbia, MO. Reminiscent of the early nineteenth-century in Boone County, the festival is held the third weekend of September and features handcrafted items, storytelling, old-time games and entertainment, and tours of the historic Maplewood Home and Boone County Historical Museum. (573) 874-7460; www.visitcolumbia.com.

Boonslick Traditional Folk Music Festival, Arrow Rock, MO. Regional musicians perform a variety of folk music at this exciting annual event, held on the second Saturday in September. (660) 837-3335; www.arrowrock.org.

Capital Jazzfest/Balloon Race, Jefferson City, MO. The soulful sounds of jazz, blues and Dixieland are celebrated in conjunction with a children's expo. (800)-CHILDREN; www.jeffersoncity.org.

Cider Days, Topeka, KS. Held the last weekend of September at the Kansas Expocentre, this celebration rekindles the pioneer spirit with Wild West shootouts, fresh-pressed apple cider, living history demonstrations, and an arts-and-crafts show. (785) 272-9290; www.topekacvb.org.

Columbia Festival of the Arts, Columbia, MO. On the last weekend of September, visitors can attend this cultural event, which features fine arts and crafts demonstrations, display and sale of original works of art, entertainment, dance, and musical performances. (573) 874-6386; www.visitcolumbia.com.

Concordia Fall Festival, Concordia, MO. In early September, the town celebrates its German heritage, complete with brass bands, parades, cattle shows, arts-and-crafts shows, and plenty of German-style food. (816) 463-7056; www.concordiamo.com.

Downtown Twilight Festival, Columbia, MO. Every Thursday evening of the month there are free performances of local artists, musicians, clowns, and children's activities in the downtown area. (573) 442-6816; www.visitcolumbiamo.com.

Fall Festival, Liberty, MO. Liberty Square is the site for a crafts show, a carnival, a car show, a parade, and a trolley tour. (816) 781-5200; www.ci.liberty.mo.us.

Fall Knap-In, Sibley, MO. Fort Osage offers a glimpse of days past as skilled artisans from across the nation gather to provide demonstrations and discussions on the art of knapping. (816) 650-5737;

www.historicfortosage.com.

Fort Osage Rendezvous and Trade Fair, Sibley, MO. Traders and merchants, archery competitions, tomahawk throwing, music, demonstrations, and children's games are part of the fun at this event held the second weekend in September. (816) 650-5737; www.historicfortosage.com.

Heritage Day "Step Back in Time" Festival, Jamesport, MO. Lost arts and skills are demonstrated on the grounds of the bicentennial "Little Brick House" in downtown Jamesport. (660) 684-6682; www.jamesport-mo.com.

Jesse James Festival, Kearney, MO. Arts and crafts, a rodeo, a parade, a carnival, period reenactments, and other activities take place at this event in mid-September. (816) 628-4229; www.jesse jamesfestival.com.

Lake Garnett Cruisers Annual Auto Show, Garnett, KS. For persons who love nostalgia, this show, held the last weekend in September, brings more than 200 classic and custom cars and trucks to town for a daylong show that includes games, entertainment, food, door prizes, and awards. A special cruise around the lake follows, with a cruise night at a local fast-food drive-in where '50s music is played and prizes are awarded. (785) 448-5496.

Leavenworth River Fest, Leavenworth, KS. This annual festival, held the second weekend in September, celebrates the city's diverse history and heritage. It includes a parade, a craft show, a fine arts show, food, entertainment, and more. (800) 844-4114; www.lvarea.com.

Little Apple Festival, Manhattan, KS. The last weekend in September, Manhattan holds an arts-and-crafts festival, complete with entertainment, food, and much more. (785) 587-2757; www.manhattan.org.

Little Balkans Days, Pittsburg, KS. This annual September event celebrates the ethnic culture and heritage of this former mining town with boccie ball, a parade, polka music, arts-and-crafts booths, and a number of ethnic foods. (800) 879-1112 or (620) 231-1212; www.morningsun.net/cvb.

Old Drum Days, Warrensburg, MO. Held the third weekend in September, Old Drum Days features a carnival, classic car show, petting zoo, baby pageant, live musical performances, regional crafts, and food, all in honor of Old Drum, the dog that made Warrensburg famous. (660) 747-3168; www.warrensburgmo.com.

Old Marais River Run Car Show, Ottawa, KS. The third weekend in September, more than 400 custom rods and restored vehicles are showcased. (785) 242-5799.

Ozark Ham and Turkey Festival, California, MO. This wild and crazy event, held the third Saturday in September, features free entertainment, a diaper derby, car show, barbecue contest, horseshoe pitching, stock car races, hog-and-turkey calling contests, antique tractor pull, washboard competition, historical events, and plenty of food, including the building of the "world's largest" turkey submarine sandwich. Nobody leaves this event hungry or bored. (573) 796-3040.

Power of the Past Antique Engine and Tractor Show, Ottawa, KS. The second weekend of September, the town gets its motor running with a show that features tractors and Warner engines, manufactured here, plus music, a free ham and bean supper, horse-drawn rides, and homemade ice cream. (785) 242-1411.

Renaissance Festival, Bonner Springs, KS. Weekends in September and October, festival entertainment includes Highland Games, Irish music, minstrels and storytellers, food, drink, and plenty of fun. Pets allowed for a fee. (800) 373-0357 or (816) 561-8005; www.kcrenfest.com.

Santa-Cali-Gon Festival, Independence, MO. This Labor Day weekend festival celebrates the days of the Santa Fe, California, and Oregon Trails with crafts, entertainment, and other activities. (816) 325-7111; www.santacaligon.com.

The Vintage Homes Tour, Lexington, MO. Held in September of odd-numbered years, the tour allows the public a glimpse of the interiors of elegant historic structures. Lexington has four historic districts on the National Register of Historic Places, and there are more than 120 antebellum and Victorian homes and buildings listed on the register. (660) 259-4711; www.historiclexington.com.

Wake Up to Missouri U.S.A. National Powerboat Championship Boat Races, Marina Bay Resort, Osage Beach, MO. Spectacular powerboats flex their muscles as they race in excess of 140 miles per hour. (800) 386-5253; www.funlake.com.

Waterfest, Excelsior Springs, MO. There's plenty of entertainment, arts and crafts, kids' carnival games, food, and fun to be had here on the second Saturday in September. (816) 630-6161; www.exmo.com.

OCTOBER

Apple Fest, Weston, MO. Apple-butter cooking, cider pressing, a parade, and lost-arts demonstrations are held in early October. (816) 640–2909; www.ci.weston.mo.us.

Apple Festival, Topeka, KS. Historic Ward-Meade Park is the setting for the early-October celebration of pioneer life in Kansas. You can view crafts made by local artists, taste brown bread and ice cream, and tour the Victorian home, cabin, schoolhouse, and train depot on the premises. (785) 368–3888; www.topeka.org.

Arrow Rock Craft Festival, Arrow Rock, MO. This popular event, held the second weekend in October, is a showcase for regional artists and craftspersons. (660) 837–3335; www.arrowrock.org.

Haunted Homes Tours, Atchison, KS. During Halloween week Atchison hosts a weeklong series of nightly tours aboard the Atchison Trolley to learn about the ghost-filled homes of this historic town. (800) 234–1854; www.atchison.org.

Maple Leaf Festival, Carthage, MO. Held the third weekend of the month, the festival features southwest Missouri's biggest parade, concerts, a car show, arts-and-crafts shows, and more. (417) 358–2373; www.carthagenow.com.

Missouri Town 1855 Fall Festival, Fleming Park, Blue Springs, MO. The first weekend in October presents a great time to visit Missouri Town. The festival offers period dancers, musicians, period games, arts-and-crafts demonstrations, historic reenactments, woodworking demonstrations, storytelling, music, food, and fun. Admission is $7.00 per vehicle. (816) 795–8200, ext. 1260; www.co.jackson.mo.us.

Octoberfest, Hermann, MO. Hermann hosts special fall fun celebrations throughout the month. Visitors can tour wineries and sample award-winning wines or dine on German food, dance to polka music, and enjoy a variety of entertaining events. (800) 932–8687; www.hermannmo.com.

Oktoberfest, Atchison, KS. This annual outdoor arts-and-crafts festival, held on the first weekend of the month, features more than one hundred booths, German foods, a beer garden, and entertainment along Atchison's downtown pedestrian mall. (800) 234–1854; www.atchison.org.

Pioneer Harvest Fiesta, Fort Scott, KS. On the first weekend in October, Fort Scott celebrates its early pioneer days with entertainment, antique gas and steam engines, food, and more. (800) 245–FORT; www.fortscott.com.

Pony Express Pumpkin Fest, St. Joseph, MO. Live entertainment, children's activities, homegrown pumpkins, decorating contests, and more can be found at this fun family event. (800) 785–0360; www.stjomo.com.

Renaissance Festival, Bonner Springs, KS. On weekends in September and October, festival entertainment includes Highland Games, Irish music, minstrels and storytellers, food, drink, and plenty of fun. Pets allowed for a fee. (800) 373–0357 or (816) 561–8005; www.kcrenfest.com.

River Rendezvous, Jefferson City, MO. Held the second weekend in October, this fall arts and heritage festival includes juried arts and crafts, authentic mountain men reenactments, a children's crafts tent, and much more. (573) 761–5355; www.jeffersoncity.org.

Wamego Fall Festival, Wamego, KS. Held the first Saturday of October, the festival offers a large crafts show, entertainment, and food. (785) 456–7849; www.wamego.org.

NOVEMBER

Annual Christmas Lighting Ceremony, Carthage, MO. More than 750,000 lights, free holiday music, entertainment, and a special dinner buffet are featured at this mid-November event. (800) 543–7975; www.carthagenow.com.

Annual Lake Lights Festival and Enchanted Holiday Park, Osage Beach, MO. From mid-November through January 1, the area turns on the holiday lights as scenic displays bring out the Christmas spirit. (800) 386–5253; www.funlake.com.

Festival of Poinsettias, Lawrence, KS. This beautiful festival, which begins the weekend before Thanksgiving and runs through Christmas, complements Lawrence's traditional holiday shopping and entertainment activities. Local shops, restaurants, and hotels display more than 4,000 poinsettia plants during the monthlong celebration, which features a Christmas parade, a homes tour, an art fair, and other activities. (888)–LAWKANS or (785) 865–4499;

www.visitlawrence.com.

Step Back in Time Christmas Festival, Jamesport, MO. The last week in November, Jamesport hosts this popular event, featuring a craft show and a cookie walk. (816) 684-6682; www.ci.weston.mo.us.

DECEMBER

Christmas in Weston Candlelight Homes Tour, Weston, MO. The first weekend in December is the time to tour historic homes decorated for the holidays and enjoy yuletide entertainment with a nostalgic flair. (816) 640-2909; www.ci.weston.mo.us.

Christmas on the River, Parkville, MO. The recent winner of the Missouri Main Street Best Promotional Event, this celebration makes a great way to start the holiday season. Held the first Thursday through Sunday in December in and around downtown Parkville, it features plenty of activities, including performances by a 1,000-voice children's choir, hot air balloon liftoffs, luminaria-lit walking trails, and spectacular fireworks. (816) 505-2227; www.parkvillemo.com.

Downtown Holiday Festival, Columbia, MO. This free event held the first Friday in December affords visitors the opportunity to enjoy downtown's festive decorations, take a hayride, stroll past "living window displays" at shops throughout the area, and enjoy music, goodies, and much more. (573) 442-6816; www.visitcolumbiamo.com.

First Night Columbia, Columbia, MO. On December 31, Columbia holds a community celebration of the arts, with continuous entertainment at a variety of locations in the downtown area. A grand finale at midnight tops off the fun. (573) 817-2781; www.visitcolumbiamo.com.

Frontier Candlelight Tour, Fort Scott, KS. Candlelight tours of Fort Scott National Historic Site are offered the first weekend in December. Reservations are required. (620) 223-0310.

Homes for the Holidays, Fort Scott, KS. The first weekend in December, visitors may tour architecturally significant buildings decorated for Christmas. Arts, crafts, music, trolley rides, and food round out the fun. There's a fee for the tour package, which includes lunch. (800) 245–FORT; www.fortscott.com.

Old-Time Holiday Happenings, Topeka, KS. Historic Ward-Meade Park is the setting for this early-December vintage holiday celebration that features Victorian dinners, trolley tours, tours of the grounds, and unique turn-of-the-century decorations. (785) 368–3888; www.topeka.org.

Sparkling Arts Holiday Show, Columbia, MO. Columbia Art League hosts its annual holiday show and sale from December 1 to January 8, with open-entry works of art, a juried art show, and gifts for all ages. (573) 443–8838; www.visitcolumbiamo.com.

Squaw Creek National Wildlife Refuge Eagle Days, Mound City, MO. The event, held the first full weekend in December, includes a live eagle program, special viewing sites, an auto tour, handouts, and various other programs—every hour on the hour. (660) 442–3187; www.refuges.fws.gov.

State Parks, Historic Sites, Conservation Areas, U.S. Army Corps of Engineers Parks and Lakes

KANSAS

In the days before Christopher Columbus, most people thought the world was flat. Likewise, a lot of folks still think the Kansas flatlands are flat, too. Not so. The Flint Hills, located between Topeka and Manhattan, east to west, present a languid, flowing topography. Consult your map and take some back roads. There should be several pleasant surprises.

Fishing is a great Kansas sport, with a large variety of species to be found, including bass, northern pike, rainbow trout, crappie, and channel catfish. To fish in Kansas you need a license. Contact the Kansas Department of Wildlife and Parks, 14639 West Ninety-fifth Street, Lenexa, KS 66215; (913) 894–9113; www.kdwp.ks.state.us. The agency offers a guidebook to the state parks, provides maps, and assists with information on park services, including boating, fishing, hunting, camping, and handicapped-accessibility.

The Kansas Historical Society, 6425 Southwest Sixth Avenue, Topeka, KS 66615, has information on state historic sites. (785) 272–8681; www.kshs.org.

Campers with Golden Age Passports receive a 50 percent discount on all camping fees in U.S. Army Corps of Engineers parks. There is a modest fee for Golden Age Passports, which can be obtained at the project office by persons sixty-two or older. Contact the Kansas City District Corps of Engineers, 700 Federal Building,

Kansas City, MO 64106; (816) 983–3632.

Got more questions? Drop by the Kansas Information Center, Milepost 415 on I–70, Kansas City, KS 66112; (913) 299–2253.

MISSOURI

There are many who believe that Missouri is one of the most beautiful states in the Union. Like Kansas, Missouri has neither coasts nor craggy mountains, but it does have a rolling and often rugged terrain that no other state can claim. It's easy to get hooked on Missouri, but first you must get the feeling of the land.

Hunting and fishing are good in Missouri, and game is plentiful. Deer, turkey, quail, migratory waterfowl, and other wild creatures abound. The waterways are alive with fish, from bass to cold-water trout and catfish. Complete information on regulations and permits for hunting and fishing, plus brochures on handicapped-accessible conservation areas, is available from the Missouri Department of Conservation, P.O. Box 180, Jefferson City, MO 65102–0180; (573) 751–4115. You can also contact the Missouri Department of Conservation, Kansas City Office, 8616 East Sixty-third Street, Kansas City, MO 64133; (816) 356–2280; www.conservation.state.mo.us.

There's camping in most state parks, and some have backpacking trails, nature education centers, and primitive camping areas. For the pampered there are dining lodges, cabins, and modern motels that stay open from April 15 through October 31. Pets are welcome, but they must be on a leash no longer than 10 feet.

The Missouri Department of Natural Resources, Division of State Parks, P.O. Box 176, Jefferson City, MO 65102, has information on Missouri state parks and historic sites. Parks and campgrounds are open for your enjoyment year-round. There is a fee for camping. Call or write for a copy of *Missouri Masterpieces,* a brochure that lists all the state parks and historic sites in the state. (800) 334–6946; www.mostateparks.com.

Campers with Golden Age Passports receive a 50 percent discount on all camping fees in U.S. Army Corps of Engineers parks. There is a modest fee for Golden Age Passports, which can be obtained at the project office by persons sixty-two or older. Contact the Kansas City District Corps of Engineers, 700 Federal Building, Kansas City, MO 64106; (816) 983–3632.

ABOUT THE AUTHOR

Author, artist, and workshop presenter, Shifra Stein has written more than thirty books and hundreds of articles for magazines and newspapers.

Her many guidebooks include the popular *Day Trips*® series for The Globe Pequot Press, as well as cookbooks such as *Wild About Kansas City Barbecue* and *Vegetables on the Grill* for Pig Out Publishing. She has also written several personal-power workbooks, including *Unlocking the Power Within: Journaling for Personal and Professional Growth*.

Equally at home with computer, pen, or brush, Ms. Stein offers exciting "Art for the Health of It" workshops that combine the visual arts with expressive writing and creativity training. She teaches around the country at arts and education centers, galleries, wellness centers, colleges, and other venues.

Ms Stein is available for speaking engagements. For more information see her Web site at www.shifrastein.com or contact her at shifra@shifrastein.com.